STORED

in the

BONES

Safeguarding Indigenous
Living Heritages

Agnieszka Pawłowska-Mainville

UNIVERSITY OF MANITOBA PRESS

T0243481

University of Manitoba Press
Winnipeg, Manitoba, Canada
Treaty 1 Territory
uofmpress.ca

Cataloguing data available from Library and Archives Canada
ISBN 978-1-77284-045-2 (PAPER)
ISBN 978-1-77284-047-6 (PDF)
ISBN 978-1-77284-048-3 (EPUB)
ISBN 978-1-77284-046-9 (BOUND)

Frontispiece map originally appeared in "Manitoba Historical Atlas: A
Selection of Facsimile Maps, Plans, and Sketches from 1612 to 1969" and is
reprinted by permission of the Manitoba Historical Society.

Cover photo by Agnieszka Pawłowska-Mainville (John and Nel
Mainville at Stephen's Lake, Fox Lake Cree Nation Territory)
Cover and interior design by Sarah Wood

The University of Manitoba Press acknowledges the financial support for
its publication program provided by the Government of Canada through
the Canada Book Fund, the Canada Council for the Arts, the Manitoba
Department of Sport, Culture, and Heritage, the Manitoba Arts Council,
and the Manitoba Book Publishing Tax Credit.

Funded by the Government of Canada | Canadä

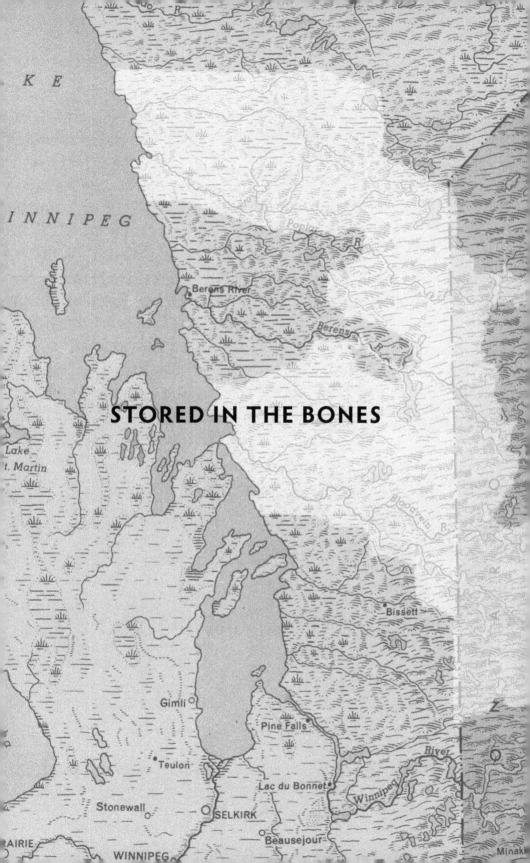

STORED IN THE BONES

Gaye giin Abelba
Gaye giin Walterba
Gaye giin Richardba
For Noah
Gaye giin John

Contents

List of Figures. ix

Glossary of Anishinaabemowin and Inninumowin Terms. xiii

Introduction 1

Chapter One: Living Heritage 33

Chapter Two: Intangible Cultural Heritage 75

Chapter Three: "The last one to know" 119

Chapter Four: "Clean energy, they say" 165

Chapter Five: "The land will stand for you". 197

Conclusion 229

Acknowledgements 236

Appendix 1: Intangible Cultural Heritage Inventory Card. 241

Appendix 2: Inventory Guidelines. 244

Appendix 3: Useful Resources. 246

Notes. 247

Bibliography 271

Index 293

List of Figures

3   **Figure 1.** Richard Morrison at his home, his hands dirty from making a pipe bowl out of pipestone. Photo © Agnieszka Pawłowska-Mainville (APM).

25   **Figure 2.** Map of *akiwenziyag* and *kitayatisuk* communities and territories. For over fifteen years, I travelled across this vast space of the boreal forest around these communities. Map design by Weldon Hiebert. Contains information licensed under the Open Government Licence–Canada.

29   **Figure 3.** Some of Frances Valiquette's notebooks given to me to "do something with." © APM.

34   **Figure 4.** The Poplar River at Poplar River First Nation, near the rapids. © APM.

36   **Figure 5.** *Azadiiwag*, poplar trees, growing along the waterways, rendering Poplar River true to its name. © APM.

40   **Figure 6.** This map shows the distribution of the 1,157 world heritage properties. Although the cultural, natural, mixed, and in danger properties are distributed all over the globe, a heavy concentration of the sites is in Europe. An interactive map of the various sites can be accessed on the UNESCO website. Source: https://whc.unesco.org/en/list/.

40   **Figure 7.** The graph illustrates the inscribed natural, cultural, and mixed properties by continent. Adapted from whc.unesco.org/list/stat. © APM.

52   **Figure 8.** Walter Nanawin, in his typical manner of running his fingers through his hair, taking a rest from his portable sawmill, which he used to start a woodworking business. © APM.

56   **Figure 9.** Walter and Jean Nanawin at their kitchen table. © APM.

59   **Figure 10.** Walter's forefather Chief Jacob Nanawin and his wife, Sarah, after their wedding, around 1900. Walter gave me a photocopy of the photo to keep and use. © APM.

59   **Figure 11.** Undated photo of Walter's family during one of the early Treaty Days. Walter is the young boy in the front holding a hat. © APM.

65   **Figure 12.** Ken Douglas looks at a map and shares stories of his trapping life.

77   **Figure 13.** Abel Bruce and I having lunch near Mukatewasipe, his trapline area.

79   **Figure 14.** Abel bringing a map to life with his stories. © APM.

120 **Figure 15.** One of the islands on Ottertail Lake where fasters may spend up to seven nights alone and without any food or fire. © APM.

125 **Figure 16.** Three generations: Richard, *ogozisan*, his son, and *oozhishenyan*, his grandchild, putting out tobacco together prior to learning about medicines, pipe making, and Anishinaabe *gigikinoo'amaagoowinan*, teachings. Photo © John Mainville.

128 **Figure 17.** In this photo, Richard is pointing across the river to a site of an old community where he spent much of his formative years before his family was moved to Nigigoonsiminikaaning. © APM.

134 **Figure 18.** Abel Bruce pulling out the medicines he collects. © APM.

143 **Figure 19.** Abel Bruce and John Mainville exchanging tobacco harvesting knowledge. © APM.

154 **Figure 20.** The process of ICH culture loss and rebuilding across generations. While community ICH in Generation A is strong because of social interactions and intergenerational transmission, members of Generation B separate due to migration, land dispossession, or other forms of community disintegration. These external factors leave Generation C with individual ICH custodians separated from each other and their inheritors. Transmission can take place in Generation B and/or C. In Generation B, transmission may occur but there are few social connections. In Generation C individuals can heal, reconnect, and revitalize their ICH. New communities and "outsider" ICH knowledge holders are created for the purpose of transmission. Note that Generations A through C may not necessarily represent three generations; the processes occurring in Generation B, C, and Generations B and/or C may take multiple generations in real time. © APM.

167 **Figure 21.** Map of the Keeyask EIS project area and heritage sites within Makeso Sakahican territory. As Noah Massan pointed out, very few dots marking a heritage site are present on the Fox Lake Cree Nation territory and on his trapline. Source: Map 1-1, "Heritage Resources and Study Areas with Registered Archeological Sites," in *Keeyask Generation Project: Environmental Impact Statement*, supporting volume, *Socio-Economic Environment, Resource Use and Heritage Resources*, part 3 "Heritage Resources" (Keeyask Hydropower Limited Partnership, 2012), 1–42. Accessed from https://keeyask.com/wp-content/uploads/2012/07/KeeyaskGP_HR_SV_1of1.pdf.

178 **Figure 22.** Noah Massan on the Kichi Sipi, pointing to an old campsite. © APM.

179 **Figures 23 and 24.** Erosion of the shorelines prevents local people from accessing traditional campgrounds or even going on shore, rendering water travel nearly impossible for Noah and others. © APM.

184 **Figure 25.** Photo of a fox dismembered by a Hydro worker, found by Noah near his trap. Photo © Noah Massan, used with permission.

189 **Figure 26.** Photo of the stuffed animal that was put in Noah's trap by Hydro employees. Photo © Noah Massan, used with permission.

190 **Figure 27.** Photos of the construction of the Keeyask Generating Station (Figures 27–33), show the impacts to Noah's trapline, before flooding and the building of the dam. Note that in this image of a quarry, there are spruce trees in the background, and the sign that says "Danger: Sudden Drop." The quarries are built alongside the road on the way to Keeyask. © APM.

190 **Figure 28.** Transmission lines from previous dams tower over the trees and the local landscape. © APM.

191 **Figure 29.** Construction work: new facilities, loud trucks, and other vehicles replace the boreal forest landscape. Note the dense spruce in the background, as well as the dug-up and torn trees ripped from the soil, commonly known as a slash pile. © APM.

191 **Figure 30.** Construction cranes and permanently damaged shorelines at the Keeyask rapids. This will be the site of the Keeyask Generating Station. It is probably one of the last photos of the *Keeyasko* (gull) rapids in their natural state. After the dam blocks the river, they will forever disappear. © APM.

192 **Figure 31.** An army of trucks stand like soldiers to construct the dam. Note the ground: the pounded rocks and gravel replace the swamps of the northern landscape. © APM.

192 **Figure 32.** Construction alters the landscape, exposing rock and filling the air with dust, noise, and machinery. © APM.

193 **Figure 33.** Not too far down this main road to the Keeyasko rapids, Noah points to a place on the right, stating that the beaver have built their own dam and flooded a large space of the forest adjacent to this road. Laughing, Noah says that "the beaver are fighting back." © APM.

195 **Figure 34.** Noah's trapline is scattered with different types of signs, many of which insist on authorization or no access/no trespassing to the area.

220 **Figure 35.** Richard Morrison putting out tobacco prior to harvesting sweetgrass to show respect and appreciation for the plant. Photo © John Mainville, used with permission.

Glossary of Anishinaabemowin and Inninumowin Terms

To help with the terminology, below is a list of several Anishinaabemowin (Ojibwe) and Inninumowin (Cree) words. In many cases, translations are provided immediately after terms where they are used within the text. Although there are different dialectical pronunciations and varying spellings of some terms, I used the Double Vowel or Fiero orthography, which is becoming widely recognized as the spelling system to use.* In some cases, I have retained the original spelling, as that is how community members have used it.

aadizookaan(ag)	a sacred story, myth, legend, spirit, oral history; "teaching(s)"
achimowin(an/ak)	story(ies) (Inninumowin)
aki(ing)	land/earth/dirt; "land and all living beings"; landscape

* Many Anishinaabemowin and Inninuwak speakers have instilled in me much of the vocabulary and language used in this book. I am especially thankful to my Anishinaabemowin teachers Pat Ningewance, Roger Roulette, and Lloyd Swampy, who introduced me to the language, and I am forever indebted to the *akiwenziyag* who spent time waiting for me to learn the language, especially Richard Morrison, who had a passion for showing me the "Old Ojibwe." Stuart Roy has been fundamental in helping me to work in and to appreciate the intricacies of the language. I also relied on language books to ensure terms are spelled correctly and translated using the Fiero orthography. My Anishinaabewibii'an skills are significantly stronger as I can work on the language by myself at home; since I don't have a lot of opportunity to speak in the language with language-speakers, my Anishinaabemotaw is significantly weaker. I take full responsibility for any mistakes and any misconceptions about the meanings of the terms.

aki gikendamowin	land-based knowledge
aki(iwi) miijim	"land food," which I identify as the Anishinaabe food system. While all food was traditionally "land food" (i.e., just food), with the introduction of store-bought food, the distinction between the two sources of nutrition has been created and, linguistically, people refer to harvested diets as "land food" or "our food."
aki mazina'igan(an)	maps; "earth books"
akiwenzi(yag)	literally, "man of the land/man who walks the land," but often used in the context of "Old Man" or "man who knows his land." I use this Anishinaabemowin term interchangeably with knowledge holder, culture keeper, and ICH custodian.
Anishinaabe(g)	human beings; Ojibwe person(s)
Asatiwisipe Aki	"Poplar River earth/land/dirt/landscape and all living beings," the homeland of the Asatiwisipe Anishinaabeg or Poplar River First Nation (also referred to as Asatiwisipe Anishinaabeg, Azatiiziibing Anishinaabeg, Asatiwisipe First Nation, Azaadiwi-ziibi Nitam-Anishinaabe). When italicized, *asatiwispe aki(ing)* refers to the bush or to the traditional territory/traplines.
asemaa	tobacco; one Anishinaabeg member interpreted the term to signify "link to the Spirits"
bimaadiziwin	life or "way of living"; "living the people's way of life" or "conducting oneself like the Anishinaabeg"

Binesiiwapigon Zaagai'gan/ Pinesewapigung Sagaigan	Weaver Lake; literally, "Thunder Mountain Lake"
dibaajimowin(an)	story(ies), narratives that are true; "stories heard and passed on"
dibaajimowininiwag	storytellers who use their knowledge and experience to teach, usually Elders of the community *dadibaajimowininiwag*
doodem	clan
Gete-Anishinaabeg/ Gichi-Anishinaabeg	the Old People, Elders, People of Long Ago
Gichi-Ginebig	Big or Great Snake
gikendamowin	knowledge, "way of knowing" or process of knowledge creation; an aggregate of wisdom gained from personal and life experience on the land as well as from the collective culture
gikinoo'amaagoowin(an)	teachings, education, a lesson; also spelled *ikino'amaagewinan*
inaakonigewin	law/protocol; a system of authority for the way people perform certain practices or conduct themselves on the land
Inninu(wak)	enthonym for the Cree living in Northern Manitoba; some individuals used the term Inninu, others used the term Cree to articulate their identity.

ji-ganawewndamang Gidakiiminaan	land stewardship approach, "we look after the land"
kitayatis(uk)	(Inninumowin) land user(s), harvester(s), an equivalent of the Ojibwe term *akiwenzi*, knowledge holder/ICH custodian
madoodoswa(a)n	generally translated as sweatlodge [structure], but Richard Morrison shares that the term can literally mean the "space under your mother's breast". *Madoodoo['iwe]* can be translated to "participating in a sweat[lodge] ceremony [s/he runs]."
Makeso Sakahican Inninuwak	Fox Lake Cree, also Fox Lake Cree Nation
manoomin	northern (wild) rice
mashkiki inini	medicine man
mashkikiwan	medicines
Memegwesiwag	"Little People who live in rocks in/near the water and who control the wind"
mino-bimaadiziwin and mino-pimatisiwin (Inninumowin)	the good life, the balanced life, living a healthy live; "continuous rebirth"
Mukatewasipe	Black River; "river that is black"

onjinewin and oohcinowe (Inninumowin)	"consequences from bad actions and decisions or from inappropriate conduct, especially when done to/ on the landscape
opwaagan(ag)	pipe(s); literally, "you blow through"
Pimachiowin Aki	name of the World Heritage Site; "the land that gives life"

Stored in the Bones

Introduction

We are driving down the main highway in Northwest Ontario to Richard's home area. Richard Giigwegiigaaboo Morrison is a *mashkiki inini*, Medicine Man, and today we are going to look for *opwaaganisin*, pipestone. Right now, we are passing through Couchiching First Nation, and Richard identifies an old brick building that used to be his residential school. He follows up with a story about an encounter with an old man in a restaurant. The man had been a pilot who picked up children and took them to the residential schools. Decades later, the former pilot recognized Richard in the restaurant, came up to him, and apologized for his role in the residential school system. Richard thanked him for offering those words of remorse.

As we approach the immense bridge that connects Richard's Treaty 3 territory to Fort Frances, the closest town, the landscape changes from swamps and wetlands to that of the Canadian Shield. With exposed boulders descending into dark waters and windblown pines anchored to massive rocks, the view is exemplary of the "Canadian North." The area is recognized for its prime fishing and hunting, with many back-country opportunities offered to American tourists. Deep-green spruce, pine, and cedar trees dot the hilly landscape, and the smell of fresh cedar occasionally mixes with the odour of the International Falls (Minnesota) paper mill located across the border. Treaty 3 territory in Northwest Ontario is a discursive crossroad, where the same Canadian Shield landscape is constructed in dichotomous ways: simultaneously dirty and pristine, at once an ugly reminder of colonial legacy and an example of pristine wilderness. Steeped in the forces of political economy, power relations, and the "northern experience," these treaty lands are constructed and perceived as both a resource-rich hinterland and a deeply political "Indian land." This area, what local people call "the bush," is also the centre of the world for local Anishinaabeg like Richard and his family.

We continue driving for some time, the forest landscape blurring by. We drive attentively: if we focus too much on the endless highway, we will miss the sign for Nigigoonsiminikaaning, Richard's community. The mouth of Red Gut Bay is at the centre of the reserve, but Richard's parents raised him, along with twelve siblings, on a trapline further down the lake. This is where we are heading. From the truck, Richard points to some tall poplar trees along the highway and says that when their leaves tremble like that, it is as if they are waving at him, welcoming him home. It makes him happy to see the warm welcome. We go past the community and turn onto a dirt road. As the truck weaves left to right on the meandering path, my two-year-old daughter giggles at the bumpy ride. Enjoying the sound of her laughter, Richard exaggerates the truck's movements.

We stop in the middle of an isolated area and walk uphill through tall grasses. Richard guides us through the bush confidently and looks behind some boulders to find the specific spot for *opwaaganisin*, pipestone. As we walk, he indicates a few trees, identifies them in Anishinaabemowin, and explains what ailments they are used for. He picks a few plant leaves

Figure 1. Richard Morrison at his home, his hands dirty from making a pipe bowl out of pipestone.

and puts them in his pocket. He reveals a patch of healthy sumac, and we pick a straight branch to be cut and hollowed out. "This will be good for a pipe stem," Richard says. "It is soft on the inside but strong and straight. Good for a pipe." We climb behind a few rocks and put *asemaa*, tobacco, on the ground before we dig into the exposed hillside with a small stone and then with our fingers. Richard takes a chunk of bluish-brown-black rock from out of the ground near the surface and declares that this piece "is smooth and does not have any veins in it. It will make a nice, strong pipe." He points out that black pipestone is the most prized and scratches its surface to show us the powder's distinctive tint. I ask if many people still make their *opwaaganag*, pipes. Richard replies that very few people can identify pipestone and even fewer people know where to find good *opwaaganisin*: "Not a lot of people make pipes anymore because not a lot of people smoke 'em," he says. "They just get it from someone or buy it from the pawn shop, and never use it. Me, I light that pipe up every day. It's good to do that 'cause it keeps you connected to . . . to everything."[1] We take a rock the size of Richard's foot and return to the truck.

Back at his house, Richard takes out his power tools (Figure 1). With water splashing around and chips of rock shooting out, Richard uses a power bench-grinder to cut the rock into a small rectangle. He then uses a small rotary tool to cut a rough shape of the pipe bowl. Once the appropriate size is reached, the next step requires using delicate leather to smooth down all the edges. It is a laborious task that takes my husband and me a few days to complete. We take turns polishing the stone and begin making the pipe stem. To make the stem, the centre needs to be carefully taken out of the sumac so that the smoke can pass through. The ends are then shaped to fit a person's mouth on one end and the pipe bowl on the other. Because these actions must be done patiently and in a specific order, this time-consuming process takes us over a month. Richard reminds us that following the proper technique is important so that an individual does not get burned or choke on smoke from a congested pipe. It takes skill to make a good pipe.

At one point during our work, a Treaty 3 community member inquires into what the stem and the polished rock are. When we tell him that we are polishing the sharp edges of a pipe bowl, he replies that if he were to make a pipe, he would do it traditionally. The notion of "traditional" is often used to describe Indigenous activities and knowledges, and for this man, making pipes "traditionally" probably included an old man chipping away at the rock using bones, rocks, or a knife. His comment confirms the complexity around the term "traditional" and the oft-unspoken reality that knowledge holders like Richard rely on power tools and "modern" materials to carry out "traditional" activities. Using machinery to make pipes, air compressors to skin animals, and aluminum wiring to make traps only proves creativity and demonstrates that skills and knowledge are alive rather than frozen in time. Later, laughing at the man's comment about his pipe-making skills, Richard observes that "it would take someone a *really* long time to use a rock to shape a rock."[2]

For Richard, it is not how a pipe is made that is important, but that the practice of pipe-smoking exists. Sharing that smoking every day gives him energy and "strengthens his bones," Richard discloses that his Elders insisted on smoking the pipe every day because the ceremony connects people to the spirits as well as to the *dibaajimowinan*, stories/narratives, and *aadizookaanag*, sacred stories/sacred teachings. He continues, explaining that

> for us, each new pipe must be lit up from another pipe, *opwaagan*. It's a ceremony. You take someone's pipe and light it up so that the fire from the pipe can be used to light up the new pipe. That pipe will light up another [new] pipe. And that pipe will be used to light up another pipe. Each pipe was lit up by the same fire. This means that each pipe [up] to now was lit up by the original pipe. That original fire can be traced up the generations to the first pipe [that was lit] by the Anishinaabeg. *Ani-shi-naabe*, "man lowered from the stars." It's where the heart sits. All the pipes come from that [original] man and from *opwaagan*, that first pipe.[3]

Smoking the pipe connects people with one another; it also connects them to their ancestors, allowing people to learn sacred stories. For Richard, the practice also signifies an exchange of stories that are lived today, stories that current generations add to the wealth of knowledge about his cultural traditions. While he interprets *dibaajimowinan* to be "like the spirit travelling around," Richard emphasizes that we need stories about "the experience of life" as much as we need *aadizookaanag*, the sacred stories. Stories, all stories, are needed because "they are teachings. They energize and strengthen my bones as I walk this Earth."[4]

Like that initial spark used to "wake up" the first pipe and each consecutive pipe, the *dibaajimowinan* and *aadizookaanag* are also passed from generation to generation to "energize and strengthen bones" of the people. The Medicine Man shares that in the old language, people understood *aadizookaan* to also mean "spirit, inside. Inside my bones. *Aadizoo* is like a 'life experience of the ancestors.' People who tell stories, who know stories so well [that] they are stored in your bones."[5]

Intangible Cultural Heritage

This book is about intangible cultural heritage (ICH) and the ways that Indigenous people[6] can use the concept to "energize and strengthen their bones as they walk this Earth." Specifically, this book is a compilation of stories from the *akiwenziyag* and *kitayatisuk* who live their intangible cultural heritage elements and who can use the ICH framework to strengthen their way of life. *Akiwenzi* (in Aanishinaabemowin/Ojibwe) can be literally translated as "man of the land/man who walks the land" or "land user,"[7] and refers to a "man who knows his land" because he has spent most of his life on the trapline.[8] *Kitayatis* (in Inninumowin [Cree]) refers to a similar idea, and the Inninuwak frequently refer to local harvesters/land users and knowledge holders as *kitayatisuk* (plural).[9] This book centres *akiwenziyag* and *kitayatisuk* lived experiences within the discourse of ICH. For the men presented in this book, certain "in-the-moment" actions are a form of cultural performativity.[10] Performed naturally, "like a fish in water," cultural heritage elements of individual knowledge holders are revealed not only through tangible elements gathered and stored in certain places but also by living experiences that are practised and transmitted "to the bone." The moment Richard Morrison ceases the gesture of putting down a spirit plate, the opportunity for his sons to transmit this relational activity to their children is erased; the moment the Poplar River trapper Abel Bruce stops the practice of putting down tobacco, his nephew and trapping helper, Willie, will stop performing the act when harvesting. When Noah Massan, an Inninu trapper whom we will meet in Chapter 4, no longer monitors Manitoba Hydro's work on his trapline, the woodland caribou and the squirrels will not be cared for on the project site. The ICH discourse tells us that the processes of cultural heritage are fragile, and if they are not maintained, they disappear. Cultural viability and transmission are thus the focus of ICH work and the goal of this book.

After the destruction caused by the two world wars, the United Nations Educational, Scientific and Cultural Organization (UNESCO) pursued numerous state-driven efforts at cultural preservation. Substantiating people's ability to rebuild after conflict in the twentieth century, the organization developed various legal instruments to protect humanity's diverse heritages. These instruments were devoted to tangible cultural expressions following a time of armed conflict, and the evaluation of heritage was based on "an objective and standardized perception of their artistic, aesthetic, architectural, visual, scientific, and economic value."[11]

More recently, cultural diversity and distinct traditions of humanity have been recognized as progressively and dangerously tending toward uniformity and disappearance.[12] Globalization, rapid processes of industrialization, migration of peoples, and the abandonment of traditional employment, practices, and livelihoods have contributed to the disappearance of many cultural elements.[13] Technological developments, socio-political dynamics, linguistic exclusivity, and the destruction of resources tied to culture have likewise contributed to the alarming diminishment of human innovation. Indigenous peoples have been especially prone to colonial fascination, which has led to large-scale confiscation of their cultural products for museums, study, and romanticized aesthetic value.[14] Fearful of the "vanishing Indian" yet motivated by the precepts of "civilization," Christianity, and assimilation, state representatives, anthropologists, and missionaries stole or bought

Indigenous artifacts and sacred items. The state also prohibited Indigenous cultural and ceremonial practices.[15] While injustice rooted in colonialism still affects Indigenous peoples, the enduring diversity of Indigenous cultures and languages in Canada also indicates their resilience against forces of assimilation and homogenization.

Cultural uniformity and disappearance of diversity signify "not only loss of cultural heritage—conceived as the totality of perceptible manifestations of the different human groups and communities that are exteriorized and put at the others' disposal—but also standardization of the different peoples of the world and of their social and cultural identity into a few stereotyped ways of life, of thinking, and of perceiving the world."[16] Since ICH is based on people's interaction with nature and their history, and constantly recreated by communities and groups, preservation of ICH also safeguards intellectual processes and world views. Although ancient tools as well as ceramics, masks, human remains, and structures found in museums remain important sources of heritage, the ICH discourse permits viewing living expressions of culture as the idiosyncratic traits of communities and nationhood. As a socio-cultural process tied to the legacy of tangible things like artifacts, ICH brings such objects (often museum-held) to life and provides modern-day context on their significance. Protection of ICH, therefore, includes safeguarding the immaterial, meaning the processes and conditions of heritage as well as their associated cultural products.

While ICH has existed as long as human society has existed, the international legal framework for its protection only emerged in 2003 with the UNESCO Convention for the Safeguarding of the Intangible Cultural Heritage (hereafter "the ICH Convention" or "the 2003 Convention"). Emphasizing the idea that heritage is "living" because it is performed by people and communicated from one generation to another through lived experience, the ICH Convention serves as an important instrument for the protection and enhancement of humanity's cultural heritage. Because it is mediated by humans, ICH exists and transmits in real time: the moment tobacco is offered to an Elder, who then imparts wisdom; the brief period when a powwow side-step song is sung and listened to; or when a Dakelh ghuni proverb is recited and heard. ICH transmission is a two-way process: if something is to be transmitted, there must be someone there to receive and absorb the transmission. Informal social interactions shape the way people experience and reproduce cultural memory and performativity of their heritage,[17] and the ICH Convention helps safeguard these interactions.

Broad in scope, UNESCO's 2003 Convention offers an intentionally vague definition of intangible cultural heritage as "the practices, representations, expressions, knowledge, skills—as well as the instruments, objects, artifacts and cultural spaces associated therewith—that communities, groups and, in some cases, individuals recognize as part of their cultural heritage."[18] UNESCO proposes five broad domains through which ICH is manifested. I have also provided several examples to illustrate the immense diversity of elements that can fall within each domain. The domains include

1. Oral traditions and expressions, including language as a vehicle of the intangible cultural heritage (for example, songs, stories, proverbs, orations, linguistic oral expressions, narratives of experience and memory, ritual recitals, prayers, lamentations, speeches, customary oral transactions, animal calls, soundscapes).

2. The performing arts (for example, musical performances, vocal and instrumental sounds, dances, dramas, operas, concerts and displays with an audience, musics, and soundscapes).

3. Social practices, rituals, and festive events (for example, life rituals and coming-of-age ceremonies such as vision quests,

name changes, baptisms, weddings, funerals; local and ecological rites, spells, religious and/or spiritual ceremonies, seasonal acts, games, recreation, folklore, governance systems, social organization, philosophies, intellectual traditions).

4. Knowledge and practices concerning nature and the universe (for example, cultural and local knowledges [also referred to as "traditional ecological knowledge"], citizen science, weather and seasonal rituals, cultural medicine, cultural meteorology, star knowledge, informal pedagogies, epistemologies and ontologies, customs and practices associated with the world and relating to it).

5. Traditional artisanship and craftsmanship (for example, skills and use of technology associated with creating, building, artwork, harvesting; production and improvement of something, innovative ways to create; musical instruments).[19]

Although many elements, such as music, overlap or can be included in every domain, the domains are helpful in categorizing cultural elements for the purpose of safeguarding. The domain list is very flexible, and countries and communities may add other domains or create different categories for their ICH.

To promote their unique heritage elements, State Parties may place elements on national registers and even nominate elements to UNESCO's Representative List of the Intangible Cultural Heritage of Humanity, or the UNESCO List of Intangible Cultural Heritage in Need of Urgent Safeguarding. While the first list is a collection of cultural expressions and practices that exhibit humanity's cultural richness and to raise awareness, the latter list identifies items that require urgent measures and assistance from stakeholders to sustain ICH vitality.[20] The Register of Good Safeguarding Practices contains projects and activities that best reflect the objectives of the Convention. Between the Convention's adoption in 2003 and 2023, there were 677 elements corresponding to 140 countries inscribed on the Representative List and the List of ICH in Need of Urgent Safeguarding, making the Convention one of the fastest UNESCO documents to be ratified by State Parties (the 2003 Convention currently has 180 States Parties among the 193 UNESCO member states).[21] In 2023 alone, sixty nominations are being considered by the Intergovernmental Committee for the Safeguarding of Intangible Cultural Heritage at its eighteenth session. With countries compiling their own national lists/registers, the number of cultural elements inventories throughout the world is even higher (Brazil, for example, has over 1,000 elements inscribed on its national registry). The ongoing cultivation of the UNESCO and numerous state lists across the globe (including the work of states that are not party to the ICH Convention) reveals that concern over the wealth of humanity's diversity is growing worldwide. The ICH discourse has consequently increased the awareness of the immediate need for heritage protection.

The ICH elements registered at the international level provide a glimpse into the global richness of people's ways of life. Examples of elements on the two UNESCO lists include the gingerbread technique from northern Croatia, the craft of Alençon needle lacemaking in France, the cultural space of the Semeiskie community in Russia, and the places of memory and living traditions of the Otomí-Chichimecas people of Tolimán in Mexico. While needle lacemaking in the Basse-Normandie region of France is a symbol of Alençon identity passed down from generation to generation,[22] the Otomí-Chichimecas places of memory encompass the symbolic and spiritual meanings and practices related to nature that are rooted in the value system of the community, thus constituting an important part of its social life and providing the people with a sense of identity and continuity.[23] The UNESCO Representative List of the Intangible Cultural Heritage of Humanity [hereinafter Representative

List] also holds Korean lyrical folk songs, the worship of Hùng kings in Phú Thọ, Viet Nam, and earthenware pottery-making skills of the Bakgatla ba Kgafela community in southeastern Botswana. The Chinese Zhusuan, a time-honoured traditional method of performing mathematical calculations by moving beads along the abacus rods according to defined formulas, was added to the UNESCO Representative List in 2013. Italy forwarded Neapolitan pizza making to the UNESCO Representative List in 2016, and Cambodia listed the martial art of Kun Lbokator as an intangible cultural heritage element in 2022. In 2021, a group of sixteen nations had Arabic calligraphy inscribed to the Representative List. German theatres and the Danish custom of snuggling in fuzzy sweaters by the fire—known as *hygge*—were added in 2017, and Uganda has barkcloth making on the Representative List and five other elements inscribed on the List of Intangible Cultural Heritage in Need of Urgent Safeguarding.

In 2020, the United Arab Emirates placed Al Aflaj, the traditional irrigation system with its associated knowledge, construction skills, and equitable water distribution on the UNESCO Representative List of the Intangible Cultural Heritage of Humanity. That year, the traditional knowledge of the Indigenous peoples of the Putumayo jungle in Colombia associated with mopa-mopa wood was also added to the List of ICH in Need of Urgent Safeguarding. In 2021, a collective of twenty-four nations nominated falconry as a living human heritage, demonstrating that vastly different cultures relate to the same practice and the falcon in their own way.[24] This is also the case of throat singing, which was inscribed by Mongolia (where this art is called Khoomei), and by Denmark, who identified Inuit drum dancing and singing as symbols of equity and equality in Greenland. Finally, in 2022, four safeguarding practices were nominated to the Register of Good Safeguarding Practices. In all these cases, while governments may be promoting the elements internationally, it is the communities and individuals who identify and ensure their cultures continue.

Working at the national and international level, the ICH Convention promotes, protects, and brings awareness to cultural heritage across the world through the identification and safeguarding of ICH elements. The Convention interprets safeguarding as measures "aimed at ensuring the viability of the intangible cultural heritage, including the identification, documentation, research, preservation, protection, promotion, enhancement, transmission, particularly through formal and non-formal education, as well as the revitalization of the various aspects of such heritage."[25] ICH work can be understood in three ways: (1) ICH safeguarding (protection, revitalization, at-risk heritage preservation), where specific steps are taken to sustain the practices; (2) ICH education, where attempts are made to transmit the ICH through diverse programs and institutions; and (3) ICH in everyday life, where a grandmother plays music and dance with a grandchild, or a family member transmits a skill such as carving, calligraphy, or cooking in the home. In this last expression, the activities are often done for leisure or livelihood, but they can incorporate tourism when they occur during cultural festivals or as part of workshops in established cultural zones. For instance, I have seen girls teach their younger cousins the techniques of a shawl dance at a powwow in Manitou, Ontario, and I observed old women in the tiny Kashubian village of Chłapowo in Poland sit in front of their homes and churn butter in traditional oak-plungers while summer tourists walked by, making their way to the beaches of the Baltic Sea.

Documenting ICH elements allows communities to enhance the survivability and revitalization of their cultural heritage; however, along with its Operational Directives and Ethical Guidelines, the ICH Convention also provides some foundational principles associated with safeguarding. This includes the recognition of human rights and respect between people as well as environmental sustainability. Similarly, while encouraging State Parties to respect the "dynamic and living nature" of ICH,[26] UNESCO warns that concepts like "authenticity" and "exclusivity" can become obstacles to safeguarding.[27] Safeguarding "does not mean fixing or freezing intangible cultural heritage in some pure or primordial form."[28] On the contrary, safeguarding measures consist of strengthening and reinforcing the "diverse and varied circumstances, tangible and intangible, that are necessary for the continuous evolution and interpretation"[29] of ICH, as well as for its transmission to future generations. To survive, ICH must be relevant enough in a community that it is continuously recreated. As we saw in the opening paragraphs of this Introduction, this may mean accepting things like power tools for the purpose of ICH continuity. Richard's response about the inefficacy of "using a rock to shape a rock" (the pipestone) demonstrates that expressions like "primordial and pure" and "authentic heritage" or "doing things traditionally" significantly limit the transmission of living heritage.[30] Rather than a custom perishing along with its "traditional" means of existence, safeguarding occurs the moment generational transmission takes place.

The community-centred understanding of heritage is what makes ICH and the 2003 Convention unique: communities and families choose and define their ICH. More often than not, individuals working to transmit their culture are not even familiar with the concept of ICH or the term itself.[31] The technical term "intangible cultural heritage" helps identify cultural expressions in a systematic way, but this also means that there is a barrier between scholarly and institutional definitions and jargon, and lived experience, where ICH and living heritage are not classified the way UNESCO has attempted to do. In working with ICH custodians and in my own attempts at transmission, my experience is that practitioners focus their energies on cultural expressions they find important. These can be a part of their everyday life or a part of expressed efforts at transmission, such as a skill or cultural food that is a component of daily life in a non-dominant language environment. These embodied dispositions and habiti[32] are non-conscious and constant.[33] In other circumstances, cultural foods and skills can be emphasized in a household or community through taking or offering language classes or workshops and cultural "camps" on culinary traditions or a specific expertise. Safeguarding can also be both non-conscious and deliberate, such as learning or teaching a parental language through conscious efforts (repeating key commands) where cultural food is regularly consumed.[34] In all these cases, because the elements have been identified as important to maintain, transmission of cultural expression occurs—and usually without knowledge of UNESCO terminology and ICH.

The ICH discourse aims to enhance the conditions for cultural transmission. It helps communities establish protective measures over elements they find important and which require extra effort on their part to attain viability. Communities and families can decide which cultural expressions to transmit, and by engaging in safeguarding measures, it is communities that determine the extent of the meaning, value, descriptions, and steps to be taken for protection. This means that rather than the top-down approach associated with heritage "experts," a community-centred approach characterizes all activities that deal with protection.[35] This includes consent and participation of members, promotion, as well as continued access to the objects, artifacts, cultural landscapes, and places of memory they may need to express their ICH.

Because the ICH Convention is the best international instrument to identify and protect cultural heritages of the world, it is my argument that the ICH discourse can likewise become an instrument for mobilizing cultural heritage policies in Canada. Canada has not ratified the 2003 Convention, and although I explore some of the reasons why that is the case in Chapter 2, I believe that the ICH discourse is an attestation of the principles outlined in the 2007 United Nations Declaration on the Rights of Indigenous Peoples (UNDRIP), which Canada adopted in 2016.

Recognition of ICH can serve as a direct response to the Royal Commission on Aboriginal People's (RCAP) 1996 recommendations for a multi-stakeholder heritage network and "comprehensive inventory" of heritage sites[36] and to the Truth and Reconciliation Commission's (TRC) Calls to Action 6 through 16, which demand the establishment of "effective measures" for the protection of Indigenous languages, cultures, and culturally relevant pedagogies.[37] After UNDRIP, RCAP, and the TRC, the ICH discourse (and the 2003 Convention) can serve as the next step in truth and reconciliation: as Canada acknowledges its role in cultural disruption and ruptures in transmission, we can move to the initial step of reconciliation, where Indigenous peoples determine their own cultural values and mechanisms for conveyance. In the context of ICH, attaining reconciliation signifies intergenerational transmission of Indigenous languages and diverse cultural practices "to the bone." While the onus of transmission is on communities, tangible support from different levels of government toward ICH-related work and policies reinforces the avenues for transmission.

There is debate over the definitions, meanings, and preferred terms around "intangible cultural heritage."[38] In Canada, Quebec uses the term "patrimoine vivant" (living heritage) and the Canada Council for the Arts uses the term "expressions culturelles [traditionelles]" (cultural [traditional] expressions) to refer to ICH.[39] Some scholars dislike the term "intangible cultural heritage" not only because the term feels too technical but because it seems to separate heritage into tangible and intangible forms; for others, the term "living heritage" appears more accessible to the public but implies too much flexibility.[40] Certain countries employ terms such as "folklore" or "people's heritage" or "national heritage," or rely on specific cultures and nationhoods to express the term, such as "Latvian heritage" (Latvia) or "oral heritage of Gelede" (Benin, Nigeria, and Togo). I use "living heritage" and "intangible cultural heritage/ICH" interchangeably. Intangible cultural heritage is the term UNESCO uses, and while it helps to have consistency I also love hearing the word "living" in living heritage, illustrating culture as alive, living, and continuing. I also interpret living heritage as both a verb and a noun, with the latter referring to individuals who are the living embodiment of heritage, who merit the title of "Living Heritage."[41] These individuals are the bridge; the bodies that make the intangible tangible. The concept of living heritage requires us to consider the daily experiences of individuals from different social, cultural, and linguistic backgrounds, and the diverse strategies they employ to ensure intergenerational transmission, knowledge revival, and reconciliation. In my work with knowledge holders, however, definitions of ICH are less important than practical applications. Without debating the issue, many of the *akiwenziyag* and *kitayatisuk* interpreted heritage to be simply their "inherited history."

Although I discuss some of the complexities around the discourse of ICH, it is important to recognize that numerous terms in the discourse are "floating signifiers," meaning that words like "heritage," "culture/ nature," "tradition," "community," and "resource management" carry multiple meanings and interpretations.[42] The ICH framework does not cover these terms in a comprehensive way, and we must take into consideration multiple dynamics. It is impossible to articulate all obscurities and contradictions of these foundational concepts in one book. These different interpretations create opportunities for scholarship, and it is important to recognize that semantics should not undermine the importance ICH has in cultural heritage safeguarding. Similarly, while the focus of this work is on the intangible, cultural heritage is indivisible from its counterpart, tangible heritage. The two are inherently connected, as ancient buildings, bones, instruments, or other artifacts have much more meaning with their assigned values; this will be explored later in the book. Intangible heritage *creates* tangible heritage. Richard's pipe-making skills and his knowledge of a pipe ceremony are examples of intangible elements (skills and knowledge are immaterial) interwoven with tangible heritage (the pipe). Likewise, for this man and the other *akiwenziyag* and *kitayatisuk* in this book, land is the foundational source of ICH–based livelihoods and the space where their heritage performativity and narrative memory live.[43] By highlighting *akiwenziyag* and *kitayatisuk* lived experiences, I illustrate that their territories (tangible) give rise to the process of culture like knowledge systems, skills, and relationships (intangible). While this land-culture connection is extremely relevant to Indigenous peoples in Canada, numerous cultures and countries across the globe also use this socio-ecological relationality to identify and safeguard their ICH.

Conversely, many ICH elements are portable and can be lived out in different places. A recognition of ICH and the ICH framework highlights the evolving and living nature of culture though migrant or relocated communities. While many cultural elements are tied to particular landscapes, forced or preferred migration caused by war, economic or environmental circumstances, oppression or emigration for an improved quality of life also illustrate human resiliency and creativity. For this reason, many diverse and vibrant cultures exist in cities, and often within the same neighbourhoods. The ICH framework illustrates that culture moves with people: music and dance, for example, travel easily with migrating communities because they are portable and can be transmitted orally. And in instances where musical instruments cannot be transported, musical genres and styles can be transmitted and re-enacted—often with music making merging new migrant experiences and landscapes with commemorations of the homeland. In this regard, ICH custodians who merge socio-linguistic elements (e.g., an English-language song on an Anishinaabe-style hide drum) or historical circumstances (e.g., African-derived cultural traditions in Cuba in the Spanish language) offer new insight into how communities, families, and individuals practise their living heritages. While I explore some of these complexities elsewhere,[44] this work focuses on *kitayatisuk* and *akiwenziyag* narratives and their territories. Ultimately, the ICH discourse highlights the multiplicity of understandings of heritage and the need to safeguard the human intellectual processes that make up the diversity of living cultures.

By exploring the discursive range of ICH through the experiences of *akiwenziyag* and *kitayatisuk*, this book provides Indigenous people in Canada with another tool to safeguard and transmit their cultural heritages. An aim of this book is to bring the ICH discourse to Indigenous communities and their leadership. Land- or water-based wage earners, resource users, and culture keepers can find that the narratives of the *akiwenziyag* and *kitayatisuk* resonate with their lived experiences. The examples of ICH safeguarding and transmission efforts from across the globe presented here will hopefully inspire families, communities, and individuals in Canada to explore new ways to seek assistance and connect with other families and communities to safeguard their heritage.[45] Heritage practitioners, government officials at all levels, and scholars will benefit from the broad introduction to ICH and be equipped to participate in creating a new dialogue on cultural transmission. Interest in learning about the past and family ancestry is growing around the world,[46] so im/migrants, families, and individuals with an interest in cultural diversity and cultural transmission—their own or in general—may also find the ICH framework useful. Families and communities cannot afford to wait for governments to hold "cultural exhibitions" when they can be transmitting living cultures as part of their daily lives.

I will not wait.

Niin Miikanaang Akimazina'iganing, *"My Road Map"*

Cultural spaces permit Indigenous land users to live their heritages. This is the case for *asatiwisipe aki*, "Poplar River earth/land and all living beings," the homeland of Poplar River First Nation, a community that rarely gets placed on maps—and often gets misplaced. With a population of 1,200 people, this Northern Manitoba First Nation relies on its cultural and natural wealth to ensure sustainable livelihoods. Illustrating the power of small numbers, Chapter 1 examines the world heritage discourse through Poplar River's participation in the Pimachiowin Aki UNESCO World Heritage Site nomination.[47] In this chapter, I show that procedures and theoretical formulations around "world heritage" need reconfiguration to better accommodate land users and Indigenous people of the boreal forest landscape. Using an ICH lens to view the *asatiwisipe aki* cultural space, I demonstrate how the Anishinaabe cultural element of *ji-ganawendamang Gidakiiminaan*, "keeping the land approach/resource stewardship system," grounds territoriality and merges the nature/culture, tangible/intangible divides. In this space, *akiwenziyag* ICH is manifested in specific stories and traditions, actions, and utterances (some communicated without a word) that occupy the landscape, enabling many Asatiwisipe Anishinaabeg knowledge holders to read it like a book.

Chapter 2 looks at the 2003 UNESCO Convention for the Safeguarding of the Intangible Cultural Heritage and its importance to the safeguarding of Indigenous and all cultural heritages. Acknowledging the uniqueness and plurality of Indigenous societies, this chapter presents the framework for community-based ICH inventorying, also referred to as documentation. Canada's relationship to the ICH framework is discussed here; specifically, Canada's lassitude toward the 2003 Convention, as well as some examples of the incredible ICH-based work carried out by several provinces, municipalities, and organizations in the country. As ICH policies and programs are gaining momentum, they need careful evaluation, and in this chapter I also address some guidelines to consider when carrying out ICH work, including the benefits and challenges of inventorying and promoting ICH-related programs.

Epistemic conventions that root the *akiwenziyag* and *kitayatisuk* land-based social order across the territories include responsibility over, and relationship with, the cultural landscape. Drawn from heritage and shaped by time and history, the *akiwenziyag* and the *kitayatisuk* offer additional teachings to their living heritage. As they take on a helper, the *akiwenziyag* add their knowledges, traditions, and skills to a continuous livelihood. By using *Anishinaabewi aki miijim*, the local "land food" system, as an example of ICH, Chapter 3 highlights the immersive pedagogies used to transmit cultural livelihoods. Illustrating the complexity of this sovereign food system, I show how cultural protocols associated with the production, distribution, and disposal of food within *aki miijim* enhance heritage and land-based pedagogies. The exploration of this unique Anishinaabe food system illustrates how teaching *for* heritage can be implemented in many different instructional contexts. Relying on ICH pedagogies and *akiwenziyag*-inspired education, this chapter supports the plethora of voices advocating for ICH transmission through culturally relevant education in formal and non-formal settings. The ICH discourse provides an interpretation of lived experience that shapes the overlapping and multifarious ways of understanding intergenerational transmission; thus, ethical and retrospective deliberations are essential to cultural revival, human rights, and diversified economic pathways.

Discussing my experience of working with several Makeso Sakahican Inninuwak and *kitayatisuk* on the licensing of the Keeyask Generating Station in Northern Manitoba, Chapter 4 illustrates the need for ICH policy making, especially in environmental impact assessments. Drawing from my work at the Clean Environment Commission of Manitoba hearings with a grassroots group led by Inninuwak, I show that the metanarrative of consultations on resource development is not consistent with *kitayatisuk* lived experiences with Hydro Manitoba's infrastructure. From epistemological disagreements to limitations in the acknowledgement of Inninuwak knowledge and concerns, this chapter discusses how recognition of ICH can help to evaluate impacts more thoroughly and empower communities to better navigate their negotiations with industry.

I use examples and personal stories from my friendship with one *kitayatis* to help provide some context to these arguments.

Building on the need for more effective measures needed to safeguard Indigenous ICHs, Chapter 5 elaborates how ICH recognition broadens the Indigenous cultural rights discourse. The Supreme Court of Canada's emphasis on integral "customs, practices and traditions"[48] brings ICH elements into Canadian law through the Constitution, and this chapter highlights the need for re-interpretation of cultural processes in jurisprudence. In this spectrum of rights, I show how specific practices, skills, and knowledges embedded in intentional practices such as *ji-ganawendamang Gidakiiminaan*, the customary land and resource governance system, help sustain local economies and ecologies. The ICH framework can inspire meaningful reconceptualization of natural resource management practices and policies to include ICH transmission and sustainable livelihoods.

Recognizing that this book focuses on the *akiwenziyag*, the men, I acknowledge, recognize, and assert the immense and important role of women, the *[min]dimooyeyag*,[49] in cultural heritage safeguarding and transmission. In many instances, both during domestic labour and especially outside of it, women represent the first source of heritage for their children;[50] this is why gender-based violence (sexual, physical, and emotional) is frequently used as tool of oppression, war, and genocide.[51] The role of women in ICH transmission and safeguarding is so important and rich that it deserves its own book.[52] I briefly address my perspectives of women's role outside the domestic sphere in this work, but a broader analysis of women and gender in the ICH discourse is needed, and this is a task I aim to take on next.

Finally, as Richard shared in one of our conversations about resource management, the *akiwenziyag* and *kitayatisuk* are "just doing what they are supposed to."[53] By doing what they are supposed to, these men demonstrate that their cultures are present and living; by sharing what they do, this book attempts to re-present *akiwenziyag* living heritage as implicit acts of resistance against cultural homogenization and totalization.[54] My hope is that these *dibaajimowinan* (Anishinaabemowin) and *achimowinak* (Inninumowin)—stories or narratives—can capture gaps in current scholarship and political frameworks about natural and cultural heritage policies and management. This book is also a platform for the *akiwenziyag* and the *kitayatisuk* who rarely, if ever, go to professional conferences and government meetings to discuss the protection and transmission of the customs and traditions housed in their "bush museums." Consequently, this book is based on four main arguments: (1) Indigenous communities can fruitfully apply the ICH framework to safeguard their cultural and natural heritages; (2) the ICH discourse relating to "practices, customs and traditions" can enhance the current interpretation of *sui generis*, Aboriginal/Indigenous,[55] and treaty rights to mobilize territoriality; (3) attention to the ICH elements found in communities can effect tangible improvements in environmental and cultural policy making, especially in impact assessments; and (4) by providing the conditions for cultural and linguistic transmission for all Canadians, acknowledgement of the ICH framework by the federal government can be a step toward reconciliation and linguistic competencies. Recognizing cultural diversity as part of the public interest will enable our generation to ensure that intangible cultural heritage elements are "stored in the bones" of future generations.

The Rationale

This book has been written by a first-generation émigré from Poland. My own heritage impacts how I interpret my role as a Polish woman and mother in Canada: simultaneously colonizer and formerly colonized; White[56] yet with unique cultures and languages; indigenous/autochton-ous to Poland but not an "Indigenous person" in the Canadian legal understanding.[57] As an outsider and immigrant, I approach the topic of cultural heritage carefully, aware of the limits of my own cultural experience. Yet I am also aware of the opportunities for knowledge exchange between Indigenous communities and immigrants. Although our struggles are vastly different, individual attempts to pass on our cultures and languages in a largely homogenizing world bring us closer together.[58] Through my position as a Polish-Canadian woman, I have foregrounded land use as a platform for political struggle and "homeland" identity, and relied on the belief that both Indigenous and non-Indigenous people participate in and experience the colonial context. As *biiwide*, a stranger or cultural outsider in Anishinaabemowin, I have attempted to work within the existing political and legal situations in a way that brought forth positive change for the *akiwenziyag* and *kitayatisuk* I have grown to care for. I interpret *akiwenziyag* and *kitayatisuk* "grounded normativity"[59] as a vehicle for their living heritage and perhaps even a form of resistance; hence, this book is not about "Indigenous cultural heritage" but rather about *how* Indigenous people can use the ICH discourse to safeguard their heritages.

I was born in Toruń, Poland, and much of my upbringing was on the beautiful sandy beaches of the cold, navy-coloured Baltic Sea and its surrounding wind-blown landscapes. Poland endured two world wars, Stalinism, and a communist regime before finally joining the European Union; I am constructed from that history. As a young girl who did not speak a word of English upon arriving in Canada, I learned English and French in school and from books, one of which was *The Terrible Summer* by Richard Wagamese. The book was my first text on "Indigenous issues," and it fashioned my understanding of Canada. While speaking multiple languages permits me to peek into other world views, it has also excluded me from them, obscuring my notion of "native tongue" and "mother culture" as a singular manifestation. The foundation for this book, therefore, is the multiplicity of cultural values I hold and the outcome of

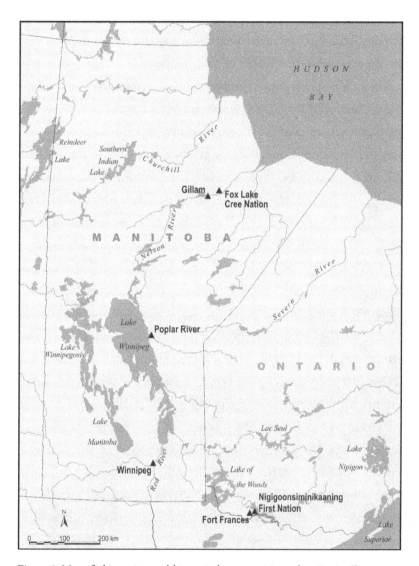

Figure 2. Map of *akiwenziyag* and *kitayatisuk* communities and territories. For over fifteen years, I travelled across this vast space of the boreal forest around these communities.

my decade-long relationships with several *akiwenziyag* and *kitayatisuk*. My fifteen-year involvement with community members from Poplar River First Nation, with Richard Morrison and his family, and with several Makeso Sakahican Inninuwak provide the basis for this work. While my involvement with the people of *asatiwisipe akiing* began when my collection of oral histories and land use stories served as part of my master's and doctoral work as well as a component of the community's "Plan B," the legal back-up plan for ancestral occupancy if the land protective measures were not achieved,[60] my grassroots work with the Makeso Sakahican *kitayatisuk* at the Manitoba Clean Environment Commission hearings for Keeyask extended from my employment with the Fox Lake Cree Nation Negotiations Office. I met Richard and his family as a master's student, and our friendship led to his becoming *nizinis*, my father-in-law.

This book represents travelling knowledges; it is a work that merges multiple cultures, perspectives, experiences, and geographies.[61] Figure 2 shows the home communities of the *akiwenziyag* and *kitayatisuk* with whom I travelled across this area of central and boreal Canada for almost fifteen years. From Nigigoonsiminikaaning through to Poplar River and Gillam, the knowledges I gained from one *akiwenzi* moved with me to another Anishinaabe knowledge holder in a different community or to the *kitayatisuk* in Gillam. Then some perspectives were sent back via another route. The continuous back-and-forth permitted the *kitayatisuk* and the *akiwenziyag* to learn about each other and from each other. At some point, Richard Morrison from Nigigoonsiminikaaning made the *opwaagan*, pipe, which made its way to Noah Massan in Gillam with tobacco harvested with Abel Bruce in Poplar River. My own heritages and immigrant experiences, and eventually children, contributed to our shared adventures, all of which permitted us to sprinkle our mutual stories across the boreal forest like autumn leaves.

Like the irreplaceable cultures of the Anishinaabeg *akiwenziyag* and Inninuwak *kitayatisuk*, Poland's languages and landscapes, its heritage and diverse ethnic customs are one of a kind. As a State Party to the 2003 ICH Convention, Poland is also striving to protect the diminishing diversity of cultural elements inside its borders, including those of sub-national entities and minority groups. My own attempts at maintaining and transmitting my culture and languages to my multiheritage children are similar to the struggles of other families in Canada. Supporting living heritage and engaging in a push for effective cultural safeguarding policy is what I research; practising resilience against cultural and linguistic loss, and finding persistence in transmitting cultural heritage to my children is what I live.

"Jako Polka, staram się przekazać język oraz kulturę polską i nasze wspólne tradycje swoim dziecią, nawet za granicą." As a multiheritage and multilingual family, we strive to transmit as many heritage elements to our two children as possible. *Agnieszka niin a'da noswin, Agnes*[62] *ndizhinikaaz Zhangaashiimo. Niin niswi nijaanisag dago ninaabem Anishinaabe. Zaagadikiing*[63] *niin d'onji minawaa 'waabishki miigizi' nin doodem. Niin a'da giigid aadizookaan Zaagadiiking/Poland*:

Mewinzha, gwa inini, Lech a'da noswin, biitaang wiigawaam matigwaaking wiiji-niizh osayenyanwag. Gwa giishik nakwek, omaamaayan a'gii naan: "A'pakadewag bemaadazijik. Gaawiin gegoo gii wiisinisii megwaa. Maajizh niizh gisayensag miinawaa mikan a'giyiiw." Ziigwan, niiw gwan a'gii ozhitaa, a gii'debanaak ningodwaaswe ganozhek, a'gii ziitaaganowaak miinawaa a'gii zagakanaak mashkimuting. Memdage gowendam, a'gii mi'pakwemaa giigoohn endaat. A'gii mi'naap osayenyan pimeyii kiikanaamade gamgong, biitokanaa giigoohn. "Waabang ani-maajaadaa gichi gizheb, a'da minwaate" a'gii kida. Naano diba'iganek shi aabita ishkwaa name giizhigak, a'gii maajad. A'gii zhagade'osek maatigwaakiing gwa mise miinawaa waayiikaa gaashakaawag, bootch niibaa. Aazhoo waabang, apii a'gii goshkozinwaad, a'gii waabaamawaad makwa. Gwa osayenyan a'noswin Rus, a'gii kida: "Ganabach a'ga biminizha'waa makwa." A'gii zhaa waabanong. Lech miinawaa osayenyan Czech, a'gii baabaamosewag ishkwa name giizhik [apii] a'gii waabamaan waawaashkeshi. Czech a'gii kida: "Niin a'ga biminizha'waa a'wa waawaashkeshi maadjiigaade'ose wajiwang." Czech a'gii patome zhaawanong awasajiw. Lech a'gii zhaame waabanong biinish a'gii izhi-zaagadikiing: "Miikawaadad waakapiming, ajina a'nii gaashakaa miinawaa bekaayaa." Lech a'nii nep naame maangat mitigomizh. Gezika a'gii naap waabishko-migiziwazison miinawaa made-babaamise waabishko-migizi. Ingwana Lech a'gii danaadizi gibe-niibin. A'gii nandawenjige miinawaa a'gii ogaake. Biichin a'gii godamowaa ode'iminan jiikaakwang swe dabagiiswaan. Dibikak a'gii waabaamaa waabishki-migizi apii a'gii gitiget. Gegapii, a'gii nidiza: "Aabadek pimachiowin aki. Niin a'da gichi zhiyaa maampi. Gaawiin pakadesii miinawaa niibana booji'waa'aaskwanewag maampi. N'ga ganonaak bemaadazijik bi-izhawag." Wiiwenh bemaadazijik a'gii zhaa'ok zaagadikiing miinawaa n'da gabegandaan waabishki-migizi odoodeman. Niin a'kii nin aadizookaan Poland'ning onjibaa minaawaa Russianing gaye Czech Republic'ning.[64]

Abel Bruce from Poplar River told me that since I have begun to understand some language and *akiwenzidiziwin*, the old way of life, I need to ensure the "*dibaajimowinan*, the stories that I tell you, here, now, are heard, passed on."[65] The narratives shared with me were frequently interwoven with Anishinaabemowin terms (and some Inninumowin and Oji-Cree terms) and I have built on them to articulate some concepts to the readers. I have kept the raw elements in numerous quotes—the pauses, repetitions, and hesitations—as they reflect the speakers' personalities and linguistic intonations.

In addition to the *dibaajimowinan*, I also received "unofficial archives"[66] from community members; these contributed to the work as well. In Poplar River, these archives consisted of notebooks that were compiled by one of the local Elders, Frances Valiquette. Frances, an elegant woman with earrings that always matched her outfits, was an avid collector of local histories and community events. In

Figure 3. Some of Frances Valiquette's notebooks given to me to "do something with."

the years 1974–81, she set out to summarize some of the changes the community went through since around the 1950s and wrote them in little spiral notebooks. One winter day after lunch, Willie Bruce, Abel's nephew, dropped off a box full of these notebooks so I could "do something with them." The handwritten notes recorded the thirty-year community history with dates, annotations, facts about local life, proposals for development, and diabetes prevention, as well as some personal reminders (Figure 3). Willie believed that these notebooks might have valuable information, and the people whose names are in the notebooks had all agreed to my reading of these journals. He wanted to see if I could include these journals in my research. Entrusted with the information, I "did something with them" by sifting through the seventeen notebooks to include data on *asatiwisipe aki* life for this book. Likewise, Elder Noel Bruce would hand me little handwritten notes with brief stories, facts, thoughts, and messages on what I could include in my research; I also regularly corresponded via mail with Walter Nanawin, a local Elder, who would send me elaborate letters with photos, stories, songs, and lists of Inninumowin terms I should know. It was the stories and poems in particular that he wanted me to "put in a book or somewhere," and I have met that promise by including Walter's many stories in this book.[67] The notes and letters were often written on loose ruled paper, on hotel stationary or on scrap paper; I even received notes on a paper napkin and on old photocopies of historical photos. Many of these are included here as well.

Similarly, my friend, Elder, *kitayatis*, and Makeso Sakahican Inninuwak trapper, Noah Massan, gave me his "files," which were essentially a large black plastic bag filled with documents from all the Hydro meetings he attended, the pamphlets he received, and the copies of legal arguments Manitoba Hydro presented to him about the benefits of more hydro development on his trapline. He told me to "see if anything is useful." Sifting through the papers, I found some maps and flyers outlining the details of the project(s)—all which were representations of "meaningful consultation" with the community. I found some contracts promising Noah more money and extra benefits for the damage to his land from development, all presented to him (and some signed) without a lawyer ever by his side. Noah and I examined many of these papers for evidence of Manitoba Hydro's dismissal of his voice opposing certain strategies. Despite attending almost all Hydro meetings for the past thirty years, and despite being openly opposed to much inappropriate behaviour by Manitoba Hydro and its workers, Noah never wrote anything down on paper; it is not what many *kitayatisuk* do. Of course, unlike many Hollywood movies with a montage and a happy ending, we did not find anything incriminating. But we did not need documentation delineating the Hydro-inflicted carnage to his trapline; the destruction of his family's trapline (twice!) was evidence enough.

When Poplar River was asked to submit "more evidence of their culture" to UNESCO, it made me think; when none of the rich elements of intangible Inninuwak culture were mentioned in the environmental assessment and in the hearings for the Keeyask hydroelectric project in 2013, I jotted down some notes. And when I examined this further and noticed evidence of unawareness (or ignorance) of ICH elements of Indigenous peoples of Canada in programs, traditional knowledge studies, land-occupancy maps, and especially in environmental regulatory policies, I began to write this book more passionately. Similar narratives on the need to find better cultural and environmental safeguarding measures came from Dakelh friends and colleagues in central British Columbia where I reside,[68] and kept me writing. The 2003 UNESCO Convention had been in existence for twenty years now, and most of the world had been working actively to protect cultural, Indigenous, folk, and human heritage; yet Canada was still not paying attention. Thus, I became determined to get the voices and living heritage of the *kitayatisuk* and the *akiwenziyag* "out there." In arguing that heritage be "stored in the bones," my hope is that communities and heritage practitioners will consider the ICH framework as an avenue for cultural safeguarding and transmission.

The notion of "stored in the bones" implies that culture lives through individuals and communities, not objects. In other words, the ICH custodians whose stories enrich this book represent the living heritage of their communities; that heritage is unique in the world. Culture lives and is transmitted through them. Exploring how territoriality and self-determination is founded on social, political, and economic practices as well as on individual efforts, in the twenty-first century, this work aims to provide Indigenous communities with a tool to "energize and strengthen their bones as they walk this Earth."

Chapter One
Living Heritage

Flying to Poplar River First Nation[1] in Manitoba, Canada, in a seven-seat plane during the hot summer is a different experience than driving eight hours to the community on an icy winter road during the cold months. Each way of travelling there is unique and, along with boat access in the summer, these are the only ways to reach *asatiwisipe akiing*, "Poplar River earth/land/dirt/landscape and all living beings." The drive to the community on the winter road allows one to see the morning frost at that special time right before the sun comes up, when snow-covered trees glitter with a hint of blue. In the winter, the whiteness that covers this enormous space parallels the splendour of the absolute silence of the night. Flying into the community in the summer months and seeing the "empty wilderness" beneath the plane's wings, one can appreciate the vastness of eastern Manitoba's boreal forest. Smelling like fresh pine, dry dust, and muskeg after a rainy day, the boreal forest covers about 53 percent of Canada's surface and at *asatiwisipe akiing*, it is among the last undisturbed boreal forest spaces on the planet. Numerous lakes, meandering rivers, and streams dot the thick greenness, freckling the vast surface like a human circulatory system that supplies air to the large, brown, lung-shaped Lake Winnipeg.

Figure 4. The Poplar River at Poplar River First Nation, near the rapids.

The sound of swishing water and wind is heard upon landing in the homeland of the Asatiwisipe Anishinaabeg.[2] The First Nation is a small fly-in community located on the east side of Lake Winnipeg at the mouth of the Poplar River. The natural landscape around Poplar River is exquisite with different shades of green, ranging from the penumbra of pine trees to the light green lichen on the exposed igneous boulders (Figure 4). The bright lushness of the wild grasses and reeds on the river shores adds to the range of colours that speckle the community. The "uninhabited" space that one flew over in the last hour is alive with plants and diverse four-legged and winged creatures that roar, play, splash, grunt, and bite. People occupy this "wilderness" too: relying on the waters and the forest for vital resources, the Anishinaabeg interpret *aki* as "the land and all life that emerges from and flows across the land. *Aki* includes all of the Creator's gifts of sun, water, wind, rain, fire, rock, soil, plants, and animals. *Aki* is also the source of life; all of the features, beings, forces, relationships, and processes that together make up the Land That Gives Life. For Anishinaabeg, the land is everything with which they share life; it is everything that Anishinaabeg depend on for survival and well-being."[3] The territory that surrounds Poplar River appears never-ending in every direction. The wind amplifies this spaciousness by rustling the poplar trees lining the main roads and rivers of the community and beyond (Figure 5). With a population of over twelve hundred people and a trapline territory that covers 8,617 square kilometres (800,000 ha), Poplar River is a unique landscape furnished with a rich heritage.

Asatiwisipe Aki *Cultural Landscape*

In the past decade, Poplar River First Nation has made a significant impact in Manitoba at the political and economic level. When the community wanted to protect its territory from logging and mining interests, members looked to their Anishinaabe and Oji-Cree values and laws; when the people collaborated with the Province of Manitoba to establish some form of permanent protection over their lands, they asserted their self-determination and customary governance. When in 2007 the Crown corporation Manitoba Hydro presented its plans to run a 500 kilovolt (kv) high voltage direct current transmission line along the east side of Lake Winnipeg, there was little consultation with local First Nations, including Poplar River.[4] Surprising many Manitobans (including Manitoba Hydro), the Anishinaabeg communities on the east side of Lake Winnipeg united and decidedly put a First Nations face on the boreal forest that year: they publicly announced their desire to protect their lands through a UNESCO World Heritage Site nomination called Pimachiowin Aki, an initiative

Figure 5. *Azadiiwag*, poplar trees, growing along the waterways, rendering Poplar River true to its name.

they had been working on since 2004. Over a decade later, UNESCO designated the area as a heritage site in 2018.

The UNESCO World Heritage Site is a program by which member states designate specific places to be of "outstanding universal value"[5] for their cultural or physical significance. A natural place warranting protection can be a mountain, lake, park, island, ecosystem, and a cultural site can be a building, complex, city, or monument; a heritage site could also be a combination of both. There are currently 1,157 World Heritage Sites across the globe, including the Statue of Liberty in the United States, the Great Wall of China, Mount Kenya National Park, the pyramids of Egypt, the Aborigine-inscribed Uluru-Kata sandstone monolith in Australia, the old town of St. Petersburg in Russia, and India's historic mountain rail line. Each of these sites is unique in its own way and recognized worldwide for its value and importance. Canada's World Heritage Sites include Wood Buffalo National Park in Alberta and the Northwest Territories, the Rideau Canal in Ontario, L'Anse aux Meadows National Historic Site in Newfoundland and Labrador, Head-Smashed-In Buffalo Jump in Alberta, as well as SGang Gwaay on Haida Gwaii in British Columbia, among others.[6] The twofold nature of Pimachiowin Aki as a natural and a cultural site makes it the first of its kind in Canada and only the second in North America, after Papahānaumokuākea Marine National Monument in the United States.

Meaning "the land that gives life" in Anishinaabemowin, the Pimachiowin Aki World Heritage Site is a 29,040-square-kilometre area of boreal forest that encompasses Poplar River's ancestral traplines as well as the traditional territories of Pauingassi, Little Grand Rapids, and Bloodvein First Nations in Manitoba. Included in the site are also Atikaki and Woodlands Caribou Provincial Parks, which straddle the Ontario and Manitoba border. Numerous organizations supported the nomination, as did the Ontario and Manitoba provincial governments. The Province of Manitoba has committed over $14 million to the initiative and passed new legislation, the East Side Traditional Lands Planning and Special Protected Areas Act (2008), which ensures that First Nations on the east side of Lake Winnipeg play a key role in protecting, managing, and developing their traditional lands.

But there is another side to this successful First Nations–led endeavour, which tells a different story—a story that speaks to the difficulties Indigenous peoples may encounter with the nomination process and the challenge the heritage discourse poses in attaining community self-determination. With respect to Pimachiowin Aki, the story also speaks to Anishinaabeg sagacity in using all tools at their disposal. In the summer of 2013, a few days before UNESCO's initial decision on Pimachiowin Aki, those involved in the nomination sat on pins and needles. If the area was recognized as a World Heritage Site, the recognition would be inspiring; if the decision was negative, the disappointment would be immense. In June of that year, at the 37th Session of the World Heritage Committee in June, the decision regarding Pimachiowin Aki's status as a UNESCO World Heritage Site was announced as . . . inconclusive. The World Heritage Committee had deferred its decision until more convincing evidence of the area's cultural value would be presented. The committee alleged that although the natural wealth of the area was clear, the "outstanding cultural value" of the area was not. The communities driving the nomination were consequently asked to further elaborate on the Anishinaabeg relationship with nature "to satisfy one or more of the cultural criteria" of the World Heritage Convention.[7] In 2016, the communities resubmitted their amended nomination with the cultural criteria emphasized, and the area was designated as a UNESCO World Heritage Site in 2018. Though their bid was ultimately successful, the request for further evidence of cultural value was hurtful for many community members and indicates a gap in how cultural heritage is understood.

The cultural and natural values of one property are currently evaluated separately. By asking the Pimachiowin Aki Corporation[8] to address how the site was of outstanding cultural value,[9] the World Heritage Committee demonstrated a lack of familiarity with Indigenous values and the conceptualization of heritage as outlined in a sister document, the 2003

UNESCO Convention for the Safeguarding of the Intangible Cultural Heritage (even though the ICH Convention had been in existence for more than ten years back then). The request for evidence also illustrates how Anishinaabe perspectives on heritage, identity, and belonging do not fit with the World Heritage Committee's approach to culture, particularly its emphasis on the "authenticity" and "integrity" of a site.

There is an identifiable division in the global heritage discourse about the way hunting-gathering-fishing and formerly "nomadic" peoples of the northern forests are perceived and understood. The Pimachiowin Aki experience brought attention to the fact that perspectives of Indigenous and land-based peoples of the boreal areas of world are largely excluded from World Heritage Sites, from the process of establishing them, and from the larger discussion surrounding world heritage.[10] With a substantial percentage of World Heritage Sites located in Europe and the Global South, the inclusion of Indigenous peoples in the Global North is limited. The map on Figure 6 shows the distribution of the world heritage properties across the globe, highlighting that almost 50 percent of the 1,157 world heritage properties are in Europe. Figure 7 shows all the sites inscribed on the World Heritage List separated by region and categories.[11] The reader can see that there are significantly more cultural sites than there are natural and mixed-heritage sites (as of 2023, there are 900 cultural sites, 218 natural sites, and 39 mixed-heritage sites). The statistics are evidence of the value placed on a certain type of heritage but also on valuation of the property itself: from the almost 449 European cultural sites on the register, only 46 are natural sites, illustrating a higher valuation of cultural places. Some countries in the Arab States and African States regions have zero natural heritage nominations; some nations, like Cameroon and Kiribati, only have natural sites. Canada has 10 cultural sites, 12 natural sites, and only one mixed site, illustrating a higher valuation for the natural sites within its borders. The reasons for the large number of cultural sites across the globe (900 as opposed to 218 natural sites) can

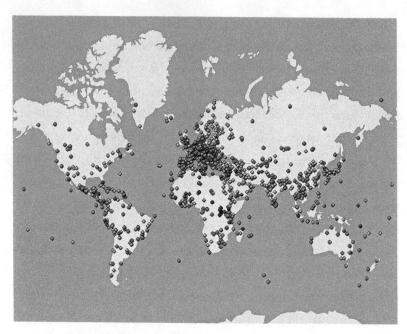

Figure 6. This map shows the distribution of the 1,157 world heritage properties. Although the cultural, natural, mixed, and in danger properties are distributed all over the globe, a heavy concentration of the sites is in Europe. An interactive map of the various sites can be accessed on the UNESCO website. Source: https://whc.unesco.org/en/list/.

Figure 7. The graph illustrates the inscribed natural, cultural, and mixed properties by continent. Adapted from whc.unesco.org/list/stat.

be attributed to both the recognition of human-made heritage as well as the increasing concern for the loss of cultural innovation (with the protection against loss as highly valued). The numbers highlight the global valuation of anthropologic sites over natural landscapes (and consequently a devaluation of natural spaces as an element of human heritage). The numbers also accentuate a heightened valuation for natural spaces that directly contribute to human use (i.e., natural "productive resources"). With several nominations in the works, I believe that these values and the understanding of heritage as both natural and cultural are changing and that nations will start to have more mixed-heritage sites. Canada will also have more cultural sites submitted in partnerships with local Indigenous nations.[12]

The two figures point to a few important considerations in the current heritage discourse: (1) more value is placed on built/tangible or "man-made" heritage, particularly in Europe; (2) the low number of mixed-heritage sites highlights the disconnection between culture/people and nature, or suggests that the relationship between people and nature is less valued; (3) the high number of cultural sites in some areas (and correspondingly, the elevated number of natural sites in other areas) underscores the assumption that cultural heritage does not exist in natural spaces—and similarly, that natural heritage does not exist in many cultural spaces.

The high number of European designations could stem from the simple fact that there are more countries in Europe than there are in North America. It also alludes to the possibility that Europe values its heritage more than North America does (or at least submits nominations to the World Heritage List more routinely), and/or that North Americans do not see cultural heritage (or value it) in their natural or "wilderness" spaces. Italy, for example, has fifty-eight properties on the World Heritage List, thereby being recognized as a country with the "richest traditions,"[13] a "cultural superpower" and a popular destination for more than forty million tourists each year.[14] The World Heritage statistics indicate that material heritage—architecture, buildings, art, historical places, and clearly defined physical sites—is more likely to be identified and valued as heritage within the heritage discourse. This understanding of globally valued aesthetics is problematic in that cultural wealth is interpreted to be unique to certain *specific* places and cultures. World Heritage Sites are meant to be areas of universal significance, hence the term "outstanding universal value" as the key criterion. The problem with the disproportionate designation of World Heritage Sites, however, is that ecologically balanced sites like the boreal forests of the Global North and the Indigenous cultures within them are perceived as continually *terra nullius*. As "empty" lands, in order to become places of heritage they must be *transformed* into cultural sites.

UNESCO bases its current criteria for selection of the type of World Heritage Site on a culture-to-nature spectrum, where criterion 1 is on one end and criterion 10 is on the opposite. Criterion 1 refers to "a masterpiece of human creative genius" and criterion 5 designates "an outstanding example of a traditional human settlement," whether land- or sea-based, but which is representative of a culture(s) or the human interaction with the environment. Moving further along the scale, criterion 10 involves "the most important and significant natural habitats."[15] Within this understanding, biological diversity and threatened species, as determined scientifically, possess Outstanding Universal Value under criterion 10. It is on this spectrum that sites must fit to belong on the World Heritage List.

It was difficult to place Pimachiowin Aki within the spectrum, and the criteria changed during the nomination process (African nominations likewise struggle to gain expert approval for their cultural sites[16]). To fit into the criteria, the nomination committee for Pimachiowin Aki finally selected three that represented a balance of the differing values at play: criterion 3, where a unique or exceptional testimony to a living or disappeared cultural tradition is evidenced; criterion 6, where diversity is associated with living traditions and beliefs of outstanding significance; and criterion 9, where outstanding examples representing significant ongoing ecological and biological processes in the evolution and development of terrestrial and water ecosystems and communities of plants and animals are exemplified.[17] The choice of these three criteria led the Pimachiowin Aki committee to emphasize their site as a "cultural landscape" in the final nomination.

As one moves from one end of the spectrum to the other, properties of culture or nature diminish, disappear, or increase; thus the more "natural" a site is, the less culture (or anthropologic presence) is accounted for. So while a biologically diverse and intact natural site ought not to have culture, a site of "human creative genius" appears to leave little room for nature. Yet humans are an integral part of ecosystems, and the separation of humans from nature to understand heritage excludes the human-nature relationship. Assigning cultural and natural places to opposite sides of a spectrum also limits cultural expressions. The dichotomy restricts the reality that environments shape cultures and that relationships with ecosystems characterize a people's use of, and relationship with, a space. As the narratives of the *akiwenziyag* in this book show, the disunion within the World Heritage Site criteria clashes with Anishinaabeg (and with Inninuwak, as we will see later) values, which view humans as being a part of nature, living from nature, and living in nature rather than opposite of it.[18] Of course, none of the *akiwenziyag* ever used the term "nature" as if it were something outside of human experience; rather, the land users argued for "a way of life" that consisted of an understanding that we *are* nature.

The nature/culture dichotomy reflects the tangible/intangible heritage separation as well. These binaries show a specific value system wherein "pristine" nature is devoid of (contemporary) human presence and where culture necessitates evidence of man-made cultural products (tangible artifacts or antique relics) or human remains. While the immaterial cultural wealth present in an ecologically balanced space is absent from the criteria, the *akiwenziyag* and *kitayatisuk* reveal that local knowledge systems are in fact a "masterpiece of human creative genius" that qualifies a site under the World Heritage Site criterion 10. Even though people may not physically change a landscape, "a rock outcropping, for example, may be linked to origin stories and create a linkage between a society's identity and a landscape," thereby illustrating that while a rock may be a mere rock to some, it is the sacred home of other-than-human Beings to others.[19] What the criteria for "outstanding universal value" fail to recognize is that the most "pristine" or "biologically intact" natural places on Earth are biodiverse *because* the values and practices of a group of local people have ensured they remain so.

The World Heritage Site nomination process becomes more convoluted when vague and subjective concepts like "integrity" and "authenticity" of a site exist in the definitions. These suppositions are more problematic when they are further affixed to a definition of "universally outstanding" heritage sites. If heritage has a universal characterization across the globe, the question arises as to whose values and conceptions of integrity and authenticity make some sites outstanding and others not. Arguably, the terms are part of the criteria for the competition; the predicament in relying too much on terms such as "authenticity," "integrity," and "universal value," however, is that their interpretations are often *not* universal and hence create obstacles for decontextualization and temporal blending. The use of terms like "authenticity" and "integrity" might evoke multiple understandings for a kind of value and, depending on who is in charge (a community or a government), these will have implications on the outcome of the nomination. Not only are perceptions and contrasting value systems problematic here, but the merging of numerous *fixed* concepts, often with opposing definitions, are dubious in their applicability to Indigenous contexts and land-based cultures.

For the Poplar River First Nation community members with whom I spoke, exhibiting evidence of cultural authenticity and integrity is perplexing. Many Indigenous people already balance "modern" and "traditional" through forms of hybridity and merging.[20] The contextual and practical applications of "integrity" and "authenticity" to groups with multiple layers of historical overtones, identities, and homelands with the concept of "outstanding universal value" may be epistemically impossible. Dependent on perceptions and individual meanings, the categories of "authenticity" and "integrity" used by the World Heritage Committee illustrate that the evaluations "do not belong to the canons of rational science. What is more, no objective parameters exist for their measurement because they are dependent on contexts and meanings, necessitating a procedural and non-defining approach."[21] Rather than linking authenticity to "uninterrupted human engagement and intergenerational commitment," communities may be more inclined to seeking "historical authentication and confining heritage to a distant past."[22] Richard Morrison, the *mashkiki inini* whom we met in the Introduction, illustrates that interpretations of heritage as exclusively "pure" or "traditional" limit continuity and intergenerational transmission. While one community member was offended at using power tools to make a pipestone bowl (and hence does not make pipes), Richard's pipe is currently in the hands of Noah Massan, the Inninuwak *kitayatis* who greatly values the sacred item. The nature/culture and intangible/tangible divides present in the global heritage discourse, then, create a perception of cultural heritage that leaves many hunting-gathering-fishing peoples of the boreal forest with a *lack* of culture.

The World Heritage Committee itself clarified that the use and application of "authenticity" and "integrity" "have not been fully adapted to the merging of the criteria,"[23] making the nomination process historically and contemporarily difficult to apply in Indigenous contexts.[24] The International Council of Monuments and Sites (ICOMOS), the organization responsible for assessing cultural elements in World Heritage Site nominations, is currently working on developing a better framework around the criteria. It created the Working Group on Indigenous Heritage in 2020 to develop concepts for site recognition that can better reflect Indigenous perspectives and values.[25] Whereas dialogue on the inclusion of Indigenous perspectives in the world heritage process is a step in the right direction, the discourse of intangible cultural heritage can further support the plurality of heritage values encapsulated in Indigenous natural and cultural self-determination.

"Keeping an eye on things"

In the summer, the community of Poplar River is alive, vibrant. The air is fragrant with the smell of white sweet clover growing profusely around the reserve. Children are everywhere and play until the very late hours of the night. They crowd onto Church Rock, jumping off and diving into the fast-moving river. Some people are washing their hair, and I can attest that hair comes out silky and soft when washed in the river. Clothes are strewn around the brown rock, a smooth remnant of past glaciers that scraped the entire Canadian Shield. Church Rock is a place to meet, a place to swim, a place of childhood. The most enjoyable thing to do is to jump far and let the current bring you back to the rock. *If* you are brave, you will dive as far out and deep as you can, and then fight the strong currents that push you out in the direction of Lake Winnipeg. During those hot summer days, Church Rock is fun, but it is also a deadly place for a poor swimmer. Bathing here is even better when boats pass by and make waves: the kids love the ripples, and the drivers of the boats love making them.

With the Poplar and Franklin Rivers separating the community, the two sides of the reserve each has its own features. Whereas the north side has a beach that is famous for swimming, the south-side beach is a hidden gem where footprints of wolves are often seen and where the setting sun glitters across the immensity of the lake. In the 1950s, many in the community lived the life of their ancestors: the homes were humble (some said poor), there were few opportunities for wage employment, and it was hard to buy things from the HBC post.[26] Many relied on trapping, fishing, hunting, and gathering; some gardened, and an attempt at bringing cows in for farming was also made. The community never went hungry and Frances Valiquette, one of the Elders, recounts that "people fished in the summer and mostly trapped in the winter. Freight was brought in by tractor trains for HBC [Hudson's Bay Company] in the winter. There was not much welfare, just the ones who were sick and under a doctor's care. It was a hard life. But it was a good life."[27] Frances acknowledges that livelihood and self-determination on the land brings a good life, but it is a very demanding life.

With the understanding that people are part of *aki* because "*aki* is part of the people,"[28] the Pimachiowin Aki World Heritage Site nomination stated that sustaining the health and cultural livelihoods of community members was a priority.[29] The name for the site, Pimachiowin Aki, "the land that gives life" in Anishinaabemowin, speaks to "life in the fullest sense: a good life in terms of enjoying longevity, good health, rewarding livelihood and freedom from misfortune. Aki ('land') includes all that is spiritual, living, and non-living: the Creator's gifts of sun, water, wind, rain, fire, rock, plants, and animals that ensure the survival and well-being of Anishinaabeg. The Anishinaabeg acknowledge that the very gift of life depends on maintaining relationships with Gaadebenjiged, the Creator, and respecting an animate association with the land."[30] Recognizing the space as a cultural landscape, the Pimachiowin Aki nomination asserted that a specific knowledge system sustains the land for present and future generations. Understood to be a "set of beliefs, values, knowledges and practices that guide the relationship with the land and all life on the land that was placed by the Creator,"[31] the term *ji-ganawendamang*

Gidakiiminaan was used to frame UNESCO's "outstanding universal value" in the nomination.[32] Maintained for generations, this cultural tradition is defined by Pimachiowin Aki communities as "harvesting sites, habitation and processing sites, traplines, travel routes, named places, ceremonial sites, and sacred places such as pictographs associated with powerful spirit beings. These attributes are dispersed widely across a large landscape and concentrated along waterways, which are an essential source of livelihood resources and a means of transportation. Anishinaabe customary governance and oral traditions ensure continuity of the cultural tradition across generations."[33] As a "compelling example of the inseparability of an indigenous culture and its local environment,"[34] *ji-ganawendamang Gidakiiminaan* illustrates the "deep and abiding connection between Anishinaabeg and the land"[35] through three fundamental principles:

1. honouring the Creator's gifts, the gift of life that is Pimachiowin Aki, through appropriate use of the land for harvesting, habitation, and travel;

2. observing respectful behaviour toward other beings, and all life on *aki*, through appropriate harvesting practices and ceremony; and

3. respecting one another by maintaining harmonious relations with other people, including through partnerships and alliances, and by respecting the guidance of Elders as bearers of the cultural tradition.[36]

Since *ji-ganawendamang Gidakiiminaan* is a combination of knowledge, performativity, and cosmologies, the Pimachiowin Aki nomination identified this customary governance tradition as an element of Anishinaabe intangible cultural heritage.

Ji-ganawendamang Gidakiiminaan, "keeping the land/we take care of our land," serves as an epistemological approach to land and resource stewardship that is sourced from cultural heritage. Rich in understandings, the term is interpreted by Poplar River community members as "caring or looking after the land," as "monitoring" the land and the animals, and as "our way of holding, of governing" the resources.[37] Because it is so comprehensive and inclusive of diverse customs and approaches, *ji-ganawendamang Gidakiiminaan* directly shapes people's interactions with the land and with each other in ways that "express *ji-gichi-inendamang* (reverence for all creation) and the understanding that all life is "united under the Creator [and] the land that is the basis for *bimaadiziwin* (the good life)."[38] This complex network of social relations, values, heritage elements, and knowledges of people in a specific geographical space is also their customary governance system.[39] The mix of Anishinaabemowin, Inninumowin, Oji-Cree speakers and non-Indigenous members living in Poplar River makes the community distinct in its socio-geographical variegation. Local knowledge, specifically, the valuable information of resident members (not all Anishinaabeg or Indigenous) about the surrounding landscape, shapes local *aki gikendamowin*, land-based knowledge, and territorial responsibilities.

The *akiwenziyag* state that *ji-ganawendamang Gidakiiminaan* arises out of Anishinaabe *inaakonigewinan*, laws, to frame *gikendam*, knowing, and *izhichige*, doing things or activities (in a certain way) when on the traplines. Abel Bruce shared that the relationship to his trapline arises out of the *gikinoo'amaagoowinan*, teachings/lessons, of his Elders and his responsibility to care for the trapline: "the Old Ones, they taught me how to protect and look after my line, and this is what I am doing now, me."[40] The now-faint clan system, *doodemag*, serves as a form of kinship politics and guides selective harvesting for some trappers. Understood as a familial and spiritual connection to certain species, the clan system limits the animals a harvester may kill on their trapline. According to *doodemag*, a harvester of a certain clan does not kill or eat the animal who is their *doodem*, clan. For instance, Abel's *doodem* is *ma'iingan*, and he would never kill or eat a wolf as "it would be like eating your family."[41] As a resource management system, *ji-ganawendamang Gidakiiminaan* denotes culture-and-nature as equal parties together, acting and providing feedback in concert with each other—an intangible and tangible relationship. Considering the intact environment of *asatiwisipe aki, ji-ganawendamang Gidakiiminaan* is a system that works.

Ji-ganawendamang Gidakiiminaan is "a masterpiece" of cultural heritage, to paraphrase UNESCO's wording of the cultural criteria in the World Heritage Site program. The cultural tradition also tells us that *asatiwisipe akiing* is not wilderness but a homeland; not an untouched landscape but a grocery store for local people.[42] Describing Indigenous philosophical traditions through a Native science approach to place, Tewa writer Gregory Cajete states that "it is the landscape that contains the memories, the bones of the ancestors, the earth, air, fire, water, and spirit from which a Native culture has come and to which it continually returns."[43] Indigenous scholars Marie Battiste and Sakej Henderson conceptualize the relationship between a specific group of people and a place where they have lived since the beginning as a web of social relations.[44] Likewise, Peruvian scholar Marisol de la Cadena discusses how place making is used to demonstrate territoriality and create "local worlds." Working with Quechua men, the author writes that the gesture of place making materializes between the men and earth beings through apprenticeship and deployment of healing practices that include humans, earth beings, animals, soils, and plants. Earth beings are not just names of places, they *are* when mentioned. The gesture known as *k'intu*, the blowing of three coca leaves from the palm of a hand, symbolizes the transference of human breath from the leaves toward the earth beings, thus "being with them in the event that requires their presence."[45] This interaction of human beings with earth beings is a conceptual practice for the Quechua and serves as a reminder that humans and other-than-humans are a collectivity inhabiting a specific territory together.

The 2003 UNESCO Convention for the Safeguarding of the Intangible Cultural Heritage recognizes the link between culture and land, and, like the Anishinaabeg, numerous groups across the world rely on this relationship for their identity. In 2008, the Kihnu Cultural Space in the Baltic Sea was inscribed as on the UNESCO's Representative List of the Intangible Cultural Heritage of Humanity. With seal-hunting, a communal lifestyle, their own dialect, and a special bond with the sand and seascapes, the Kihnu regard their small island and their relationship to it as a fundamental part of their cultural expression.[46] Likewise, the cultural space of the Yaaral and the Degal in the Niger Delta encompasses vast pastoral lands and crossing of the river during the seasonal movement of livestock (known as transhumance) as an ICH element.[47] In Kenya, the traditions and practices associated with the Kayas in the sacred forests of Mijikenda link Bantu-speaking ethnic groups with their natural space through songs.

The Otomí-Chichimecas people of Tolimán in Mexico and the Górale in Poland also interpret their cultural expressions through the landscape. The places of memory and living traditions of the Otomí-Chichimecas have been recognized as an ICH element since 2009. The traditions of this Indigenous group express a relationship with the local semi-desert ecology and topography: people pray to the sacred Frontón hills in the triangular space between Zamorano and the Peña de Bernal (Bernal Rock). Communal identity and cultural continuity is asserted through ceremonies like annual pilgrimages to pray for water and divine protection and to venerate their ancestors. For the Otomí-Chichimecas, the relationship between spiritual culture and physical space is influential in the region, where diverse art forms, including religious images, murals, dance, music, and "the traditions that embody [the space] are central components of the cultural identity of the community."[48] In the Tatra Mountains in

Poland, the Górale, a sheep-herding cultural group, are working to place their culture and associated landscapes on UNESCO's ICH list.[49] Despite heavy deforestation, massive displacement, and dispossession,[50] the practice of sheepherding that was shaped over centuries continues. Many cultivated ICH elements define the Górale cultural space, including the ceremonial *redyk* that announces the commencement (and closing)

Figure 8. Walter Nanawin, in his typical manner of running his fingers through his hair, taking a rest from his portable sawmill, which he used to start a woodworking business.

of the herding season, the smudging of sheep (to cleanse them and bring good luck and prosperity throughout the grazing season), a special relationship with the sheepherding dogs, the skills associated with living in the remote mountains, and creating cheese products from sheep milk.[51] *Baca*, the lead sheepherders, healers, and knowledge holders, are working with their Elders and other community members to use the UNESCO designation to transmit their language, music, beliefs, local food, and traditional clothing to future generations. These examples show that specific territories (many of which are not legally "owned") underpin a group's identity, and—albeit differently in each case—cultural expressions, including music, worship, and relationships, are used to express and interpret the landscape.[52]

After a satisfying dinner of fried pickerel and mashed corned beef with Walter Nanawin at his house, the local Cree Elder shares an Anishinaabe (and Cree) Creation story that reinforces my understanding of reciprocity and why land users here leave tobacco.[53] He runs his fingers through his hair and points at the recorder; I turn the machine on and place it in front of him on the kitchen table (Figure 8). The *aadizookaan*, sacred story, begins with the gift of Creation, which commences during the great flood, when there was nothing but water on Earth. While some animals were swimming in the water, they noticed a woman falling from the sky. The animals pitied her, for they knew she could not live in the water, and called on the turtle to come and "catch" her. When the woman landed on the turtle's back, she asked the animals to bring some soil from the sea bottom. The animals knew the woman was special in spirit and tried to help her, so the beaver went down first. After some time, he came up empty-handed, embarrassed that he had failed her. Then the fisher dove; he too came up without the precious soil. The marten dove afterwards, but soon surfaced out of breath and empty-handed. Finally, the muskrat volunteered, and even though all the animals laughed at him for trying to do something the stronger animals failed to do, the muskrat leaped into the water. He was gone for so long that the animals started to worry. Finally, after what seemed like a long time, the body of the muskrat floated up to the surface. When the animals pulled him onto the turtle's back, they realized that the dead muskrat was clenching soil in his tiny fist. Because he sacrificed his life, the woman breathed into the muskrat and gave him life.

Although told in many ways (sometimes the muskrat does not die but returns triumphantly), the story is imbued with diverse meanings. One of the teachings is that the gift of life—whether giving it up or breathing it into someone—is reciprocal. The muskrat sacrificed his life to present the woman with a few grains of soil; the woman in turn provided the animals with a land base upon which they could make comfortable homes. The woman was a gift to the animals; the animals in turn offered to help her live on Turtle Island. Finally, this *aadizookaan* tells me that because the animals were co-creators of the landscape, a reciprocal and respectful partnership informs the way the *akiwenziyag* look after the land.

Later, as we discuss land management, Walter reminds me that the regular spring fires north of Poplar River are a result of the *Animikiig*, Thunderers, and *Binesiiwag*, Thunderbirds, flying over the area each year. These spiritual-physical birds that travel to and from their nests after a long winter fly over *asatiwisipe aki*, creating storms and thundering sounds as they flap their wings. The story was told to me partly in Anishinaabe, partly in Inninumowin, and partly in English, and I have summarized it here. *Niin a'da bezhig aadizookaan onji-Azatii ziibing Anishinaabeg. A'gii aadizookewag Walter miinawaa Abel:*

N'gii Anishinaabebiige baamaa. Giishpin Anishinaabe mi'bimi-ayaad Weenipagamig zaaga'igan giiwedinong, gegapii dagoshin azatii-ziibing akiing geget. Mii dash maadjii-mase waabanong nonchagwa ako-mase biinish gichi wajiw. Wajiw-Binesii zhinikaade. Ajina a'daa baa danege, Animikii wazason yaad pimeyii miikaasing. Giishpin ajina a'danege niisaake, a'wii mikan a'we waawanoon Animikii wazasoning jibowaa dibikak ganimaa. Giiwenh, gabeyii ziigwaning, a'gii goshkoz a'we Animikii. A'gii onishkaa minaawaa a'dazhwaangeni. A'mii dash a'gii animibide, a'gii agawaatese noopimiing miinawaa biijibiisa endowaatch. Nangwa, a'babaamise akiing. Apiji a'animwewebide "chuut-boom" Animiki miinawaa a'gii madwewe. A'do inwaakoningwii Animikii ninda. Igaye a'baapawaageni, a'gii baashkikwa'am. Aki a'baapagishkaa zhemaag. A'gii babaamise Animikii ajina, a'waasese biichin. A'apagidaw waasamowin Animikiing misko-shkiinzhigooning. Biichin a'gii magising mitigong miimawaa a'baaginewaatig. Dowaatch a'gii nawadizo mitig naangwadanang. A'we a'ga maadji-nibigin ishkode maanda miinawaa a'ga nibigin, a'gichi-zakide noopimiing biinish angwaakide gamiing. Nomak yaad gaakina noopimiing. Maajaam awesiinh akina gwanda. Gaawiin a'wiiyaa noondawaa megwaa. Gwaataani mademooshkineyaabating mitigwaaking endaso-giizhik ziigwaning niibowa. Gaawiin geyaabii bimaadiziwin yaad.

Gegapii, a'gii baakise wazhashkwedowensag. Awashime ozhaawaashkonaagozi akiing. Biisa badakidewan waabigwaaniin. Wiiba a'da okogiwag miinan baataniino. A'bi-naagozi oshki-mitigoog. A'da bagamanaandang moozag. Mii dash moozag gaye Anishinaabeg giiwekiid. Indaawaj a'oshki-matigwaaking. A'gii nakiiwin giizhiitaa Animikii. A' zhaa-skaabii wadiswaning ji-namadab a'do waawanoon. A'mii dash a'da nowebi Animikii.[54]

In this story, humans look after the landscape, but so do other-than-human Beings like the Thunderbird. The Thunderbirds are frequently seen by the Elders, and Walter saw one in the early 1950s when he was travelling as a young man from Wasagamack to Poplar River with furs. Because the Thunderbirds create the landscape for the *akiwenziyag*, the land users leave tobacco. "The fire they created," Walter tells me, "was needed to renew the forest, you see. So, I left 'em a little something. I left 'em a little tobbaco on the shoreline."[55]

A devout Christian, Walter informs me that there are numerous Spirits and Beings on *asatiwisipe akiing* and that being disrespectful toward them is "bad politics." And so he regularly puts down an offering or "feeds the water." He maintains that Sasquatches roam the territory, "the females, with their hairy breasts swinging as they run through the land [should be] feared more than the males. They moved here from out West, you know [. . .] they ran this far, especially after Mount St. Helen's. The explosion destroyed their home, you know," Walter tells me. "That is why we bring them gifts, to welcome them. Not make them mad, you know."[56] Walter's teaching provides the underpinning for the temporal merging of story with territoriality. The Sasquatch may be unreal to many, or simply a stand-in for Nature, but to Walter it is a real Being, a co-inhabitant

Figure 9. Walter and Jean Nanawin at their kitchen table.

of the eastern side of Lake Winnipeg who will have nowhere to go if the land is destroyed.

Walter moves his finger in a circle on the map and tells me that there is a tiny island on Lake Winnipeg (the island is not on the government-issued map, mostly likely because it is too small). The island is unique in its topography, and Walter says that

> first there is water, then there is sand, and then is high land. That's where the trees grow. These stubby trees grow there because of the variation of winds and cold weather, you know. They snuggle up against the winds and cold weather [laughs]. They are not good for making lumber but [. . .] There is a kind of life in them trees. You think they are dead trees, "muskeg spruce," I guess the Old Ones would call that. Small spruces, they never grown up, you see. There's all kinds of flowers and all kinds of cranberries that grow in there, in this protected land.[57]

Walter regularly perceives such details and differences in the landscape, and constantly studies the area. I have witnessed him and his wife, Jean, go for walks to observe the river: they look at how fast the ice is melting, at the signs of seasons changing, and examine the plant distribution around them. I have often seen them stand on the shores of Poplar River on chilly winter evenings, holding hands; their tender gestures always remind me to appreciate life's intimate moments (Figure 9). Walter's vigilance over changes in the local ecosystem is something the man himself acknowledges, as he admits that he has been "keeping an eye on things" for most of his life:

> I've seen trees, the animals, the land all east of here, and I think the land should be protected. There's too much going on, take for instance in the spring, I always watch the birds, I always watch the robins. My wife and I have been interested in them and I'd say, "look, out the window, see how many robins are there this year?" This year there haven't been many [. . .] there's three there sitting up in the poplar tree [points out the window] and singing no more. They don't sing any more. They seem to have a madness about them, like they mighta have been stripped off their land down south, but they come up here and . . . we don't bother them. And we just look at them, and they go about pick[ing] up bugs. I don't know where they go from there, cause you don't see them [much], you don't see robins around in the summertime here much.[58]

For Walter, the fact that *asatiwisipe aki* is a space where the robins can escape from the "madness" caused by being "stripped off their land" is immensely prophetic. Outsider-imposed limitations to land use and harvesting frustrate the *akiwenziyag*, who are cognizant of their knowledge and expertise on resource management. Emphasizing his words by tapping on the relevant locations on the map in short bursts, Walter vehemently affirms his place in the world: "I'm talking about the land from here to Black River, where we used to travel to the traplines. 'Cause the winter road there, from time immemorial that people have travelled to Manoomin River and Black River and Bear Head River. And that road, I have travelled that road, I've waded that up to my knees in cold freezing water in spring, going back and forth on native block, on the traplines. Even before the traplines were made."[59] Walter's knowledge of the area goes back for generations of land use. Long before Manitoba created the Registered Trapline System in the 1930s, Walter's ancestors "waded up to their knees" in Inninu, Oji-Cree, and Anishinaabe territories. Walter's great-grandfather was Chief Pewanowinin, one of the signatories to Treaty 5, and a descendant of Charlie Nanowin (brother to Chief Cuthbert Nanawin) and Chief Jacob Nanawin. Walter can provide a lot of the historical context of the area, particularly around his time working at Black River with Icelandic fishermen. During our discussion, Walter tells me that Crane Creek "is called Crane Creek 'cause it has these, them special cranes, you see." Getting up to find me a few photos of his ancestors and family (Figure 10), he continues,

> My grandfathers, Walter Bruce, and Charlie Nanowin, then there's Chief Jacob Nanawin, there [points to photo]. And my grandpappy [Pewanowinin] had hunted caribou in that area. [One time] he [Walter Bruce] came upon . . . [laughs]. . . . He surprised a crane sitting on one egg. That's a big egg. And the crane got up and chased him [laughs]. He said "I couldn't find anything [that time], that crane was really aggressive, he was really aggressive, so I had to avoid that place. I couldn't get caribou," he says, "so I came home. I didn't want to disturb the crane laying its eggs." I've written down some of those stories. Since I've travelled, I've written stories [and] songs of those interesting places and the animals from where I've been.[60]

Figure 10. Walter's forefather Chief Jacob Nanawin and his wife, Sarah, after their wedding, around 1900. Walter gave me a photocopy of the photo to keep and use.

Figure 11. Undated photo of Walter's family during one of the early Treaty Days. Walter is the young boy in the front holding a hat.

Walter's extensive knowledge of the land comes to life through stories. Chronicled with events, Walter populated the seemingly empty map of the east side of Lake Winnipeg laid out in front of us with living heritage (Figure 11). With Walter's *dibajiimowinan* and *aadizookaanag*, a map of isolated clusters of green, dots, and "piles of rocks" became imbued with names and sites of cultural, personal, and historical significance.

At the conclusion of one of our visits, Walter says to me, "Yeah, I have so much to tell you. Studying is my favourite. I read and read and read. Sometimes I ignore the phone." He tells me that he'll take me to Whiskey Jack one day, where

> there's wolves running around, howling around, howling around them, the Indians. People didn't mind them at last; they seemed to be brave, [even] when the wolves are around. I guess they thought of them as guardians, eh, from that Owl, that big Owl there. I was right about Owl, how he steals rabbits out of your snare. And how you catch him? [APM: How do you catch him?] Oh! Whoohoo hoohoo hoo. And uh, he [can] swallow the rabbit head, the whole thing! After about a week, I returned, and then, nothing but rabbit bones. So, the wolves, you see, they keep your snares, they keep the snares safe.

Walter concludes by sharing that "I'm just like my grandpappy, you know, my great-grandfather used to look after everything." Now it is his role to "keep an eye" on things, like that owl, Walter continues: "Yeah, funny how that goes, eh? And she always build[s] the nest, [s]he does way up high in a tree. And they grow little ones there. And next thing, pok, pok, pok, pok, if you go near that place. Just like a cat, no? That sound they make. She, she warns. Yeah. She's so smart, she hides, you don't see her. I saw her, I know she's there, but I don't tell nobody! [laughs] She has been there about three years now. I make sure no one bothers her, you know. Like the wolves, I keep an eye on 'er."[61]

Storied Lands

As we share a bag of chips over a fire, Abel Bruce and I are catching up on current events in our lives and in Poplar River. We discuss recent deaths, the last fishing season, the weather changes, and married life. We are sitting near the Mukatewasipe, Black River. It is cold but I am enjoying the moment: the still silence of the remote landscape, the untouched soft and thick layers of snow against the green trees, and the distant snowmobile (here referred to as the "ski-doo"), finally silenced. Plus, winter is the only time one can enjoy the muskeg area without hordes of mosquitoes and blackflies attempting to get a piece of human flesh. Our discussion turns to life in the bush and the hard work it entails. Abel reminisces about the time he survived a lengthy trip from his cabin back to Poplar River, some 130 kilometres, by foot. It took Abel and his brother Albert almost a week of walking on snowshoes fashioned from the walls of his cabin to cover the distance. The men subsisted on one can of fish oil between them, in an exceptionally cold winter. Abel recalls going back to his cabin the following year to repair the holes left in the structure—and laughs at the experience. Admiring this old man, I tell him that this is some life story. "You have to know the stories" he responds, "[otherwise] how do you know anything about you? How do you know how strong you are? How do you know where you want to go?"[62]

The Mukatewasipe is the blood vein of Abel's trapline. It is the space where historically and continuously used trails, campsites, lakes, and rivers anchor his *dibaajimowinan*. Oral traditions are forms of teaching, and Anishinaabe stories communicate heritage. "Stories," writes the Shawnee, Sac and Fox, Muscogee Creek and Seminole scholar Donald Fixico, "are the sine qua non of Indian life and they transfer knowledge among Native peoples as well as pass [. . .] oral literacy to the next generation."[63] Fixico argues that oral traditions are "an interaction with and understanding of the world," and that people in oral tradition–based communities "think and act according to what has been said. Daily communication is imperative for the community to function successfully, and cooperation is essential. Orality is the process of the Indigenous mind taking in information and transmitting it to other people in the community. In this light, non-Indians can learn much about Indians by listening to their stories."[64] Distinct ways of knowing ingrained in oral traditions reproduce, preserve, and convey knowledge.[65] Woven from experiences and without temporal or spatial boundaries, oral stories are alive in any point in history and many reveal the conventional character of human consciousness.[66] Since they are passed by word of mouth, oral traditions and expressions "often vary significantly in their telling. Stories are a combination—differing from genre to genre, from context to context and from performer to performer— of reproduction, improvisation, and creation. This combination makes them a vibrant and colourful form of expression, but also fragile, as their viability depends on an uninterrupted chain passing traditions from one generation of performers to the next."[67]

UNESCO's definition of "oral traditions" encompasses a variety of forms, including songs, proverbs, riddles, nursery rhymes, legends, poems, prayers, songs, and dramatic performances.[68] The performance of oral traditions is a highly specialized occupation in many societies, and knowledge holders such as storytellers are often held in high esteem as guardians of collective memory. Q'um Q'um Xiiem scholar Joanne Archibald writes that a good Stó:lō storyteller needs basic oratory skills and training, a good memory, an understanding of their own abilities, as well as individualized mentoring (sometimes accomplished through competitive means).[69] While several storytellers, poets, and historians may be imperative for the collective narrative to exist, other oral traditions may be limited to a particular social group, gender, age, or family. Specific instructions as to when, how, and to whom stories are told may also play a role. UNESCO's identification of oral traditions and cultural expressions as one of the five ICH domains (as presented in the Introduction) helps distinguish how culture exists through stories and sometimes through gestures. Because gestures are forms of physically embodied communication, they could be a part of the "social practices and rituals" ICH domain, and/or the "knowledge and practices concerning nature and the universe" domain, or/and "oral traditions" domain. Domains are helpful for identifying and recognizing ICH, but they also highlight how one element can also be designated in multiple categories of understanding cultural heritage. Truly, in lived experience, certain acts, like the laying of tobacco or musicmaking, are holistic and combine multiple spheres, demonstrating that UNESCO's domains are just a tool to classify ICH elements for safeguarding purposes.

When we stop to look at one trap, Abel expands on our discussion of what it means to be on the trapline. "There's too many things in the, in the way that you could survive you yourself in the bush, you know. So many things," he says. As we head further into the bush, he continues,

> Even if you don't have a gun or something like that. You really want to eat chicken or something like that. You put a snare, a snare, there, you know? Like this [we proceed to set a snare]. Like this. You'll have a good trap season and all that [but] you ask him [the Creator or Gichi-Manidoo and the spirits] what you want. What you want from Him, what you want Him to do. He'll do it for you. That's what it is. That's offering. That's what we used to do. Every spring we go out [and] we used to offer there, so that everything would be good while we're trapping. You ask 'em [the animals and the spirits] to get lots of fur. Even, ah, when you get sick and all, you know healing and all that, you know. The Creator, you give Him an offering, [He will] try and help you out. Yup. My dad used to, my dad used to tell me a lot about that, you know. Offering. Even, he'd come home in the springtime, he'd have to come down Lake Winnipeg. You couldn't,

you couldn't carry a canoe right in the bush, so my dad, he'd have to go around the lake to come home. There's an offering place there. Every time we go, we want to come home, we offered tobacco there. We asked, we asked Memegwesiwag, [we] asked the Creator, to try and have a good trip home. So we could meet everybody at home nicely. That's what it is. Offering tobacco.[70]

The gesture of putting down *asemaa*, tobacco,[71] or other offerings like bullets or coins, sustains Abel's safety and his relationship with his trapline. Abel does not interpret this practice as a spiritual or religious performance. It is a relational act that is part of the routine of travelling along the Mukatewasipe: by acknowledging the Creator, other-than-human Beings, and the trappers who came before him, Abel reaffirms the established social connection between humans and others on the landscape. The performative act of relational place making across *asatiwisipe akiing* is a fundamental element of this *akiwenzi*'s ICH.

Another Anishinaabe Elder from the community, Ken Douglas, also puts down tobacco.[72] "My grandfather," he says,

before he would go up the river, he would put down tobacco. Even some people, they put things in the river. Before you go up the river, we used to do that. Some of our people, they would put things in the river, like [the Poplar] River. . . . They say there was something in the water. It's like they [people] are protected, I guess. They just put tobacco there to go across. One time, that's what happened. It was windy there one time, we were trying to go across, and this old guy put out tobacco there to calm down, and it wasn't about half an hour and the wind come down. And they went and crossed together to the other side.[73]

Ken and I are sitting at the Elder's Lodge; this is where we spend most of our time talking and it is one of the coziest places in Poplar River. The

Figure 12. Ken Douglas looks at a map and shares stories of his trapping life.

large windows overlook the wider section of Poplar River and numerous eagles that feed in the nearby rapids can be viewed here. I can see the popular Church Rock in the distance, next to the Roman Catholic Mission of St. John Bosco, which also serves as an Anglican mission. The building is cared for by those who practise one of the diverse forms of Christianity and who may also frequent *madoodoo*, a sweatlodge ceremony, or the local Bear Lodge, as it is called here. The lodge is held in the spring and summer months and, like the bear, is given time to hibernate in the winter. This highlights the fact that people adhere to numerous and sometimes seemingly contradicting sacred practices.

Over tea and blueberry-filled cookies, Ken details the community's last trip to Pinesewapigung Sagaigan by pointing to the topographic map.[74] Ken was one of those Elders who loved looking at the map. Often I laid it out in front of him to watch him run his fingers across the coloured sheet of paper (Figure 12). There were moments when he did not say much; occasionally he laughed at something and only sometimes did I ask why. Every now and then, he would "unleash" and proceed to divulge an assortment of stories within a span of minutes. Pointing his finger to an area on the map, he would tell me that here is where the fat pickerel are, and this is where people picked lots of *manoomin*, wild rice, that one year. With good humour he would often allude to his fishing adventures, like the several times he and his fishing partners had to weather out a storm deep into the night.

Retired by the time I met him, Ken enjoyed sharing the stories of his Elders and harvesting partners about the bush life. He recalls his time spent around Wrong Lake and Weaver Lake. As his finger graze over the area of Pinesewapigung Sagaigan, Ken tells me that people put down tobacco at the pictograph site and at the lake crossing. It is because "on the big high rock to Weaver Lake, you can see prints, all kinds of prints," he tells me, and, lowering his tone, says that "sometimes when you pick [there], there are all those signs of Them, of those Beings, being present."[75] He elaborates on the protocol of leaving tobacco, sharing that

> we would go on top of the mountain, on top of that mountain there, Thunder Mountain there, Pinesewapigung. We used to go there, we used to trap there. I used to trap there with John Berens [youngest son of William Berens]. All those old guys would go there, all these old guys who used to go there, are gone. It was nice to learn things from them about our way of life. Like putting down tobacco. Respect. Not upsetting things, eh. When they were there, I learned from them, and from them, I learn how to survive our way, go trapping. So that after we grew up, we [would] know how to do [things] like the old people there, those Elders.[76]

As he emphasizes the importance of this practice, Ken points to the Negginan Fishing Station and said that some of the guys still put down tobacco when they go out. We look at the horizon and Ken states that many community members work at the fishing station. Fishing, like trapping, is a demanding occupation and requires knowledge of the waters, the weather, and shorelines. Ken professes his love of fishing but also confirms my observation that it is indeed hard work, necessitating strength and familiarity, especially with ice during the winter season:

> It was stormy sometimes. We had to deal with that; you would have to wait until after dark. We used six nets about eight feet; you drill a hole and just pull it through. You use a line at the end of the net-line, and [pull to] the other side where [there] is a hole. If you use a jigger you can hear that knocking under the ice where that jigger is. [Then you] pull. Now there is young fishermen doing all the work; the old ones are gone. Sometimes there is less fish, sometimes there is lots of fish, but them young fishermen, when they know that stuff, they are making money pretty good.[77]

After sharing this story, Ken's eyes wander off into a memory. Perhaps reflecting on his own life and contributions to local stories, he has a soft smile. Like the other *dibaajimowinan* Ken told me, stories share experiences, pass on teachings, and may even transmit life-saving wisdom learned about local livelihoods.

There are many [*da*]*dibaajimowininiwag*, storytellers, in Poplar River who tell narratives of their lived experience in the bush or on the waters. Then there are also those rare *aadizookewininiwag*—the storytellers of the sacred stories, myths and legends and teachings,[78] who add to local knowledge. Walter Nanawin is one such *aadizookewinini*. Although he is Inninu, originally from the Red Sucker Lake region, Walter has travelled on the east side of Lake Winnipeg for most of his life. He knows the area's history and can share many Inninu and Anishinaabe oral stories and histories. Because of his extensive work as a trapper, hunter, fisherman, and tradesman—a *kitayatisuk* and an *akiwenzi*—he recounts great tales of his family's lineage and the history of other families in the region, including accounts of Icelandic fishermen and Hudson Bay traders in Negginan[79] throughout late 1800s and early 1900s. Some of Walter's stories are historical; some are philosophical. Others merge Cree teachings with lessons from the Bible, and, because his grandfather witnessed the Treaty 5 adhesion in Poplar River, Walter can also share some of the narratives his grandfather told him about that event.

Sitting at Walter's dinner table, with him looking out the window from time to time, we would talk about anything and everything. Oftentimes Walter would test my Bible knowledge and ask me about my favourite Bible passage, or which Christian rules guide my life. My Catholic upbringing proved useful during these inquiries and even though I could not remember many of the stories on the spot (let alone their biblical references!), Walter enjoyed "interviewing" me in the same way I questioned him.[80] As we chatted about my answers, a teaching or story would come to him. One time, Walter noticed some birds flying and said, "The little birds . . . these little birds there, you know. You don't see them much here anymore. These little birds, they are special little birds, you know. Do you wanna hear a story about the little birds . . . those little birds there, where they come from?"[81] And he proceeded to tell me the story of how the birds came to help the Thunderbird Woman live among the humans. Another time, Walter told me the history behind the Thunderbird Nest at Pinesewapigung Sagaigan. "On top of that rock [Thunder Mountain]," Walter shared, "my great-great-grandfather and grandpa, he saw them lizards, those snakes [Gichi-Ginebig] fight on top of that rock. The Thunderbirds came to stop the fight. Wind was blowing a hundred miles an hour, boom, there was this sonic boom. That's also why they call it Thunder Lake, Thunder Mountain. The Thunderbirds live there now, you see. This [the Thunderbirds] is still a great scientific find."[82]

Walter is also a recognized *debwemaaganiban*, often understood to be a historian and cultural preserver/keeper. He is one of those exceedingly rare storytellers and "tellers of truths" of our society who "has memories, miles and miles long with stories," to paraphrase a Stó:lō member cited in Joanne Archibald's work.[83] Walter tells fascinating stories of Jija'onsag, "The Little People Who Live in the Forest and Trees," the Memegwesiwag, "The Little People Who Live in the Rocks [and who control the wind]," and the Bunhahbe, "The Water People." People from outer space, other-than-human Beings, and his civic fellows also play a role in Walter's stories. His stories, especially the ones about the Wiindikaazo and the Wiindigog, teach, explain, and challenge to provide a multifaceted perspective of the Beings and their importance for bush cultures.[84]

Walter would often invite me to join his family for dinner, but when his wife, Jean, was away, his invitations had a characteristic quirk. The first time he invited me, I got a phone call in the morning to come by for dinner at 2:00 p.m. As soon as I walked in, Walter placed an unopened can of Spam (canned meat) on the kitchen table, pointed to the stove in their little kitchen and three unpeeled potatoes, saying, "There's the potatoes." Then he sat down in his regular seat at the kitchen table and began reading from that tattered plastic-covered sheet of paper I frequently saw him read from. I understood. Without hesitation, I cubed the spam, peeled and boiled the potatoes, and then fried the spam with the potatoes. No words were exchanged during this hour, but Walter ate the meal I presented to him in silence, with an occasional but brisk "mmm" (which I interpreted to be sounds of satisfaction, since I was invited to cook dinner for him a few more times after that). After his meal, Walter pushed the plate away, leaned back in his chair, and crossed his arms. He ran his hands through his hair in a manner I came to recognize as meaning he was ready to talk. I put the pot of tea on the table with two cups, and indeed, Walter began talking. Walter shared fascinating *aadizookaanag* with me, stories that challenged my rational thinking. He shared stories of Gichi-Ginebig, the "snake" that fights with the Thunderbirds, and how it formed the local landscape, and of Mishibizhiw,[85] the "giant water lynx" who used to be greatly feared, sometimes revered, by people in this region. These and other Anishinaabe oral histories and stories embody different themes and meanings, thus time, imagination, and adequate appreciation of the storyteller's skills are expected from listeners who may draw their own unique conclusions from a story.[86]

For some stories, Walter waved his hand and asked me turn off the recorder, and I did; for other stories, he wanted me to "put them in [my] book or somewhere"[87] so everyone could learn from them as well. In such moments of ethnographic interviews, trust and mutual respect are key. When Walter (and the other knowledge holders) asked for the recording to be cut off, I pressed pause on the digital recorder. This is important for building trust, but it was hard to do sometimes. In these instances, the knowledge holders would usually tell me to rely on my memory to tell their story, or they would inform me that they just did not like the stories "being in the recorder" (i.e., in the actual machine). While the process illustrates the living element of stories because I could retell them from my own summation and interpretation, it was also strenuous to remember the details and keep the original story. Sometimes, the requests for pauses followed a particular story, and after turning off the recorder, I would receive more details about the story.

Contrary to my initial belief and theoretical instruction that "off the record" would mean "traditional" wisdom, local politics, or secret community information, the pauses contained more personal (and sometimes more sexually explicit) stories. In my experience, if a knowledge holder was against a political decision or the leadership, they were openly vocal about it. But it was the intimate and affectionate details that were kept private, such as how and with whom one kept warm in a desperate time, a first menstrual period, or what the spouse was like physically. Because these intimate stories occurred after numerous visits and discussions, I concluded that I was trusted with these stories not because of my willingness to truly pause the recording for the juiciest parts, but more so because of our mutual harmony that allowed us to laugh about the details contained in them. In these moments, I learned that most people (especially older people) simply prefer not to have their very personal moments permanently embedded in a recorder, and that the interviewee's awareness of being recorded should never be underestimated (contrary to the idea that one forgets there is a camera in the room).

Working with the *akiwenziyag* likewise taught me that many culture keepers want their knowledge remembered and passed down; there is nothing secret about their way of life. Richard Morrison from Nigigoonsiminikaaning once said that he wants everything he says recorded, because those who keep cultural traditions secret do so to sell them to individuals who will pay for this "secret traditional knowledge." However, if knowledge and culture are alive, they are not secret but lived. Many *akiwenziyag* believed traditional knowledge is secret only when not enough people are living it on a daily basis. Trust and relationships are important elements in research, and, as the *akiwenziyag* and *kitayatisuk* often reminded me, some things are better learned and remembered with the intent to teach further, rather than by being recorded and kept hidden for safekeeping. Finally, full disclosure: the reason why Walter shared so many different *aadizookaanag* with me was partly because he was very hard of hearing and he frequently misheard my questions, ignored, or never heard the others, and of course, just enjoyed my cooking.

When Walter describes the Beings in his *aadizookaanag* and *dibaajimowinan*, he usually points to where they reside. Marking a few spots on the topographic map of Northern Manitoba, Walter emphasizes that it is important to leave tobacco and food for them. This is so they will not be offended and leave the land "empty," he shares. Walter tells fascinating stories and tells them well, articulating with his hands at the right moments and enunciating key words that invoke emotions at the appropriate time. Each time he would tell me a story, I felt like a child again, immersed in my imagination. It was especially fascinating with the maps, because then I became engrossed in the descriptions of places, like those that are filled with great noise alternating with absolute silence, such as when the cranes or the Thunderbirds are laying their eggs. Hearing the stories and concurrently viewing the maps helps connect story to place. Meaning making from maps functions as a stand-in for being in these places and helps to better understand people. By reading the land like a book, we can understand how people and their languages attach significance to certain places (i.e., why physical elements have names), and why cultures are tied to specific spaces (i.e., ethnonyms).

By spending a lifetime learning about and creating stories, the *akiwenziyag* read the landscape like a book. For them, stories must be continually recreated with more stories built on top: a site named after a family member, a recent interesting event, a unique feature can all become part of the subsequent oral history of *asatiwisipe akiing*. When these men say "I know the land," it is because the landscape is "a repository for the memory of past events and thus a vast mnemonic representation of social relationship and of society."[88] When Walter and I discussed the importance of telling stories, he said to me, "That story, that great story you know; that story I told you, that great tale of the Thunderbird eh, that story about Thunder Mountain. There were Thunderbird eggs in a nest, you know. But then someone built a tall radio station tower up there."[89] Offending several community members, Walter said that eventually "the tower imploded, you know. The nails and screws just flew out of the structure outwards. Now the Thunderbird eggs are back in that nest."[90] Stacked on top of each other, stories like the building of a radio station tower on the site of the Thunderbird's home, fill the "uninhabited wilderness" with new stories of familiar places. That's living heritage.

The *akiwenziyag* have come to trust memory over formal (written) history. These men believe that something lives only as long as the last person who remembers it. By anchoring their narratives to the land, the *akiwenziyag* illustrate their relationship to it. Their stories reveal that while Canada interprets "its" land with a centralizing narrative of a unified heritage and the "great Canadian wilderness," the *akiwenziyag* saturate this wilderness space (perceived as "empty") with *aadizookaanag* and *dibaajimowinan*. Stories take up space, they occupy space. And because they hold the core of a counter-memory and offer another, more human understanding associated with the places and spaces that *akiwenziyag* inhabit, stories challenge the status quo, the dominant narratives.[91] It is when the landscape does not have stories that it is an unknown, empty place. *Akiwenziyag* cultural expressions therefore challenge the notion of ownership: how does one claim and take natural resources (or even protect them) if the land is presumed an unoccupied[92] forested space without any stories, without heritage?

The claim "I know my land" is frequently asserted by the *akiwenziyag* and the *kitayatisuk*. But the claim expresses more than just familiarity with land formations and cultural stories. The stories highlight the importance of experiencing the healing *and* the painful aspects of the land. This means that as the land serves to feed, restore, and provide, it is also the space where one experiences "wading up to the knees in cold water" and "surviving on one can of fish oil" with a brother. Getting stuck in mud on a trail named by the Gete-Anishinaabeg or having one's hands bleed when opening a trap are experiences of vulnerability and *gikino'amaagewinan*, teachings, about why tobacco is put down. The *akiwenziyag* (and the *kitayatisuk*, as we will see in Chapter 4) were trained to take care of their lands and to fight for their livelihoods. Their humbling experiences have given them fiery personalities!

One of Abel Bruce's *dibaajimowinan* helped me to understand better the value of stories and *akiwenziyag* territoriality. Abel shared that

one time, there, when I was a young buck [he laughs], I was out trapping, there, on Mukatewa. I was with my dad. We were trapping and this conservation officer came to check on us. He wanted to see what we got [what we hunted]. He looked at our stuff. He stayed with us for a while; he was a nice guy. Nice guy, that guy. And we invited him, we invited him to eat with us, there. And he ate with us that time. It was that meat, that meat he ate, that [was the] meat he was looking for.[93]

While formal history may interpret this story as being about ensuring there is no "poaching" on "Crown land," Abel's narrative speaks to knowledge of the land and resources as expressions of territoriality. The conservation officer could not identify the wild meat he was looking for, even though it was literally in his mouth; Abel and his dad knew that this outsider would not be able to tell what he was eating. Consuming the meat was illegal for the conservation officer, but his acceptance of the meal with the two men and Abel's good-humoured interpretation of the experience speaks to the man's possible awareness and ignorance of what his dinner represented. What makes this a superb story is that it speaks to what makes the *akiwenziyag* stand out. It is their strength, determination, and optimistic outlook; regardless of whether they face injustice from the state or unpredictable circumstances from Nature, they never see themselves as victims and are never discouraged by the hardships they face(d). Although several of the *akiwenziyag* lived with alcohol and altercations in their youth, they got themselves "all fixed up"; they also advocated for building stamina among the youth through time on the land: "I got all fixed up. Not like today. Today, young people feel too sorry for themselves too much, and all that. I just go to my [trap]line. My [trap]line, that's me, you know. That's got me all fixed up."[94] Never losing their sense of humour, the *akiwenziyag* strongly believe that the land not only shows young people their potential but also shapes them.

Chapter Two

Intangible Cultural Heritage

In the winter of 2013, Abel Bruce took me out to Black River, Mukate-wasipe, in northeastern Manitoba to show me an old settlement and his trapline.[1] With the run-down buildings along the white horizon, the desolate area was eerily beautiful against the howling wind from the west. He pointed to a crumbling structure where one of the families had their fish house open to the community and identified the old church and the former school building. We drove out from the frozen muskeg, closer to the river, and Abel called my attention to some campsite locations and cultural grounds. This was a community before the government relocated the families to the current settlement of Poplar River First Nation in the twentieth century.[2] It was during this discussion with Abel, who was looking out into the distance, on the river he has travelled all his life, that I saw *that* look in his eyes: the look of admiration, respect, and reflection of the time he spent on Mukatewasipe. After a minute's gaze at the horizon, where the river meets the tree line, he smiled knowingly and said, "Mukatewa . . . crazy old river."[3]

On the way back we stopped along the snow route to check some traps and warm up. We had barely walked a few steps away from the snowmobiles when I fell waist-deep into the snow. Struggling only pulled me deeper into the snow, so I dragged myself out by crawling in a snow tunnel back to the path we had just made with the machines. I was glad that we had decided to stop to warm up. It was, after all, well below minus forty degrees Celsius and one of the coldest weeks that year in Manitoba. We gathered some dry branches, wrapped them in spruce tree lichen called Old Man's Beard, and made a little fire among the trees (Figure 13). We were immersed in silence, with the only sounds coming from the crackling fire and the wind blowing between the pines. We sat quietly in the stillness. Every once in a while, Abel asked if I was cold, to which I replied "no," even though I could feel a tingling numbness in my toes. It felt good to be in that moment. We sat there, me leaning against one of the thin spruce trees and Abel to the side of me, lying as if on the beach, propped up on one arm.

Then Abel started talking. He recounted stories of his trapline life, about trapping with his brother Albert and his uncle Philip along the Mukatewasipe, how he used to indulge in fried gull and duck eggs, and how much fur prices range from year to year. "This year [2013]," he said, "the marten is worth 120 bucks."[4] He mentioned that the trapping life is hard because you go out in late October and come back in March,[5] and that daily activities consist of getting wood, making meals in bush "kitchens," and checking the traps. And checking them again. And again. And sometimes, still finding nothing in the twentieth trap. Abel recalled how he used to sit down with his dad and uncle, who would tell him stories about the Old People and about Long Time Ago, an expression used to refer to the days of previous generations living *Anishinaabediziwin*,

Figure 13. Abel Bruce and I having lunch near Mukatewasipe, his trapline area.

"the Ojibwe way of life." "Just like us now, here," began Abel, "I sat listening to him tell the stories. I said, 'That must have been good for you, Dad.' And now, my grandson, sometimes he goes and asks me to put rabbit snares in the bush. Last week he wanted to go in the south in the bush by himself, you know. And [he] knows right where to go and where to set that rabbit snare. 'Cause I am always there for him to help him out and tell him those teachings."[6]

After a few *dibaajimowinan*, Abel became quiet. We watched the evening sun peek out between the spruce trees and then started packing before it became too dark. On our way back, Abel occasionally stopped the snowmobile, and over the roar of the idling machine, he would point to where a conibear trap was set and identify some old trails and where they led: to whose line, across what lake, over how many kilometres of muskeg. I am amazed by his memory: he can recall the amount of fur he captured each year, the day the ice opened up on the Poplar River in 1978, and of course, as a trapline holder, he can locate the areas where the healthy marten and unhealthy mink are. Abel is a great storyteller, but he is also inquisitive and often asks questions about my culture, wondering about the kinds of animals we have in my country and if people my age go out on the land. Stressing that it is important to learn about things the Old People did, Abel tells me that *Anishinaabediziwin*, "Anishinaabe way of life/living, customs," is what "helps prepare you for today. This is what I am doing, me. I trap. I'm living like the Old People, me. They live . . . they live though me."[7]

Abel himself merits a short anecdote. Until the year he had a heart attack, Abel was completely independent and did all sorts of undertakings in the bush; it was his belief that not doing these activities would make him an old man. When he had his heart attack at the age of sixty-seven, he was out in the bush, cutting down wood in the winter for people in the community. When his heart "snuck up on him," as he said, he noticed his left arm was not as responsive as he wanted it to be. He continued cutting wood until he felt too weak to move. At some point, he decided that it was perhaps better to go home. "I can get the wood later, I thought to myself," he says to me.[8] But he could not start his snowmobile, and so he walked home through the bush for hours. Once he got home, he tried to go to sleep, but his arm and chest were bothering him. It was only at that point that he decided to go and ask for help. He proceeded to walk to the nursing station until someone stopped to offer him a ride. From the nursing station he was flown down to Winnipeg instantly. In the city, he was boarded in a hotel near the hospital so that he could easily travel to and from his room for his medical appointments. However, no one accommodated the fact that this was an Elder from an isolated community, who, having spent most of his life on the trapline, did not know that "G" referred to the ground floor in a building. Abel told me how scared he felt when each time he pressed the numbers 1 or 2 on the elevator buttons, the doors opened—but all the floors looked the same. He could not find

Figure 14. Abel bringing a map to life with his stories.

his way out of that elevator for a long time. It was only after this incident that Abel would start of many of his stories with "When I was a young bull/buck." In my mind, this man is not old by any means. Rather, the fact that an Elder from an isolated community was left to fend for himself is symptomatic of health care bureaucracy and inexperience with land users like Abel.

Sitting with Abel at his kitchen table one morning, we exchange some family and culture stories. He especially likes the stories about my one-hundred-year-old grandma and her war survival stories: how she smuggled meat under her coat to hide from the Nazi SS-Waffen,[9] how a French man brought her family a cow that he found because he fancied her, and how she took shelter from bombs in the potato fields in a summer dress and high heels because she wanted to be elegant when the war would end after a few days (it ended seven years later). At some point in between our mutual teasing, he looks down on the map in front of him, which prompts him to chronicle another *dibaajimowin*. Almost every place on Abel's trapline holds a memory, a narrative, a teaching (Figure 14). Each important site has a specific use, and like many *akiwenziyag*, Abel enjoys looking at *aki mazina'iganan*, maps/picture land-books, and reliving his life from the bird's eye view a map offers. Abel is good at remembering the differences between rapids on the rivers, and at describing intricate details about where the Old People fished and where the best medicine harvesting sites are. Despite generations of colonial policies that continue to weigh down many harvesters here, knowledge of the area and bush skills still flourish. It is important to recognize that not all Elders are harvesters or land users, and not all *akiwenziyag* are Elders. One is not born with knowledge of bush skills. As with any expertise, to achieve the level of competency and knowledge that Abel has, one must "seek to know the land" continuously.[10] The point of the ICH discourse is to transmit *akiwenziyag* proficiency of knowledge and sophisticated bush skills.

Indigenous Intangible Cultural Heritages

The great diversity of ICH elements and ICH safeguarding approaches across the globe (including in Canada) provide interesting starting points for Indigenous communities. The historical prohibition of Indigenous peoples' cultural traditions like the *bahlats*,[11] Sundances, or Midewewin ceremonies has interrupted the transmission of ICH elements or living heritages. The devaluation by colonial governments of certain practices and territorial identity and rights has led many communities to reinterpret the recognition of their rights through court cases, collective movements like Idle No More, and individual acts of resistance. In recognition of such difficulties, the 2003 UNESCO Convention for the Safeguarding of the Intangible Cultural Heritage refers particularly to Indigenous people who "play an important role in the production, safeguarding, maintenance and re-creation of the[ir] intangible cultural heritage."[12] While the document was not written solely with Indigenous peoples in mind, it does recognize Indigenous communities as requiring special consideration.

In 2016, Canada endorsed the United Nations Declaration on the Rights of Indigenous Peoples (UNDRIP) as providing "a road map to advance lasting reconciliation."[13] UNDRIP recognizes that Indigenous peoples not only "have the right to practise and revitalize their cultural traditions and customs" but also to "maintain, control, protect and develop their cultural heritage, traditional knowledge, and traditional cultural expressions."[14] The ICH Convention pushes for the recognition of safeguarding plans and programs associated with Indigenous cultural and linguistic revitalization. What makes the ICH discourse especially valuable is that communities and organizations can start identifying their ICH elements without involving national bodies and without having any inscribed elements on the UNESCO lists. Communities can simply complete ICH inventories for their own purpose and establish avenues for transmission according to their own needs.

There is an immense heterogeneity of Indigenous peoples' cultural heritages in what is now Canada. The Anishinaabe culture alone is so rich in local uniqueness that an Anishinaabe inventory could include elements found within that specific socio-cultural group or be subdivided further into a repository of elements from a single First Nation or from regional communities. For example, an Anishinaabe *madoodoo*, a sweatlodge ceremony, can be considered an ICH element. But these cultural practices are not limited to a fixed manifestation or region and may include instances from multiple and overlapping ICH domains, including knowledge and expertise with the prayers, a specific ceremonial site, the structure itself, drumming and singing, and the use of medicines. These may differ by region, among communities, and within families, yet all variations of the same *madoodoo* ceremony can be considered an Anishinaabeg ICH element.

The medley of stories and laws, arts and skills, traditions and mementos existing in performativity illustrate that Indigenous ICH elements—the living heritages of communities—are diverse and alive. From making canoes from birchbark, cedar, and cottonwood through to moose skin boats; from storytelling and weaving to pipe ceremonies and *inuksuk* building, communities can select for themselves the identification and level of description of ICH elements they want to safeguard and document. The process is limitless within each community's needs and coordination efforts. While Inuit throat singing, the potlatch system of West Coast Nations, and the Midewewin Society of the Anishinaabeg are identifiable elements of living heritage that are already recognized and valued, other elements may not be as noticeable. Cultural medicinal rituals tied to a specific practice or plant or song may not be as noticeable within the sphere of a cohesive knowledge system. Again, cultural elements are often woven together rather than perceived as their own separate entities, and UNESCO emphasizes that identifying specifying elements of culture that communities value as their living heritage, establishes more actionable measures of protection.

Since there is a diversity of Indigenous peoples in Canada, there is a multiplicity of Indigenous heritages. When discussing Indigenous cultural heritages, I pluralize the term "heritages" to reflect the multitude of cultures within and among people, Nations, and communities. An individual (or community) may also have more than one heritage. When it comes to heritage elements, the focus on cultural plurality within the political term "Indigenous people" helps with identification. For example, in British Columbia, traditional forms of leadership and community planning through houses and potlaches represent an element of heritage that is unique to First Nations in many areas of British Columbia. Because this governance system is not found among the Anishinaabeg, for example, the element cannot be an "Indigenous intangible heritage" but is rather an instance of Nisga'a heritage. Similarly, governance and law through the Dakelh *bahlat*, potlatch, systems among certain Nations would count as an element of Dakelh cultural heritage, or of Indigenous cultural heritage*s* (emphasis on the "s"). Because it is not a feature of all cultures and the practice may be different for each Nation or community that functions through *bahlat*s, a specific socio-linguistic frame may be needed to articulate the element. The ICH discourse centres a ground-up approach, and the use of ethnonyms in heritage transmission may be more appropriate to communities than top-down terms like Indian, Aboriginal, Native, or Indigenous.

The following examples are useful to consider. Elements of Indigenous cultural heritage*s* may include the Medicine Wheel and its teachings for Nations in the prairies, as well as powwows and their associated drumming songs and push-up techniques, vocables, and dances. The powwow intercultural meeting space would naturally include powwow grounds and the "PowWow Trail." Legal concepts and governance structures can be identified as ICH elements. Oral histories, including the central figures of Glooscap, Trickster, and Raven, as well as the sacred stories that frame the diverse epistemologies of the respective Indigenous Nations, would further enrich inventory lists. Skills associated with building conibear traps, tanning moose hides, creating masks, and making tobacco could be identified by their corresponding cultures and tradition keepers. Shaking tent protocols, Christian jamborees, star cosmology, totem pole carving, languages, clan or house organizations or territorial governance systems,[15] and naming or coming-of-age ceremonies are some possibilities for communities to add their own safeguarding initiatives, especially if the practices are declining. The Thunderbird, so immensely vital to Anishinaabeg that world-renowned artist Norval Morrisseau often painted it, qualifies as an ICH element of that culture. Certainly, the distinctive style of woodland art associated with Morrisseau that blends Anishinaabe *aadizookaan* with contemporary media is an example of intangible and tangible living heritage, and vastly appreciated by art lovers today.

Whatever elements communities identify, ICH documentation should be wide in scope to allow for multiple standpoints and interpretations. Identification should not limit elements to the traditional (however this term is understood), but must consider contemporary applications and contexts passed down from generation to generation and incorporated into today's customs. For example, in Poland, the more "traditional" and "cultural" dance, the Krakowiak, is recognized as a national dance, but it is the less colourful dance, the Polonez, that is being nominated to the ICH list.[16] Since the Krakowiak is more of an institutionally taught performance and the Polonez is danced each year at school graduation ceremonies, the latter stands out as the more plausible candidate for intergenerational ICH transmission. Inventories are meant to encompass meanings and practices in which people culturally engage when with each other, so what is important is how communities and individuals make meaning of identified ICH elements *in the present.*

UNESCO recognizes the importance of cultural expressions and languages to ICH transmission. Parental language helps ground identities, and Brock Pitawanakwat writes that Anishinaabemowin "is a root that grounds us and connects us to our ceremonies, land, and to our history. Roots can also be medicinal, and the language tap-root may mitigate some of colonization's most destructive effects, and perhaps, support the restoration of mno-bmaadiziwin (good life) for Anishinaabe people."[17] Representing high value among many Anishinaabeg, *mino-bimaadiziwin* is a linguistic cultural expression tied to a specific way of thinking and behaving. The expression is often interpreted as "living a good way of life" or "living a balanced life/the right way" based on codes of conduct around sharing, respect, and, sometimes, spirituality.[18]

The *akiwenziyag* also rely on the concept of *mino-bimaadiziwin* to locate themselves in the world and to make decisions.[19] For Poplar River Elder Ken Douglas, hunting, fishing, and keeping the traplines healthy, feeds into his understanding of *mino-bimaadiziwin.*[20] Another Poplar

River Elder, Marcel Valiquette, shares the fact that "being out there," able to trap and sit in his cabin, "makes life worth living. That's *mino-bimaadiziwin*," he says.[21] Abel Bruce, too, shares that the Old People in Poplar River relied on the term not only to maintain a balance in their lives but also as something to aim for in making decisions: "You know what to do. Say you, you have to make a choice. Then you choose that [which helps maintain] *mino-bimaadiziwin*. You choose that. Simple."[22] The Pimachiowin Aki communities likewise relied on the term to describe *ji-ganawendamang Gidakiiminaan* in their World Heritage Site nomination. Arguing that the land is the source of *bimaadiziwin*, "the health and well-being associated with *bimaadiziwin* depends on maintaining respectful and harmonious relationships with all life on the land. Anishinaabeg seek to fulfill their sacred trust with the Creator,[23] and thereby pursue a good life, through the cultural tradition of *ji-ganawendamang Gidakiiminaan* (Keeping the Land)."[24]

For many *akiwenziyag*, *mino-bimaadiziwin* signifies responsibility for maintaining community balance and a coexistence with the land. For Richard Morrison, the Nigigoonsiminikaaning *mashkiki inini*, the term refers to living in harmony with Mother Earth and Father Sky. This harmony starts from birth because "when we bring children into this world," Richard says,

> our Elders, what they were saying, is that it's really important to hold the baby, feel that, [to] feel that skin between the mother and the baby. And when that skin is touching between the mother and the child, that unity, that nurturance, that sustenance, that purity of life, is at its greatest. But the energy, the strength of that baby just becomes super strong, immediately. And [it] also energizes the mother. So, what happens is, that [umbilical] cord, this is what they were saying, our Elders were saying, about that cord: there is a way to do it when you cut it. You gotta leave the

baby, just hang onto the baby for at least a half hour. Let that cord do its work. That little cord that's connected from the mother to the new life, and then once, once the baby's ready, the baby will let you know. And then, then you cut it. It's very precise. You use the hand of the mother. And it's like what I do with medicine. You use the longest finger and cut that line so [the child will] stay connected. That [umbilical cord] stays with the baby for the first year of life. So that baby doesn't look for himself; doesn't go around all over the world looking for something they already have. The essence of life is really central, it's there with the little belly button; [it] stays with them for a year. Then we put it out, put it out and hang it in a tree, *mitig*, the universe of all life. Everything from the universe connects us to this physical world we live in. We stay connected to that energy from birth, to that *mitig*, and to *mino-bimaadiziwin*.[25]

While the term does not have a unifying definition, Richard explains that we can "obtain" *mino-bimaadiziwin* today by not permitting our perceptions to separate us: "*Mino* is the universe of you and me," he shares,

that is, one is physical and one is spiritual. So, you are the universe, we all came from the universe, in a spiritual way to become physical here in this world that we live in. That is why we have to honour [...] our Mother Earth and our Father Sky. Everybody that walks the Earth is their children. We are the children of the world. There are no differences. The only difference is what we think. We can see Caucasian, we can see Black, we can see Oriental, we can see the Native American. We distinguish it that way. In reality, we're all the same. [...] we know what ugly is, we know what beautiful is. So what stops us from really feeling that *mino-bimaadiziwin* today, is judge[ment].[26]

Richard emphasizes that *mino-bimaadiziwin* is about supporting each other and "being connected" to our responsibilities as humans. He tells me that it's "aligning to all the energies of the world, the water, the trees, the birds, the elk. Taking care of them."[27]

The ontology of what it means to have a good life and what losses articulate the opposite understanding of the concept continues to guide many societies in their decisions. The *kitayatisuk* in Northern Manitoba too have an Inninumowin (Cree) term for the concept. The *kitayatisuk* have interpreted community *mino-pimatisiwin* as existing up until a point in time. The Inninuwak were living *mino-pimatisiwin* until hydropower development came in in the mid-twentieth century. Hydro destroyed Inninuwak lands, and caused ill health and community disintegration, namely, the loss of *mino-pimatisiwin*. *Kitayatisuk* struggles with hydro development are developed in Chapter 4. While *mino-bimaadiziwin/ mino-pimatisiwin* serves to articulate Anishinaabeg and Inninuwak experiences, the idea of a centralizing concept of living "a good life" is an informal socio-linguistic element found in other cultures as well. Some examples include *la dolce vita* in Italian, *dobrobycie/dobrobyt* in Polish, *buen vivir* in Spanish, *sumac kawsay* in Kichwa, 人生 (*jinsei*) in Japanese, and *aha ye de* in Twi, one of Ghana's national languages. *Buen vivir* and *sumac kawsay* play such an important role in Indigenous communities in Central and South America that the world view was institutionalized by Bolivia and Ecuador.[28] The global existence of these concepts informs us that the cosmovision of relating to each other and to the world plays a central role in many cultures, and that many societies across the world place high value on this element. Recognizing ICH demonstrates that the notion of "a good life" has manifold and culturally specific interpretations. What interests us here, however, is how the *akiwenziyag* and *kitayatisuk* world view of prioritizing harmony and livelihoods with their local environment (including humans) can serve to understand and safeguard Indigenous living heritages.

As illustrated through *mino-bimaadiziwin*, ICH depends on language and utterances (such as putting down tobacco) for its transmission. Constituting an essential part of a group's identity, heritage/parental languages are carriers of knowledges and used in ICH performativity.[29] Almost all rituals, including communication between people, rely on language. *Akiwenziyag* songs and ontologies are examples of cultural expressions. Heritage tongues consist of highly specialized sets of terms and expressions and reveal the intrinsic depth of connection between language and ICH.[30] For example, by elaborating on animate and inanimate terms in Anishinaabemowin, Richard illustrates Anishinaabe cosmovisions. He tells me that while the English-speaking positivist perspective interprets certain natural features like rocks and thunder as examples of (non-living) things, Anishinaabemowin interprets some rocks (*asiniig*) as grandfathers (*omishoomisabikoog*) and thunderstorms as the *Binesiiwag* and the *Animikiig*, Thunderbirds and Thunderers. The complexity inherent within these two languages is not meant to be comparative or generalizing; rather, the contrast illustrates epistemological diversity that languages offer.[31] The ICH discourse recognizes the importance of language in maintaining knowledges and other ways of interpreting the world, but the framework also pushes responsibility onto governments and individuals to ensure avenues for the transmission of languages.

Over seven thousand languages are spoken around the world. Most states, Canada included, are linguistically diverse.[32] It is well known that extinction is a threat to most languages, and by the year 2050 most of this linguistic wealth will see a 50 to 90 percent reduction if urgent action is not undertaken.[33] There are more than seventy Indigenous languages in Canada and the 1996 Royal Commission on Aboriginal People recommended "due attention" to the significance of Indigenous languages in "communicating Aboriginal knowledge and perspectives [and that] Aboriginal language education be assigned priority in Aboriginal, provincial and territorial education systems to complement and support language preservation efforts in education."[34] UNDRIP and the TRC also emphasize the need to safeguard Indigenous languages, many of which are at risk of extinction.[35] The British Columbia–based First Peoples' Cultural Council recognizes the urgent need for policies and programs for Indigenous language revitalization, and encourages merging language learning with land-based teaching and learning.[36] Recognizing that Indigenous peoples have "the right to revitalize, use, develop and transmit to future generations their histories, languages, oral traditions, philosophies, writing systems and literatures," UNDRIP petitions states to take "effective measures" to provide Indigenous people access to an education in their own culture and provided in their own language.[37] Correspondingly, the TRC calls upon Canada's federal government to appoint an Aboriginal Languages Commissioner and enact an Aboriginal Languages Act that recognizes Indigenous languages as a fundamental and valued element of Canadian culture and society.[38] Canada's $334 million investment toward language initiatives and the Indigenous Languages Act in 2019 galvanized language revitalization efforts,[39] including courses and degree streams in educational institutions and community-led language nests. While online workshops, dictionaries, and learning sites like First Voices build on the suggestions summoned by the TRC and UNDRIP,[40] the ICH framework can advance policies on "effective measures" of language transmission by strengthening the cultural environment in which languages naturally exist.

Despite the fact that language is widely recognized as a key mechanism of ICH, the UNESCO 2003 Convention does not explicitly recognize language as an ICH in its own right. Relating to "oral expressions and traditions" in the first domain, language is restricted to a *vehicle* of culture in the convention. Failure to recognize language as an ICH is a shortcoming of the convention and a step back from the strong link made between language and cultural identity in the UNESCO Universal Declaration on Cultural Diversity (2001) and UNDRIP (2008).[41] Communities are bypassing this technicality in creative and distinct ways, however. Some nations inscribe elements like songs and spaces on the UNESCO or national lists, thereby pursuing protection of their languages in conjunction with these elements. Countries in Africa and Latin America present languages as an ICH in their own right and not just as a "vehicle" of it.[42] Peru and Lithuania also include languages in their ICH lists, and Armenia's Law on Intangible Cultural Heritage includes language in its definition of ICH. Bolivia, Chile, and Peru are working together to safeguard the heritage of Ayamara communities bordering all three states through a program that strengthens language through formal and non-formal education.[43]

In a similar collaborative fashion, Poland recognizes Esperanto, the constructed international language of European citizens, as a cultural heritage on its national list, and Croatia honours that same language as a cultural asset in its own administration. Many universities in Hungary also accept Esperanto for language certification. Belize, Guatemala, Honduras, and Nicaragua have worked together to inscribe the language, dance, and music of the Garifuna on the UNESCO list. The Garifuna are a population that blends Indigenous Caribbean and African cultural elements. Belonging to the Arawakan language group, the Garifuna language is a depositor of traditional knowledge and oral history; merging with African-influenced drums and dances, the language is also expressed through many locally-based songs. Only one village teaches the language, and the $226,000 USD ($247,000 CDN) funding from Japan Funds-in-Trust and UNESCO toward the Garifuna language revitalization action plan in 2006 helped to create inventories and artistic archives and to disseminate Garifuna language and knowledge.

Relying on the ICH framework, nations that are party to the 2003 Convention are creating policies that strengthen existing language-development tools such as language-based daycares and tertiary education, as well as adult and family-based education in the home. Numerous efforts also take into account the restoration of fluency of non-dominant or sub-national/minority languages. In China, for example, Hezhen are an ethnic minority whose language serves as a vehicle for expressing and transmitting Hezhen culture. Based on this endangered mother tongue and the lack of a writing system, China placed Hezhen Yimakan storytelling on the UNESCO List of Intangible Cultural Heritage in Need of Urgent Safeguarding in 2011. To protect the Yimakan storytelling traditions, the country has established bilingual teaching programs in elementary and secondary schools to improve native-tongue fluency. Cooperating with folk organizations, local communities, and the storytellers, the Chinese government, Heilongjiang Province, and departments of culture at all levels also provide financial support for Hezhen Yimakan training activities, recording, and website creation devoted to transmitting the oral performances. To protect the Indigenous knowledge that is taught "from ear to ear, mouth to mouth" state funding totalling 45 million yuan ($85,000 CAD) permitted more than seventy people to receive Hezhen Yimakan training in 2006.[44]

Because communities and families benefit from clearly defined programs and policies geared toward language revival and transmission,[45] it would be valuable for Indigenous communities in Canada to identify languages as an element of their heritage in addition to their role as a vehicle for culture. With effective policy, program development, and inventorying, the ICH framework can become an "effective measure," to use the TRC's language, in language revitalization efforts. However, while it is important to recognize that collective and individual efforts at language safeguarding, revival, or transmission are critical, no single safeguarding measure can ever guarantee language survivability and intergenerational transmission. In most cases, the successful revival of a language has been achieved through classroom curricula *as well as* through families and ICH custodians who include children in everyday use of the language. When culture keepers and entire communities play a direct role in child development, children gain a more solid foundation of their language and identity.[46]

There are more young people learning an Indigenous language than ever before; however, few have an Indigenous language as their native tongue.[47] The ICH framework can help promote avenues for fluent speakers to transmit Indigenous languages naturally and can offer tools and resources for (first or second) language acquisition. The conditions for language revitalization and transmission must be priorities so that *at the very least*, a learned Indigenous language as a second language may become a mother tongue for subsequent generations.

Canada and ICH

With all the benefits the ICH discourse offers, a reader may ask why Canada, whose support for multiculturalism is federally recognized, has not signed the 2003 UNESCO Convention for the Safeguarding of the Intangible Cultural Heritage and why no Canadian policies or documentation exist at the federal level. Although in existence for twenty years now, the ICH Convention and the ICH discourse have not played any significant roles in Canada's policy making at the national level. Canada has not been a strong advocate for ratification of the Convention, either. While most countries have ratified or accepted the rights and obligations arising from the Convention (as Russia did), Canada has refrained from doing so, along with Australia, United Kingdom, and the United States. Canada "adheres" to the conceptual understanding that surrounds ICH through "the legal, financial and administrative provisions set out in multiculturalism, official languages and human rights legislation and policies."[48] In 2005, the federal government articulated its awareness of the UNESCO concept by safeguarding, preserving, and promoting ICH "directly and through" bodies like the Canadian Museum of Civilization, Library and Archives Canada, and the proposed (but never created)

Aboriginal Languages and Cultures Centre. The reason for the lack of interest in the ICH Convention is difficult to pinpoint, and present-day multicultural policies are likely viewed as sufficient for the protection of languages, ethnic celebrations, and the diverse cultural freedoms of Canadians. However, Canadian policy and perspectives on heritage need significant updates. The current Department of Canadian Heritage Act is from 1995 and it outlines the minister's powers over "Canadian identity and values, cultural development and heritage."[49] The Act also identifies jurisdiction over thirteen different sectors of society such as sports, official languages, museums, and Canadian symbols. There is not a single mention of Indigenous peoples and languages in the act except in reference to the Native Citizens Directorate, which is now largely Indigenous Services Canada.

Antoine Gauthier, the directeur général (executive director) of Le Conseil québécois du patrimoine vivant, writes that the reasons for this abstention may relate to the vague definition of ICH in the Convention as well as to the "significant obligations for the state" to create and regularly update an inventory.[50] Echoing Gauthier's suspicions, Gerald Pocius, a folklorist who worked on drafting the ICH Convention at the UNESCO level and on developing an ICH policy in Canada in the early 2000s, agrees that the limited work done by Canada is disappointing.[51] Writing about the convoluted way the ICH framework was brought into documents, taken out of agendas, ignored at policy meetings, and reduced to "traditional knowledge," he characterizes Canada's lukewarm interest in ICH as being based on "the establishment of a conductive environment for the full expression of the diversity of our nations' ICH through governance structures and value-based legislation that enshrine fundamental rights of citizens and promote the values and principles of diversity, multiculturalism, and an open, tolerant, and accommodating society."[52] According to Pocius, Canada's interpretation of the convention as "wide, ambiguous, and rushed" was the main reason for not ratifying it. The wide scope of the convention was too "difficult to interpret and implement within the Canadian context," especially in the domains of religion, customary laws, and "sacred traditional knowledge."[53] ICH elements found in the plurality of faiths and in religious customary laws of diverse ethnic groups indeed merit more attention; the subject, however, is beyond the scope of this book. Identifying entire cultures as ICH is not the point of the Convention; the ICH framework is a tool to help communities *themselves* identify cultural elements that are important to them and which may warrant protective measures and assistance. While allowable plurality is necessary to explore in the ICH legal context, it is imperative to point out that recognizing one culture's aspect of heritage does not negate another group's cultural elements.

Moreover, at the time of the debate, Indigenous ICH-based programming existed through the Indigenous Languages and Cultures Program, whose objectives were to promote Indigenous languages, strengthen cultural identity, and increase Indigenous participation in Canadian society. It was twenty years later that Canada passed the 2019 Indigenous Languages Act, and while protecting Indigenous languages is important, protecting only language is myopic with regard to its further role as a vehicle for heritage. To use Anishinaabemowin as an example again, this verb-based language entails intellectual epistemologies in many cultural expressions, thus "Anishinaabeg" is generally translated as "Ojibwe people," but the word literally means "humans [as] the light or energy of the people that are going down or are lowered [from the stars]."[54] The conceptual philosophy is lost in the English translation, and for Richard Morrison, original linguistic descriptions are immensely important as they ground people in their identity and values.[55] Richard goes further, reminding me again that *asin* is more than just a "rock," it is the oldest living relative [of humans], and in many circumstances called *omishoomisan*, [his] grandfathers.[56] Referring to the pipe-smoking ceremony, this *akiwenzi* tells me that as one smokes the pipe, that "oldest living relative" passes knowledge to the individual through thoughts, prayers, and visions.[57] Taking the drum from his medicine bag, Richard points out that protecting only language ensures the word *dewe'igan*, drum,[58] remains, but it does not provide the knowledge of arranging vocables into songs, the mastery of creating the sound and form of a one-beat melody, or even the skills with which to make a drum. This is where the ICH lens is exceptionally helpful: it brings into focus *a diversity* of elements that *together* make up a group's cultural heritage. For Richard, linguistic competencies merge with individual skills and cultural customs, and in the ICH context, Indigenous culture keepers enhance the material heritage stored in books and museums through language and living practices.

Canada's inaction on the Convention is symptomatic of the nation-to-nation relationship with Indigenous peoples. It is interesting to note that although more than 181 states were party to the Convention in 2023, three other settler states—Australia, the United States, and New Zealand—have chosen not to endorse this document. State-sanctioned frameworks to protect cultural heritage elements of Indigenous peoples have yet to be open for discussion, and very few Indigenous and treaty policies focus on ICH recognition and protection.[59] This strategic position can be further attributed to unresolved Indigenous and treaty rights as well as outstanding land claims and self-determination measures whose interpretations and scope may broaden with the implementation of this instrument; this is the position I take in Chapter 5.

Several issues stand out regarding the drafting of the Convention and the debate around ICH policy and Indigenous people in Canada in the early 2000s. One, Indigenous people across Canada were not consulted (as was the case for many other groups and folklore organizations). Two, the governments's "series of initiatives" dealing with an ICH inventory of "traditional cultures" and "traditional knowledge" point to a view that identifies "traditional" heritage as essentially Indigenous; and three, the Department of Canadian Heritage believed that First Nations would find the process of inventorying problematic as certain secret traditions may be "exposed."[60] The lack of consultation and the "frozen" approach to Indigenous cultures illustrate Canadian Heritage's limited awareness of Indigenous methodologies and Indigenous people's perspectives toward safeguarding their own heritages. Concerns over exposure of Indigenous sacred traditional knowledge also demonstrates minimal understanding of the ICH framework and the urgency of the situation. Since ICH inventorying is a bottom-up process, it is not government officials who identify and document Indigenous (and other) heritages but communities themselves. ICH custodians and communities determine their own involvement in the process and the measures of protection; they are the owners of their inventories. Any public identification of sacred traditional knowledge merely recognizes its importance to the community; what this knowledge entails can remain entirely within the community sphere. Rejecting a convention that pushes for community-based safeguarding measures based on assumptions (perhaps due to lack of consultation) unfortunately limits Canada's cultural heritage policy to outdated policy work surrounding tangible heritage.[61]

It is important to point out that like other UNESCO conventions, the 2003 ICH Convention only applies to countries that have ratified it. State recognition of the convention is both a limitation and an opportunity. In regions where minorities and Indigenous peoples are not recognized and respected—or worse, where their rights are suppressed, a state refusing the 2003 Convention has serious consequences for communities. In war-torn countries and in colonized nations there may be no interest or willingness from the state to protect certain cultural heritages; there may even be an expressed eradication of culture from the state. In Ukraine, for example, there is a widespread narrative of denigration of Ukrainian culture and identity promoted by Russian officials, and explicit efforts are made to erase local culture, history, and language. This is carried out by the destruction of cultural places such as libraries, educational institutions, cultural and religious sites as well as places of memory like cemeteries, archives, and monuments.[62] In Syria too, the country's rich tapestry of cultural heritage continues to be devastated due to fighting, systematic looting, illicit trafficking of cultural objects, and pillaging at ancient archaeological sites through illegal digs.[63] For many ethnic minorities, Indigenous peoples, and sub-national populations who cannot take advantage of the opportunities and support systems the convention offers, the state is a direct barrier.

In some instances, affirmative action, community development programs, and other grassroots strategies may be more effective than rights protection or state promotion of ICH safeguarding.[64] Because Canada has not signed the ICH Convention, the country is in an excellent place to decide if ratifying the convention brings more opportunities for communities or if the administrative and political requirements associated with ratification bring with it unnecessary and constrictive measures at protection. Ratifying the ICH Convention obliges State Parties to create ICH registers, but while the process is up to the state, safeguarding ICH is not politically neutral. In *Making Intangible Heritage,* Valdimar Hafstein elaborates on the politicization and bureaucratization of heritage to illustrate how institutionalization shapes policy and management of ICH, often taking it away from community members and placing it in the hands of bureaucrats.[65] The author exposes how power and "naturalized" logic permeate the ICH discourse which then embody belief systems and material practices that express particular worldviews and values. A state institution thus uses institutional norms and legal rules to make decisions about cultural heritage and shapes which (and whose) heritages are granted support and endorsement. The author writes that narratives of heritage and the ICH discourse conceal "a wide divergence of views on cultural production, conservation, control, and dissent" and consequently broaden the complexities of cultural history and politics.[66] ICH documentation and policy making requires reflective examination in tandem with community consultations.

ICH recognition undoubtedly extends discussions around common investments, nationalism as well as collective remembering and selective forgetting.[67] Having examined the ICH discourse for the past two decades, I can recognize an increasing need for a legal analysis of ICH as it relates to national legal systems, technicalities around community-involvement, ownership, and rights regimes.[68] Because the 2003 Convention is a relatively recent instrument, legal creativity can ensure this international mechanism is conceptually benefitting ICH custodians at a national level and that administrative capacities of the 2003 Convention and the ICH discourse are used to limit state power. Considerations around national symbols and identity, cultural rhetoric, and financial investments into *particular* ICH elements or heritages are needed. Likewise, questions about equitable support for communities and whose heritage is safeguarded, promoted, excluded, or disregarded—and who decides—are critical to legislative schemas. Because state involvement in ICH promotion through the 2003 Convention can also bring forth a remapping of ideological, historical, economic, and political landscapes to the heritage discourse, soliciting research about discursive, structural, and operational powers within policymaking will ensure ICH custodians have agency over their own day-to-day practices.

Without Canada's acceptance of the 2003 UNESCO Convention, several organizations and institutions in the country already have well-established ICH programs and policies that are recognized and praised internationally.[69] Quebec has been engaged in the ICH framework since 2003 and the province is leading the way in institutionalizing ICH work. In 2011, Quebec created the Québec Cultural Heritage Act, making it the first Canadian province to recognize living heritage at the provincial level. The province organizes numerous festivals, workshops, and programs, and also has extensive publications and guides on *patrimoine vivant* (living heritage), including the *Culture Trad Québec* magazine.[70] Le Conseil québécois du patrimoine vivant (the Quebec Council for Living Heritage) focuses on reviving and maintaining culturally sourced construction, musical instruments, and diverse activities; the Conseil works with Indigenous communities throughout the province as well. In 2023, Le Conseil québécois du patrimoine vivant organized its first professional training in artisanal milling. After more than 200 years of transmission from master to apprentice, the craft of artisan milling is threatening to disappear in Quebec, and so organizing training in this traditional skill will help with the succession and perpetuation of milling.[71]

The Heritage Foundation of Newfoundland and Labrador took on ICH work in 2008, recognizing traditional games, culinary traditions, and animal husbandry as well as places of memory as ICH. The foundation defines ICH in the Canadian context as "many traditions, practices, and customs. These include the stories we tell, the family events we celebrate, our community gatherings, the languages we speak, the songs we sing, knowledge of our natural spaces, our healing traditions, the foods we eat, our holidays, beliefs and cultural practices."[72] Through different partnerships, the Heritage Foundation focuses on identifying, inventorying, and establishing protection of the region's diverse heritages, including ballad singing, snowshoe making, fiddle playing, berry picking, boat building and much more. By recognizing and celebrating living heritage with festivals, providing support for transmission, and exploring the potential of ICH identification as a resource for community development, particularly for at-risk heritage, Newfoundland and Labrador offer tradition-bearers sustainability of their cultural activities.

Central and western Canada are also pursuing ICH work. Heritage Saskatchewan has taken a unique approach to suit its own context. The organization is an accredited nongovernmental organization to the 2003 ICH Convention and uses the framework to develop living heritage projects, hold workshops on documentation, long-term data storage, and ethics, and employs a full-time community engagement ICH officer.[73] In 2021, based on interviews with over twenty heritage scholars, practitioners, and policy makers across Canada, Heritage Saskatchewan produced a report for the Federal Provincial Territorial Culture and Heritage Table on the state of ICH safeguarding in Canada.[74] Similarly, the First Peoples' Cultural Council advocated for including ICH in recognizing Indigenous cultural heritage in the British Columbia and is increasing its programming in that area.[75] In 2022, the University of Northern British Columbia established a UNESCO Chair in Living Heritage and Sustainable Livelihoods, which will further the work and build extensive scholarship in this area.

Cities and communities, too, are exploring the ICH framework to enhance their cultural programming. I have shown in the previous chapter how the Pimachiowin Aki communities used the ICH discourse in their World Heritage Site nomination, and in northern British Columbia, Dakelh Elders have worked with higher education institutions to create experiential learning courses in cultural traditions like moosehide tanning. Similarly, the City of Calgary includes ICH in its cultural plan to recognize community stories, place names, and beliefs; the City of Vancouver included ICH in its understanding of heritage and identified "arts and culture" as its number one "endangered heritage" element in 2020.[76] These examples confirm that the ICH Convention is being used as a guiding instrument or aspiration document for many organizations, communities, and municipalities. While these entities are working within the constraints of their particular political and funding contexts, the ICH discourse is already playing a role in cultural programming and protection of community interests.

Finally, funding is perhaps the underlying matter in Canada's hesitation to engage in ICH work. Signing the Convention would not only force departments and governments to pursue programs in which they have little or no interest nor expertise, but also it require them to shift funding to "ordinary" practices.[77] The Convention's interpretation of heritage as alive and requiring community engagement directly challenges the "authorized heritage discourse,"[78] which argues that material heritage relies on authority in order to be recognized and restored. The ICH framework, however, characterizes heritage as a living legacy belonging to people: constantly changing and recreating, evolving rather than remaining "pure." The challenge behind devising new programs for living heritage is that an ICH focus "will clearly take money away from the architects and restorationists who make their living on a static past that needs to be continually rescued and restored."[79] The debate around cultural heritage, then, is one where built monuments are products of the enlightened, held up against the "ordinary expressive behaviours of the majority of the population."[80] Living their heritage daily, the *akiwenziyag*, however, illustrate that discourses of cultural "authenticity" and "integrity" of physical objects held in distant institutions and discussions of ratification and promotion have little place in their evolving world.

Documentation of Living Heritage

ICH safeguarding begins with documentation, also known as inventory-ing, and establishing measures that facilitate transmission or revitalization. Articles 11 and 12 of the ICH Convention that a State Party shall "ensure the safeguarding of the intangible cultural heritage present in its territory [and] ensure identification with a view to safeguarding."[81] The convention further states that a country shall draw up "in a manner geared towards its own situation"[82] one or more inventories that are to be regularly updated. The steps of the inventorying process include

1. identifying the element (by name or locality and culture associated with it);

2. describing the characteristics of the element (why the element is important and its significance);

3. identifying persons involved with the element (the practitioners);

4. determining the state of the element (viability of the element and threats to transmission as well as safeguarding measures currently in place);

5. gathering and inventorying data (collecting any digital or recorded and consent to access and use the data);

6. compiling references (a bibliography of items associated with the element).

While the complete documentation of an element will be very long, Appendix 1 of this book includes an Inventory Card that communities are free to use as a template for beginning the process of identifying their cultural heritage elements. Appendix 2 contains inventorying guidelines that I have adapted from UNESCO and ICH scholarship to include components more relevant to Indigenous peoples in Canada. Funding will be required to carry out documentation, but communities can begin by looking at the helpful resources included in Appendix 3 and by obtaining assistance from scholars and professionals doing ICH work. It is important to point out that not all cultural heritage professionals are familiar with the ICH framework, and not all will have the training to do community engagement in the context of living heritage.

"Collecting" ICH elements and formulating concrete safeguarding plans is time-consuming—but extremely rewarding.[83] As described in the Introduction, there are five domains that help identify ICH: (1) oral traditions and expressions, including language as a vehicle of ICH; (2) the performing arts; (3) social practices, rituals, and festive events; (4)

knowledge and practices concerning nature and the universe; as well as (5) traditional artisanship and craftsmanship. Recognizing that the boundaries between the domains are "extremely fluid and often vary from community to community," the UNESCO framework offers a wide array of variation and inclusivity of elements within its inventories.[84] Although ICH inventorying is a mandatory component of the Convention, the beauty is in the flexibility of documentation styles. Communities may add domains and/or divide manifestations of ICH elements according to their own needs. Broadening current categories or creating subcategories or new realms are also options.

Mauritius, for example, follows the domains laid out in the ICH Convention to organize its inventory, but Algeria and Haiti have separate categories for religious practices. Rather than a national inventory, Spain has elected to use Autonomous Community ICH Atlases that incorporate each region's ICH. While Kyrgyzstan created seven ICH domains and additional subdivisions, like "pastoral and nomadic knowledge," Venezuela's categories include "nature with a cultural significance" and "individual heritage bearer" as elements.[85] Poland recognizes regional "herbalism and plant [traditional] medicine" as its national heritage that is passed down in the home. Some State Parties explicitly mention "music and dance" rather than using the term "performing arts"; still others consider music separately from dance. Inventories are not meant to be exhaustive or limiting. Drawn up as written catalogues and/or digital collections, inventories are a classification and education system used to help organize information for community purposes.[86]

Since documentation is a community-based process, practical competency-based skills make it an empowering experience for members. Training workshops as well as technical and applied expertise in data management build capacity. Many communities undertake safeguarding activities without assistance from outside agencies, but policy planning in cultural heritage transmission is beneficial. Structural provisions about the value and diversity of ICH occur through education and advocacy. Governing bodies that guide adherence to local or cultural ethical standards and protocols as well as other scientific, technical, legal, and economic studies help manage divergent community views on safeguarding measures. Maintaining and updating inventories is advantageous for local development, and planning may involve working cooperatively with other organizations to promote understanding about an ICH element in daily life. Those in charge of implementing concrete safeguarding activities can be trained in ICH recording and coordinating ICH-related activities. In Brazil, the government has created "cultural reference centers" across the country to assist communities in ICH-based work. Hungary employs regional coordinators who act as a bridge between local communities and the state, and Venezuela established 287 community councils to help with safeguarding and promotion of the 687 groups representing diverse ICH elements.[87]

For Indigenous peoples in Canada, documentation of living heritage elements has the benefit of becoming a staple of Indigenous-led programming that puts natural and cultural heritage management at the forefront. ICH education and inventorying can become a component of the "culture camps" and community events already being organized by numerous Indigenous groups. If done effectively, such initiatives can play a role in enhancing land- and water-based skills and knowledges, thereby revitalizing sustainable livelihoods and "geo-linguistic expressions," oral terms a culture uses and which are anchored to a specific locale, environment, or activity. ICH custodians can share their cultural expressions in schools, during community and national or provincial events, and through other partnerships. By strengthening cultural programs and ICH-based economic development, documentation empowers self-governance initiatives. For communities who wish to nominate an element to a UNESCO list, the Intangible Cultural Heritage Fund offers technical and financial help worth up to $100,000 USD ($136,000 CAD) to support capacity building and preparation of inventories; unfortunately, only countries that have signed the ICH Convention are eligible for this funding.[88]

A recognition of intangible cultural heritage provides communities with not only a sense of identity and continuity but also creativity and control of their future. In the face of globalization, the ICH framework recognizes heterogeneity and reinforce communities' attempts to maintain their cultural richness. Without imposing rigid definitions, the ICH framework stresses that communities need to focus on today's cultural traditions. Traditions can be maintained in the high-tech era, and despite some groups' regarding their ICH as "unchanging," there is a general recognition that change is normal, natural, and ideally effected by communities themselves rather than imposed from the outside. In that regard, UNESCO specifies that there is no minimum duration for how long practices need to be established and transmitted between generations for them to be considered elements under the Convention. With the focus being revitalization and *living* heritage, it is up to a community to include an extinct heritage element in an inventory and determine what plans can be made for its revival.

Documentation does come with several challenges, with one being that ICH elements are intangible. Determining how to capture something without physical form or that only occurs in the moment of happening can be perplexing. But as I show through my work with the *akiwenziyag*, the intangible materializes through its custodians, ecosystems, and practices. Inventorying is also not limited to the intangible: Lithuania, for example, integrates tangible elements associated with a tradition bearer or with archives, including elements that are no longer exercised; Belgium includes elements of cyberculture and virtual experiences in its digital ICH classificatory system.[89]

I too sometimes struggle with "seeing" the intangible cultural elements. When I travelled with the *akiwenziyag*, it was not difficult to distinguish the obvious elements of cultural heritage: listening to a teaching or a song, eating a specific food, watching a dance, or sitting at a ceremony. It was easy to say: Wiindigo story, or *manoomin* (wild rice), or powwow—yup, elements of heritage, got it. But it is the deeper examination of the cultural impact and mechanisms of safeguarding that presents the challenge in inventories. It is how the Wiindigo permeates other teachings, behaviours, and perspectives among people today; how *manoomin* is valued, harvested, and processed by families in the modern world. It is also about determining how powwows are the foundation for an immense range of other characterizations and behaviours (how amazing it would be to nominate this vibrant intergenerational element to UNESCO's Representative List of the Intangible Cultural Heritage of Humanity as a cultural element of multiple nations![90]). Distinguishing something that is already part of everyday life and composing a detailed description with the intent that it can be re-enacted is very demanding. It is one thing to identify a certain type of dance, for example, but another thing to document the dance and establish compelling avenues for transmission in such a way that it can be successfully performed by future generations. This can be more challenging with cosmovisions, laws, or customary governance like *jiganawendamang Gidakiiminaan*.

It is vital to call attention to the fact that transmission goes beyond documentation. ICH elements are not meant to be documented and shelved. When ICH elements like stories, for example, are removed from the landscape, they are difficult to distinguish and often do not hold as much meaning. What makes the stories and the places compelling is seeing the places like Thunder Mountain, the trapline, Weaver Lake, and other spaces the land users discussed. The maps and the words on this page are what the *akiwenziyag* shared with me over the kitchen table or over a beaver home, and even as I bring these narratives to share with readers, they ultimately belong to the lands from which they originate—the lived heritage. What is important is that younger generations of community members can have access to these stories from the tellers themselves, not just from reading them. Personal transmission of living heritage supercedes documentation, and inventorying brings to light the fact that cultural heritage must fundamentally be *lived*.

Documentation summons questions around textualization and ethics, especially if a tradition is described and recorded in English or in a language other than the one through which the element is transmitted. Language poses a challenge when an oral expression or story is inscribed because there may not be any native speakers anymore to do recordings and further conveyance in a particular language. Similarly, if the youth do not speak the language but are interested in the stories to understand their world, the community must determine if stories can and should be translated to English or another dominant language or if the stories have more value in their original language. This, however, is complex as it raises the issue of either creating archival recordings of stories and practices, or completely overhauling avenues for cultural knowledge transmission.

A narrative or performance may also be ontologically transformed if secrecy, limited audiences, or other protocols accompany it. Richard Morrison explained that many Anishinaabe *aadizookaanag* and songs are shared only in specific seasons; some are told to certain people or clans only. This means that knowledge holders who do not wish for such stories or other elements to be audiovisually recorded need to be respected. Richard shared a thought-provoking anecdote about ethics and recording the *madoodoo*, sweatlodge ceremony. The *madoodoo* is a key cultural and spiritual element for many Anishinaabeg, and protective measures around the ceremony are important to many people. Richard laughed as he told me about the time someone attempted to make an audiovideo recording of a sweatlodge ceremony he was leading. The man was surprised that Richard said yes. Perhaps because it is a spiritual activity or maybe due to the moist environment, nothing was captured by the camera. Arguing that people should not worry too much about a ceremony being disrespected like this, Richard claimed laughing that it is "just the spirits' way of keeping things from being recorded."[91]

Inventorying can also lead to disputes between communities and among community members. Communities that regard an element as originating from them rather than from another group may feel a sense of ownership over the element. Because it is difficult to establish how many generations a tradition has been practised, particularly where language has traditionally not existed in written form, the need to pinpoint the origins of heritage may be desirable. This was the case for Indonesia and Malaysia, where Indonesians were urged by their president to wear batik clothes as a form of insistence that Malaysia had stolen the practice of creating batik fabric (and other Indonesian traditions). Batik, a method of making and decorating cloth by dipping wax in dye, was added to the UNESCO Representative List in 2009. The bitter cultural feud, which made international headlines, continues to raise issues of ownership, authenticity, official recognitions, alleged theft, and accusations of appropriations (this will be addressed shortly), but one UNESCO culture specialist has argued that Indonesia's batik traditions do not preclude other countries from claiming batik as well.[92] The argument points out that attempting to find an originator is nonsensical (especially if the cultures are very close), and that it is perfectly acceptable that two different nations nominate the same ICH element as representative of their identity. Imposing a source or age requirement contradicts the spirit of the Convention, whose goal is continuity of an element.[93] While UNESCO cannot enforce any legal measures to sanction protection of the identified elements within nations, it can refuse to place an element on its ICH lists or remove it.

The batik case illustrates that national, provincial, and regional borders do not always match cultural borders. Communities themselves need to decide what to recognize as their ICH, but they must also be aware that those elements may exist in multiple regions. I have already noted the multiplicity of Nations that participate in powwows, rendering this element important in many Indigenous cultures, and on both sides of the Canada–U.S. border. Indigenous communities, thus, have the option to document their ICH elements according to nationhood, territories or landscapes, or provincial and territorial boundaries. However, specific administrative divisions (like those of treaty lands or provinces) may not coincide with borders that were traditionally occupied by different ethnolinguistic or otherwise definable Indigenous communities, but communities can work together to support each other in the process. Documentation could be unique, too, and take the form of a list or inscribed research or maps with all the different ICH elements in Canada present in each Indigenous cultural area or territory. How interesting it would be to see a First Nation-led inventory of all the cultural elements—immigrant, Euro-Canadian, and other Indigenous cultures—present in their territory! Another creative option could be to list ICH elements according to natural features and ecosystems—or simply by domains. Haiti, for example, uses national borders to organize its heritage inventory, but Venezuela, Colombia, and Poland divide their inventories along internal lines. Ultimately, ICH is not about boundaries or tenure; it is about the transmission of an element a group finds important to their identity.

Since inventories obligate communities to pick elements of culture that they want to safeguard, one may ask whether ICH "itemizes" culture. While humans naturally categorize things (edible vs. non-edible berries; rubber boots vs. work shoes), identifying separates elements and emphasizes difference (e.g., a Mushkego Inninu spiritual song is not an Anishinaabe Bear Song is not a Syrian Jewish *pizmon* song). Nevertheless, ICH inventorying helps organize knowledge so that it is easier to navigate for a specific purpose (such as for education or for an impact assessment statement) and establish a concrete measure of protection. For example, if a community identifies powwow dancing as an ICH element of their culture, it is because it is a vibrant and living practice that is passed on from generation to generation, and because communities already devote resources to ensuring it continues, such as building powwow grounds and holding powwows. Identifying dancing emphasizes its uniqueness; it is not *manoominekewin*, ricing (knowledge), or *madoodoo*, a sweatlodge ceremony. In identifying different elements, inventorying points to already existing categorizations where certain members of a community are recognized ICH custodians because they have gravitated toward certain elements more than others (e.g., some opt to dance while others may be more interested in learning about plant medicine or language instruction; some may do all three).[94] This means that inventorying (powwow) dancing offers the opportunity to learn more about the different dances (Crowhop Dance, Men's Traditional, and Grass Dance, etc.) as well as about the regalia for each type of dance or person, drumming styles and techniques, philosophies and values, and other domains associated with that element. By speaking with different community members such as singers, drummers, regalia makers, Elders, observers, harvesters, and masters of ceremonies, inventorying permits everyone to exchange knowledge on a wide range of features (some seemingly unrelated to dancing) that *together* make up the identified element. When all community members participate and demonstrate the myriad of cultural elements that represent their community, inventorying deepens knowledge of culture.

Therefore through documentation, the ICH framework offers a constructive approach to cultural heritage. It brings forth the understanding that different temporal and historical contexts, hybrid and transnational identities, and fluid national boundaries and migration impact its form. ICH inventories also offer a powerful tool when a community is approached by outsiders or when its members want to learn about their own heritage; documentation places communities in a position to make decisions at the local level. ICH inventorying has even led to building and rebuilding peace, as in Papua New Guinea, where ethnographic records have assisted communities in reconnecting with their disrupted heritage, and in Rwanda, where traditional court systems are used to build justice and peace. In Canada, the ICH discourse can be used as a human rights instrument to build mutual respect and social cohesion among communities. Other countries' active engagement in this work also shows that recognition and promotion of ICH bolsters environmental sustainability and reinforces cultural identities, practices, and well-being.[95]

Protecting Living Knowledges

During the drafting of the 2003 ICH Convention, UNESCO decided that the document would not affect any existing intellectual property (IP) rights.[96] The organization addresses the issue of conventional and *sui generis* intellectual property regimes by relegating the responsibility and options for safeguarding to State Parties. Referring to international agreements such as the World Trade Organization's Agreement on Trade-Related Aspects of Intellectual Property Rights (TRIPS)[97] and the Berne and Paris Conventions,[98] UNESCO states that the framework of IP protection can support safeguarding by promoting a community's benefits from and stewardship over its ICH. Because IP rights can help owners "control access to and use of certain knowledge, representations, and practices, they [. . .] can help prevent the misappropriation of ICH from communities concerned and ensure that benefits are channeled back into communities."[99] In considering the relationship between ICH safeguarding and intellectual property, communities need to balance ways of maximizing protective or beneficial outcomes with any potential negative effects associated with IP regimes. While IP regimes are not the only options for ICH protection, ICH policy making should consider IP-related issues carefully.[100]

Addressing the question of agency and representation, ownership, and IP regimes, Australian law professor Lucas Lixinski writes that one of the primary issues with community control is the question of "who gets to register the manifestations of heritage on behalf of the community, and who administers and controls the rights of the community to attribution and even royalties."[101] Rendering details of music, an art form, or a knowledge public (especially of medicinal plants or healing ceremonies) may lead to appropriation by and economic benefits to others. It can also spearhead increased tourism to sacred or culturally relevant spaces as well as commodification of craftsmanship or a skill. Exposure of elements brings with it an array of issues, including disagreements with IP regimes as well as need for protection from outsiders, even the state itself.

Restrictions and limitations to public access of an element are understandable and need to be included in an inventory. Elements that are too personal, spiritual, or not appropriate for the process do not have to be described. The ICH Convention emphasizes that safeguarding measures and any descriptions, details, images, or digital recordings are determined solely by the community. In 2011, for example, Colombia inscribed the traditional knowledge of the jaguar shamans of Yuruparí from the Pirá Paraná River. The sacred cosmological structures that make up the traditional knowledge of the jaguar shamans are based on ceremonial rituals to draw the community together, to heal, to prevent sickness, and to revitalize nature. The rituals feature songs and dances that are believed to be inherited from an all-powerful, mythical Yuruparí, an anaconda that lived as a person. This story is embodied in sacred trumpets fashioned from a particular palm tree, and male children learn these practices as a part of their passage into adulthood, known as the Hee Biki ritual. Women learn food preparation as well as nursing techniques for children and pregnant women during this ceremony.[102] Other than the ten-minute introductory video of the jaguar shamans preparing for the Hee Biki on the UNESCO website, access to the digital content is restricted and permission must be obtained from the copyright holder, the Asociación de Capitanes y Autoridades Tradicionales Indígenas del Río Pirá Paraná.

This case study demonstrates that knowledge holders and communities will need to cooperate with institutions or governments to determine protocols around access, protection, and intellectual property–related issues.

At present, IP regimes, intellectual property, and the rights of traditional knowledge holders are pushing the limits of existing intellectual property laws.[103] The ICH Convention encourages states to explore and extend conventional IP regimes but also recognizes that communities should hold ownership of their intellectual property.[104] Communities considering commercializing their cultural practices or elements should look to the World Intellectual Property Organization (WIPO) and explore patents, the Ownership, Control, Access, and Protection (OCAP) principles, as well as the principles of free, prior, and informed consent (FPIC).[105] These resources are included in Appendix 3. In the Philippines, for example, in tandem with customary laws and practices, the Indigenous Peoples' Rights Act (1997) requires free, prior, and informed consent of communities prior to ICH use by third parties.[106] Although this approach to knowledge does not fully fit with the community's world view, a *sui generis* solution is developed for each case after community negotiations.[107] In Madagascar, Betsileo community members register their art work with the Zafimaniry trademark on all woodcraft products. The Zafimaniry are a sub-group of the Betsileo, living in remote forest regions in the highlands of southeast Madagascar. To guard their body of practical proficiency in forestry and wood sculpting, the Zafimaniry use cultural motifs representative of community life to protect their creativity from commercialization. Abu Dhabi, on the other hand, took a more formal route and established the Zayed Complex for Herbal and Traditional Medicine Research Centre, recognized by the World Health Organization as a centre for alternative medicine in the Middle East. The Zayed Complex manages a database of traditional knowledge for IP protection.[108] Placing a community practice, knowledge, or music on the UNESCO register also protects these elements from theft, as they are publicly recognized and chances for misappropriation are very slim.

Some communities look to using their own governance structures for protection. To date, these strategies include communities separating their knowledges and skills among members, providing access to information to members by demand only, having many caretakers of inventories, and giving "access keys" under strict guidelines.[109] Two examples illustrate community resistance against exploitation. In Varanasi, India, exquisitely embroidered fine silk Banarasi sarees are handmade by traditional crafters. To distinguish these sarees from Chinese-made synthetic sarees (misrepresentation), the producers have registered a geographical indication for their clothing. A geographical indication is a sign used on original products that have a specific geographical origin and possess qualities or a reputation arising from that origin.[110] To distinguish their products from the fakes, the indication helps market buyers to recognize that the hand-made silk qualities of the reputed product are owing to their Banarasi origin. Similarly, the Sápmi have relied on IP regimes to shield their ritual drum from appropriation. Decorated with religious and cultural symbols, the drum was taken from a Sápmi shaman in 1693 and placed in a German museum, where it still is today. A jewellery company registered a trademark using the sun symbol from the drum in 2009 and attempted to stop Sápmi craftspeople (artists and poets) from using the symbol (that is, misappropriating or taking without permission). The Sápmi crafters filed a complaint to the IP office in Norway and the government subsequently invalidated the company's mark. The Sápmi are now working to get their drum back.[111]

Customary laws offer IP-like opportunities to help with access, enforcement, damages for infringement, or other forms of indemnity of a cultural right. In some Dakelh communities, for instance, access to and singing of songs is inherent within the hereditary traditions like the *bahlats*, meaning that only family members control the use of certain sounds, texts, and musical compositions.[112] Richard Morrison also argues that only the Creator or dreams can "gift" certain ceremonial drum songs. This means that someone cannot (and should not) play a Bear Song on social media as their own and a group would unlikely play a Food Song at a powwow.[113] Unfortunately, because Canadian copyright law limits ownership to one individual for up to fifty years after the death of the copyright holder, the law does not account for the collective and intergenerational transmission of many Indigenous songs and artistic expressions. To overcome this limitation, the Kwakwaka'wakw Nation, for example, looks to its own self-determination to protect their performances. Collective in nature, Kwagiulth performances are inherited from one person to another, sometimes intergenerationally but not necessarily. To address IP-related issues, the nation asks all outsiders who are interested in Kwakwaka'wakw culture to deal with them directly. As part of any collaboration, rules and guidelines about ownership are determined by the nation and partners must abide by them.[114]

Third-party assistance becomes important when inventories offer incentives for community members and when attributions do not sufficiently aid in safeguarding.[115] This is extremely useful when ICH custodians capitalize on their ICH elements and fellow community members expect moral and material benefits to be shared.[116] Protecting knowledges and cultures from exploitation is a serious consideration for communities. At the same time, extremely stringent protective measures can counteract ICH safeguarding. Safeguarding measures are meant to ensure viability and not to hide an element from other community members. In the Introduction, we met a man who criticized Richard's use of power tools to shape his pipestone bowl. Ironically, this was also the same individual who, to the dismay of his own (and neighbouring) community Elders, uses a jet boat to harvest *manoomin*, wild rice. What's worse, the man promoted the rice as being harvested by a "traditional knowledge holder" . . . and sold it back to community members and outsiders at extremely high prices. Making a living from heritage while safeguarding ICH is a balancing act for communities, but as case studies from around the globe show, when safeguarding measures are carried out in an equitable way, communities can benefit from their ICH-related goods and services to ensure sustainable livelihoods.[117]

His hand pointing at the horizon, Abel tells me there are several rapids along the Mukatewa and that one of the portages is as long as from his house to the Northern Store (about 300 metres). He pauses and we listen to the silence for several minutes. I hear him chuckle and look over at him. Smiling, he explains how one time he and his trapping partner found a red balloon along the river. It was stuck in a tree, and the novelty of coming across this odd find incited the men to cut down the tree and bring the object down. Abel thinks it was a weather balloon and a transmitter of some kind. The men examined it and took it apart, very amused at their discovery. I also laugh at this story and say how fun it must have been to inspect such an un-ordinary item, to which Abel responds, "Oh, we travelled all along that [Mukatewa] river. My line is down the river there. Ah, there are all of them . . . stories. We always see some thing or other."

In this vastness of the open muskeg, I acknowledge the experience that a trapper must have in order to live eight months on the trapline with a nod and a mm-hmm. Alone or with a partner, this is a tough life. I think about how resourceful and skilled an *akiwenzi* like Abel is; how much knowledge he has. I think how much learning I would have to go through to live out a year (or even two months) on a trapline by myself or with a trapping partner. As if reading my mind, Abel stretches his hand out in front of him and tells me this story:

> Oh, we travelled all along that [Mukatewa] river there. I go further [down the river] to my line. I used to trap with my dad. We never used to have these [points to snares]. We could not afford to buy it, you know. One time there, we trapped a, whatcha call it, an

otter. My dad and me, we caught a mink too. My dad used to have braces you know, he had these braces. He cut off a piece [points to his shoulder] and we made a snare out of that. I couldn't believe it, myself. I watched him do that. ["It worked?" I asked.] It worked. Those Old People long time ago, they would do that. They would take the overall[s] . . . they made a snare there. I couldn't believe it myself, there. You gotta talk to those Old People, to my brother next door. The young people, they gotta know how to do work like that, to work like that, to work like those Old People.[118]

Standing side by side, Abel and I are almost the same height, but I feel so humbled. Everything is covered in a thick fluff of white. The snow is inviting in appearance. Some distance beyond, the endless chain of pines and poplar trees descends into the winter sky; other than for the few clouds floating just above the horizon the sky is clear. Everything seems to be in order, at peace, in this little corner of Abel's paradise on earth.

Later, I realize that none of the *akiwenziyag* have ever expressed concern about someone stealing their knowledge. The land-based skills and experiences of these men cannot be stolen, appropriated, or co-opted. They cannot be learned from books. What "gives" the *akiwenziyag* that "sacred traditional knowledge" everyone seems to be looking for is their lifetime on the land. Any individual who decides to spend their own lifetime learning and working (hard) alongside an *akiwenzi* can also earn the gift of that knowledge.

Chapter Three
"The last one to know"

I am driving to Nigigoonsiminikaaning with Richard Morrison again. This year, I am helping him "put out" fasters, that is, people who will fast or participate in a "vision quest" ceremony (Richard never uses the term "vision quest"). One time, as we were organizing materials for the autumn fast, he mentioned that the ceremony is not just about seeking visions. As *mashkiki inini*, Richard has been putting out fasters for decades, and he shared that many people tend to expect a magical and guaranteed spiritual or paranormal experience. He was often amused at individuals who fasted competitively, to see who could stay out the longest and in the most extreme conditions, or who had the most extraordinary visions. Rather, Richard argued, some visions or moments of realization "come to you if you are ready" and this could be years later. Having put out many different fasters, for Richard, fasting is as much about the character of the faster as it is about visions.

Figure 15. One of the islands on Ottertail Lake where fasters may spend up to seven nights alone and without any food or fire.

We drive from Winnipeg and pick up people as well as a boat along the way. En route, we visit some communities to get helpers for the ceremony. About five adults are fasting this year, and each of them will be put out on their own island in Ottertail Lake (Figure 15). They will be alone and without food, water, or fire for a few days. Some individuals have brought a sleeping bag; some come with a backpack filled with tools or sacred items; one person is going to fast with nothing. I have already fasted a few years prior, so now is my turn to help. While the participants are enduring the challenges that come with being alone and stripped away from all human conveniences, I assist with the arrangements, the preparations, and all the other backstage activities that need to occur. Richard and other Elders will hold a sweat ceremony each day to pray for the fasters, and to give them strength and perseverance. I help by getting the firewood and doing the cleaning. I also prepare snacks and do the cooking, and there is a lot of food to make: Richard and four of his brothers are all six feet tall and over 250 pounds, so serving them food is an unending task. In an attempt to satisfy the perpetually hungry men, I am creative and serve them an exquisite Polish meal of hand-picked wild mushrooms sautéed in cream; only Richard eats the "slippery" dish with satisfaction.

A few days after the fast, Richard and I meet up for breakfast at a Winnipeg restaurant. He sprinkles lots of pepper on his plate and his eggs are blackened by the spice. Although never calling himself Medicine Man (he always says that he is "just a human being"), Richard enjoys working with academics in that role. He has travelled extensively across central Canada and into the United States to share his Anishinaabe teachings, with several of them ending up on the internet later. As we eat, Richard tells me how his Elders would frequently meet with university professors from different disciplines, including physics and chemistry, to have long and engaging conversations about topics like the cosmos and about one's purpose in life. Richard tells me that science is a common language between the two seemingly opposing groups and shares a Four Directions teaching his Elders taught him about human connection:

> In those teachings, those Four Directions, we say *waabanong* [to the East], and then we say to the West, *ningaabii'ianong*, the North Star. But really [*waabanong*] doesn't just mean East, it also means "a light," the eastern star. A gathering of lights. That's what it is. Like all the stars are one big ball of light. So, all the stars in every universe, they're all together [. . .] even though to us, they're billions of miles apart. So, the thing is, they're actually together. *Dibinawe inaangoomidiwag* [they are directly related to each other] so, there's no distance between them and they all energize each other.[1]

For Richard, the East Direction teaching informs the role of humans in the universe and how we all relate to each other. Stating that we may appear to be "billion of lights apart" as human beings from different areas on the globe, we actually energize each other and learn from each other. Elaborating on that collective human energy, Richard tells me that "in our language we say 'Mide'[wewin].' *Mide* means the universe at heart. *Ode*, the heart, is the universe. So, when we think about it, when we put the heart as our centre [of decision making] we can slow things down. We can feel, emotionally, and we can understand emotions of others. We can understand each other."[2]

While energy in physics is understood as a process or transfer of "work" from one body to another,[3] Richard uses this capacity for doing work to help fasters learn about the Anishinaabe understanding of the concept of energy. Writing down several Anishinaabemowin terms on a paper napkin, Richard tells me that the sound *ode* refers to a type of energy, like a heartbeat: *ode*, heart, is the energy, our hearts. *Giiwedinong* [the North Star] is the energy, "the heartbeat" of the north. Richard then explains his understanding of fire, *ishkode*, is the same *ode*, that energy that creates fire, hence *ishk-ode*. He continues, "When we say *noondeskade* hungry, *noondeskade*, *noonde-*, to need, in need of, is also 'short of energy in the heart.' And when we say *mino-*, that universe of I and me, there's an energy in my heart that we carry. And now *bimaadiz[i]* means 'alive.' It's energy, like a living cell, like a ball of water. There's that little energy inside of you [that is filled] from that need."[4] As a member of the Midewewin,[5] Richard states that *mide*, from Midewewin, can be understood to be "the fire in the heart of the Midewewin [society]," and that many Elders have "fuelled" collective Anishinaabe knowledge with new experiences, innovative skills, and personal lessons. In Richard's view, the Elders and the physics professors were able to have hour-long conversations because they were exchanging knowledges "from the heart." Like the physics professors who networked with the Elders, Richard believes that everyone can learn from Anishinaabe teachings because "we all live the Four Directions." He explains:

The essence of life, the beauty of it, it's there. [. . .] When a baby is born, we put out their belly button and hang it in a tree, *mitig*, because *mitig* is the universe of all life. Everything came from the universe to come here to this physical world we live in. And that's so we stay connected to that energy of the tree. We can't see it, we can't hear it [but] we can feel it. I tell fasters all the time "Put your hands straight out and pivot." You can feel that heat, that energy from the four directions. You can just feel that. That's the energy I'm talking about. We align ourselves [when] we own those, the good and the bad. [Richard pulls out a feather.] Like that feather, life is decided for us [runs his fingers along the spine of the feather], but we carry the good and the bad . . . it's just less [remarkable] as we get old [points to the tip of the feather]. That philosophy, to balance things with our hearts, to balance ourselves as we travel in all those directions [points to the soft parts of the feather] . . . everyone can learn and benefit from that.[6]

Having taken many learners under his wing over the years, Richard worries that "many young people today are no longer interested, they just prefer to watch TV than do that hard [cultural] work. Who's gonna learn the culture then?"[7] For this *akiwenzi*, the teachings of his Elders need to be passed down so all humans can benefit from Anishinaabe *gikendam-owin*, knowledge/way of knowing.[8]

Immersive Pedagogies

In 2015, the Truth and Reconciliation Committee (TRC) released its *Calls to Action*, a document outlining a path of reconciliation for Indigenous and non-Indigenous communities. The Calls to Action are a response to the imposition of Euro-Canadian world views on Indigenous oral traditions, cultural knowledges, ontologies, and linguistic expressions.

To address the ongoing impacts of residential schools and the rupture of cultural transmission, the Calls to Action detail recommendations across a wide range of areas, including child welfare, education, health, justice, language, and culture. In Call to Action 62, the TRC addresses the need to make appropriate curriculum about Indigenous peoples' "historical and contemporary contributions to Canada."[9] The call foregrounds the integral role funding plays in educating future teachers on how to integrate and utilize Indigenous knowledge and cultural teaching methods in classrooms.[10] In a similar vein, the UNESCO ICH Convention addresses the loss of ICH elements by Indigenous and other groups through colonization, migration, technology, and globalization. Many young people today spend much of their time in school or on social media, away from other community members, leading to the erosion of informal ICH education that is passed down in the home.[11] With non-formal education interrupted or constrained, formal education systems of schools and universities are being conscripted to fill the gaps.[12]

Highlighting the vital role of education and of formal learning in safeguarding ICH, the views of the ICH Convention and the TRC align on the methods of instruction and support for cultural revitalization efforts. Traditionally, intergenerational cultural knowledge, much like all ICH transmission, occurred informally by watching, listening, participating, and repeating (Figure 16).[13] Families and communities often used social institutions and recognized Elders to train young people. Apprenticeship with a carving expert or a *mashkiki inini* meant spending significant time with a knowledge holder to learn their skills. Relying on the immersive pedagogy he experienced as a child, Richard welcomes individuals to dark room ceremonies, shaking tents, fasts, and naming ceremonies. He teaches the sweatlodge ceremony beginning with the preparation for and building of a sweatlodge through to the taking down of a *madoodoswaan*, illustrating that heritage education can take place through ICH elements.

Figure 16. Three generations: Richard, *ogozisan*, his son, and *oozhishenyan*, his grandchild, putting out tobacco together prior to learning about medicines, pipe making, and Anishinaabe *gigikinoo'amaagoowinan*, teachings.

The ICH Convention encourages State Parties to institute educational programs and interventions related to cultural transmission.[14] These include promoting multilingual education, developing curricular resources, and training teachers in ICH. Involving parents and practitioners, arranging participatory or place-based pedagogical experiences, and integrating ICH into vocational training are some innovative examples of pedagogy already used in classrooms around the world. Malaysia, Poland, and Korea integrate living heritage into their national curricula, and Mauritius promotes traditional games among schoolchildren through extracurricular activities. Latvia receives municipal support for ICH education and uses the funding for folk costumes, traditional instruments, rehearsal spaces, and travel to cultural events. China and Lithuania both integrate living heritage into non-formal education by embedding music and dance groups in tertiary education and by teaching traditional craftsmanship and art as part of state curricula. Multiple countries, including Canada, also offer training courses and workshops in ICH management and inventorying at the post-secondary level.

With the intent to move toward achieving reconciliation and to support safeguarding of cultural heritage, the ICH framework provides an opportunity not only to respond to the TRC's Calls to Action and RCAP's recommendations on Indigenous language education systems[15] but also to adopt UNDRIP's principles on education systems. Residential schools overtly interrupted the chain of cultural transmission in the attempt to assimilate Indigenous people.[16] Affirming that Indigenous peoples have the right to "education in their own languages, in a manner appropriate to their cultural methods of teaching and learning," ICH-responsive pedagogies can build on existing curricula and develop innovative pedagogies. In Canada, primary and higher education systems already rely on land immersion to foster learning about cyclical environmental knowledge, land skills, leadership, and life skills.[17] Post-secondary institutions are also designing courses that bridge Indigenous knowledges and academia. My own courses are geared toward ICH pedagogies, and, in collaboration with two Dakelh Elders, I offered a course entitled "First Nations Cultural Heritage through Moose Hide Tanning" in 2016 at the University of Northern British Columbia. Taking place over a span of three weeks, the course merged the practice of moosehide tanning in the Dakelh way with diverse issues in cultural heritage. The course was unique in the sense that the natural process of working with the hide guided the in-class components, so when the hide was soaking or "resting" to absorb grease, the students learned about ICH scholarship. The key goal of the course was to have the students experience both Dakelh and academic teaching methods simultaneously, as well as to illustrate that informal training mechanisms such as listening, hard work, attention to detail, and perseverance exist in both pedagogical settings.[18] The course was a means for teaching about ICH transmission, and the moosehide tanning component highlighted the fact that learning about Dakelh cultural safeguarding occurs best *through* Dakelh heritage.

The recent post-TRC move to restructure education in Canada illustrates an evolving approach to heritage. Conceptualizing heritage in ways where multiple stakeholders interpret its significance and value more openly has led to an emergence of innovative ways to include Indigenous lived heritages as something that goes beyond authoritative and objective understanding of "cultural artifacts." Working in a European context, Tim Copeland and Angela Labrador distinguish between education *about* heritage, education *through* heritage, and education *for* heritage.[19] In the first instance, when students learn about heritage, only cognitive competencies are engaged. In the second, students draw on their cognitive and affective competencies when heritage is used to learn another subject. When learning *for* heritage, that is, comprehensively linking heritage across disciplines and abilities, action-oriented competencies are employed along with cognitive and affective competencies. Education *for* heritage *through* ICH elements permits critical pedagogy and awareness of one's own (and others') cultures to build capacity for intercultural understanding, empathy, linguistic compentency, and mutual respect.[20]

Part of the struggle to include ICH and Indigenous knowledges in education curricula is the problem of "undoing" standardized curricula. In *Pedagogy of the Oppressed*, Paulo Freire advocates for students to become "co-investigators in dialogue with the teacher" and solve real-world problems relating to their own experience.[21] Freire's influential work aspires to include action-oriented heritage competency, and his argumentation accompanied the Dakelh moosehide tanning course discussed above. In the classroom, the students were introduced to ICH identification, artifact repatriation, and language revitalization policies; this teaches about heritage. Subsequently, the students were shown how archeology and heritage scholarship can enhance Dakelh knowledge and land claims; this is teaching through heritage. Finally, having the students pull, stretch, and scrape the hide as they discussed the readings actively exhibited to them not only how context-based Indigenous cultural practices

Figure 17. In this photo, Richard is pointing across the river to a site of an old community where he spent much of his formative years before his family was moved to Nigigoonsiminikaaning.

can become a form of sustainable livelihoods but also that it takes a community (or at least twelve people) to ensure such a practice survives; this is teaching for heritage. In this pedagogical context, a more active and collaborative participation enriched didactic lectures, while at the same time formal-and-Dakelh-together teaching styles geared instruction for heritage *through* living heritage. Having gained competency in university-level curricular standards, the students built their curiosity around Dakelh heritage, language, and tanning skills, and developed the commitment required to inspire transmission.[22] The experience, therefore, placed students in an active role of "articulating their own ethical obligation toward heritage and applying heritage knowledge to solve a contemporary problem."[23]

Richard also demonstrates his teaching for heritage through different Anishinaabe cultural elements. He takes out fasters to teach them about ecology, Anishinaabemowin, and spiritual values through what he refers to as *giikendamaazo*, "to know things by way of sense, to take knowledge on." In tandem with the surrounding soundscapes, Richard uses a multisensory teaching style to instruct the fasters about the ability to focus (on the experience and not their hunger) and to absorb knowledge (from the spirits, the animals, and their own emotions). Answering my question about experiential pedagogy, Richard states:

> Well, we gotta go back to the beginning of life. When we say *waabamaawaso* [it] means "to see in and at [birth]."[24] When we came here, we didn't know anything. We didn't know language, we didn't know the difference between the colour of human beings, the way that a human being looked like. We all heard the heartbeat for nine months. That's what we're all, we're all trained, to do. We were all trained to feel the essence of that heartbeat. When we hear a drum, we can calm down real quick. When we hear a rattle, that rattle takes away our thoughts. We call it *zhinawishin* [rattling, it rattles to me]. *Zhinawishin*, [it] cleanses the way that we, we keep this light-energy at its most pure. This light, like when we shake a rattle, [it] helps your mind [to] just slow down. [It] slows down. Pretty soon your mind just focuses on that sound, on that sound. What happens is, [then] we're not thinking. Then we relax, and we can learn. [This] calms me a thousand times faster than therapy.[25]

Richard uses "immersion in everything" as his pedagogy. He tells me that emotions, sounds, and energies help us grow, develop, and be better human beings. While the sound of a rattle helps Richard get rid of distractions, the sound of a drum connects him to his feelings and thoughts. This is true for the fasters who are left alone on a small island, with the sound of the water and the shaking of trees in the wind accompanying them on their journey. The solitude of the fast provides fasters with perspective and strengthens their endurance; sometimes the gift of *mawadishiwe*, a visit by an animal or spirit, can make the experience more meaningful. Being alone in the bush without food, water, or even fire teaches about one's role and responsibilities in the world, and indeed can work "a thousand times faster than therapy."

For many individuals across this boreal landscape, spending time on the land was not a pastime; it was their childhood (Figure 17). Although interrupted during the residential school era, many of the men affirm the value of a land-based upbringing. Some 600 kilometres north of Nigigoonsiminikaaning, in Poplar River, the former chief of the community, Russell Lambert, acknowledges that spending time on the land was not only emotionally meaningful but also taught him the value of long days and hard work: "When I came back from [my] first year of university, I went out with my dad to his trapline. And we spent about three or four weeks there. And it was something very dear to me, because it was a big change for me; none of this nine-to-five thing—because sunrise to dusk, that's when your day ends. And we were on the go for about twelve, maybe fifteen hours a day. And of course, there was no hydro [electricity], so when you came back, it was almost bedtime. And when the sun rose, is when the day started."[26] Life on the trapline started at daybreak and ended when the sun set. Responsibilities were not determined by abstract time; rather, work was performed until it was done. Russell maintains that it is good for the youth to experience the life of a trapper and the industriousness that goes into this activity: "We want them to know who they are, to work, to be responsible. But also, that they have a future here," he tells me. Rose Klippenstein, a nurse born and raised in the community, agrees with Russell. She shares that "if you get the young people in there [in the bush], to educate the smaller ones [. . .], they can proudly say that 'this is my home.' I work hard to keep my home."[27]

Patience and a strong determination to do what needs to be done despite hunger, physical discomfort, and stiff fingers comprise the demanding work of a land-based livelihood. For the land users, the land teaches survival skills as much as it shapes individual character and respect for *aki*. The traplines also reinforce the emotional bonds between a head trapper and his helper, who are generally family. Abel Bruce's stories about Mukatewasipe, for example, are often about his father, uncle, and his nephew, Willie. His stories not only prolong the memory of those individuals and keep *their* stories alive but also extend *akiwenziyag* pedagogies. Cultural landscapes are the training ground for living heritage transmission, and immersive pedagogies teach through stories about fathers and sons, uncles and nephews, daughters and grandmothers, all who are learning from each other about what it means to be... Anishinaabe, "human."

"It's good to eat"

We are out on the land south of Poplar River in 2010, and Abel Bruce has not said anything for a while. He is driving the snowmobile; I am again in the home-made plywood trailer attached to the back of the snowmobile. I can film freely, but I must also endure the extremely loud sounds of the engine and the fumes that escape it. We have been driving around for some time now, and I am certain he is as hungry as I am. Every so often, Abel stops and disappears into the trees. He comes back a few minutes later and, without a word, starts the machine up again. In some places, he stops for a longer period, and I see him checking something near the ground or picking at a tree. He gestures when he wants me to join him, so I usually wait until I get the go-ahead. In one spot, he puts up his arm to the sky, and offers tobacco. After what seems like a long time of this, he stops, turns off the snowmobile, and starts unloading our equipment. I understand this to be a stop for us both and help. Without talking, we start a fire and open our lunches. "It's good to eat," he finally says.

Abel has spent much of his trapping life consuming *aki(iwi) miijim*, land food.[28] His dad and uncle taught him how to harvest, and now he teaches his nephew and grandson this livelihood. The Asatiwisipe *akiiwi miijim* is one of many diverse Indigenous diets consisting of plant and animal resources that have cultural meaning as traditional food. Reflecting the larger pattern of relationships between community members and the structural organization of land, the food system is another element of this *akiwenzi*'s intangible cultural heritage. Similar to the diversity of Indigenous ICHs discussed in the previous chapter, there exists a plurality of Indigenous peoples' food systems. Indigenous food systems reflect not only the environment in which people live but also the local and cultural knowledge that guides practices surrounding food production. These food systems are integral to community and individual well-being, health, and development.[29] They are also a part of a larger framework that incorporates self-determination, customary governance, and resource stewardship into social relationships.[30]

What distinguishes Indigenous food systems is that they have been in existence for generations and are formed around socio-environmental organization. They define cultural epistemes that exist within a nation in a comparable environment. Whereas some Inuit eat seals, others rely on caribou as their main diet; likewise, some Anishinaabeg eat black bears, others do not.[31] The Anishinaabeg extend over a large geography around the Great Lakes, ranging west from what is now the Ottawa area to as far as Northern Manitoba. This large portion of land suggests that Anishinaabeg in different areas may have a different set of food and customary practices surrounding food. Cultural variation is an important part of foodways and Asatiwisipe Anishinaabe *aki miijim* exists as a sovereign process based on complex consumption patterns arising out of unique cultural traditions and maintained through *akiing ondaaji'idizowining*, customary and land-based livelihood practices.[32] As an identifiable ICH element, the Asatiwisipe Anishinaabe food system roots people to a particular geography. Consumed in tandem with store-bought food, this bush diet illustrates the ongoing and contemporary nature of living heritage.

One Poplar River Elder, Alex Mitchell, states that:

local people would use birch-bark baskets to collect sap, a very sweet drink from birch trees [and] collect red leaves or in Saulteaux terms (*kakegaypugoon*) which the people would pick from the muskeg to make tea. [. . .] There used to [also] be a lot of Indian carrots that grew in certain places [and people] would use the carrots for cooking stews and soup. After picking the carrots people would replant them near their homes for future use. Another delicacy called lichen (*ateinewackunuck*) that they would use for fish soup and moose stew. Pemmican was also another food that they ate. First, they would dry the meat and then they would mash or pound it, then afterwards they would mix it with oil and fat from the moose meat.[33]

Alex points out that local knowledge and the ability to identify plants to make bush food such as pemmican secures a livelihood, speaking to the fact that one cannot eat if a harvest is unsuccessful. Another Poplar River Elder, Ken Douglas, shared similar stories of local knowledge. Until his passing in 2014, Ken's *dibaajimowinan*, stories, informed my grasp of the narratives surrounding this food system. Patting his stomach, this *akiwenzi* frequently asserted that he had always found joy in eating and appreciated being so well fed at the Elder's Lodge. Ken said that it made him "feel good" to eat food from the land because it is what he had always eaten during his trapping and fishing days: "I like to eat pickerel, jack fish. We used to eat mariah.[34] Jackfish livers, even whitefish livers, they are pretty good. Mix them with flour . . . Pretty good. I miss eating [land] food. I used to like beaver and muskrat. You sell the [beaver] fur . . . and the[ir] meat is soft and has lots of fat. But muskrat does not have fat [. . .]. I like beaver smoked and boiled. We used to smoke and we used to boil them, same as [musk]rats."[35] Knowledge of edible products on the trapline can mean life or death, and Ken exhibited that with beaver knowledge:

Figure 18. Abel Bruce pulling out the medicines he collects.

"They [the beaver] have good meat in them. They taste good, but not when it's hot. Beaver, it can make you sick when it's not cooled off. That's when you eat it [or] it can make you real sick, real bad. Because it [the beaver] has lots of fat on him, you'll have to wait till it's cooled off, then you can eat it. If somebody brings it to me, I'll eat it same as moose meat [but] it's gotta be cooled down."[36] Ken's comment illustrates that skills are needed to harvest, but that another layer of knowledge is required to turn the animal into food. Whereas many *akiwenziyag* knew everything about the bush life, Ken was saddened that people are "not learning [as] much today. They are not learning [because] they are not out on the land much. Not like we used to be, us, in the old days."[37] *Aki miijim* then, serves as a pedagogical element through which local ICH elements are transmitted.

Many *akiwenziyag* interpret *aki miijim* as a form of medicine that nourishes both the animals and the harvester; it is the connection of all living things on *aki*. When Abel and I ventured out on the winter road to Berens River in 2010, we were discussing beaver—its taste, its fur, and how best to catch it. As we walked along a frozen stream, Abel kept pointing to sites and exclaiming that *this* was the best place to set a trap. Later, from the road he signalled and said, "No good [beaver] here. Not too good, those ones."[38] When we stood alongside the snowmobile path to this trapline a few weeks later, Abel once again pointed with his hand and emphasized that *here* is where you find *good* beaver. It was then that

I understood what he was trying to tell me. As a component of *aki miijim*, beaver is medicine because *mashkikiwan*, medicines, exist through land food. It is common to assume that medicine and food are separate: one is something to be eaten, like steak or potatoes, and the other is something that heals, like mint tea or aspirin. From talking to the *akiwenziyag*, it becomes clear that those who rely on *aki miijim* view the harvested resources such as beaver and muskrat as a source of medicine.

Pulling out his collection of medicine jars filled with *okandimoo* (water tuber), *wiike* (rat root), *mashkodewashk* (bison grass), and *miskwaabiimag* (red willow) a few days later, Abel tells me that he takes these to supplement his diet (Figure 18). Poor health no longer permits Abel to trap as frequently so he relies on *mashkikiwan* to keep him well. It was Abel's father who taught him about medicines: which ones to ingest, which to inhale, and which to grind into powder to place with flour. But "if I eat a muskrat or beaver, I do not need this medicine because that medicine is already in them," he tells me.[39] Abel acknowledges that the reason he was "strong enough to go to [his] line at Mukatewa[sipe] almost every year" is because he has been eating muskrat, beaver, moose, and rabbit most of his life.[40] So while mainstream society may buy medication and "healthy" food in specialty shops or marked sections at the grocery store, *akiwenzi* like Abel eat food that is already healthy and full of medicinal properties. Illustrating this process at work, Abel continues:

> Even lynk [lynx],[41] people used to eat hides from the lynk long time ago. I remember my mom used to feed me hide from the lynk. That's food. But those other ones, marten and mink, it tastes different, different kinds of meat, even though they eat the same kind of root from the ground and all that. Beaver is good to eat. Beaver eats *wiike*, that's medicine. You can eat it from the beaver, cause the beaver eats that, it's good for your health, nothing wrong with that. Even muskrat eats *wiike*, that's medicine. And

when you eat that muskrat, it's good for your health. [. . .] In the bush, you don't go and inject [with hormones] those animals. That is why our food is healthy.[42]

Abel asserts that muskrat, beaver, or deer taste different because these animals carry the medicinal properties of *miskwaabiimag*, *okandimoo*, *wiike*, or other plants. "This is why our Old People were always healthy; they knew where to find good animals," he concludes.[43]

Walter Nanawin echoes Abel's words about the Old People's familiarity with medicines. One of the reasons he is so active is because he eats *aki miijim*, grows his own vegetables, and cultivates a medicine garden around Crane Creek. "The Indian, he knows the richest kind of medicine. My wife recognizes them," Walter explains, revealing that his wife, Jean, looks after an old medicine patch: "And we protect these medicines and trees in the willows. We even have some out here, on Pickerel Island, the wife is looking after them, [those] that my grandfather had dumped out of his medicine bag years ago! Some of them growing, it's a small enough [patch], but we will pick them after it grows. Remember that on the beach? [he asks his wife, Jean; 'I guess,' she answers.] And these flowers that grow, muskeg flowers, our medicines grow there, you know. This is our protected land that we are talking about."[44] Noel Bruce, another *akiwenzi* from Poplar River, concurs: "It makes sense when you think about it," he says. "Because traditional food made people strong and healthy, people who ate wild foods were very strong and never got sick."[45] He informs me that "moose, beavers, muskrats, and waterfowls, and other animals ate plants that were healthy and medicated. [. . .] And when the people ate these animals, they were healing from the medicated plants the animals ate. It was tough to get food, and people sometimes went hungry, but we had a good life and healthy people."[46] Noel elaborates that to prepare for illnesses like the flu, "people would gather ginger root in the fall. They would gather other [medicinal] plants and specific tree barks for the common flus that are associated with fever. Women used to get up as soon as [possible] from giving birth to a child, that's how strong the women were in the old days. And because there was all that work [laughs]! We can see why 'living off the land' is still important today, then."[47]

Because *aki miijim* procurement exists on the principle that the land and hence the food are gifts from the Creator, there is a sense of responsibility and sacredness in "keeping the land" and in maintaining good relationships with the animals. Driven by explicit *akiing ondaaji'idizowining*, land-based livelihood activities, harvesting demonstrates gratitude for the Creator's gifts. Not using the animals would be disrespectful and would suggest that people "no longer need or respect the Creator's gifts, [which] might lead to the declining availability of those gifts."[48] In return for good stewardship and sound harvesting practices, the *akiwenziyag* say, the animals will "do their job." Abel explains that "every living thing, including the smallest insect, was given jobs to do, to make sure the life our Creator made will always be there. Plants and trees, for example, were given many jobs, cleaning the air, medicines, [and] as food for the birds, animals, fish, and people. Some of the animals, birds, and fish were given the job to feed us and much more. Our job, as given to us by the Creator, was to take care of all the life on the earth."[49] Honouring the Creator's gifts ensures kinship between people and the ecology, and with other-than-human Beings in a way that makes "everyone responsible toward each other and to what connects everyone on the land."[50] In an ecosystem enriched by *ji-ganawendamang Gidakiiminaan*, *aki miijim* is sustained. Indigenous foodways and resource management systems are therefore interdependent ICH elements.

At another supper at the Nanawin home, the family and I feast on the plate of boiled moose meat that was stacked high on one plate and brought to the table. I dust the tough grey meat with salt and pepper, and eat with delight. Stories of past moose hunts or the phrase "we used to only eat moose meat like that in the bush" accompany the meat as lard is spread over it. That night, in response to the comment made by her granddaughter about preferring store-bought meatballs, Jean, a community Elder and Walter's wife, recalls, "I once went up south to visit. Someone gave me a burger to eat. I couldn't eat it. It made me sick. It was too greasy. Yeah, it just made me sick because it was so greasy."[51] Undeniably, having a great amount of harvested food like pickerel, moose, rabbit, caribou, or duck is a source of wealth here. A few days later, during one of our regular visits, Ken Douglas agrees with the Nanawins that *aki miijim* is healthier and better tasting: "When you take food from the land, it is better, yeah. It's more healthier when you eat wild meat—it's tasty. You got that strong taste. And even fish, when you fish from Lake Winnipeg, it's tasty, it's good. But if you go someplace else, like in Winnipeg, if you buy those fish [sticks], it doesn't even taste like a fish [laughs]. Not like fresh fish from the lake."[52] Harvested food is important not only because of taste and nutritional factors but also because it represents for many community members "our" food, namely, food that is more symbolic because it represents *mino-bimaadiziwin*.[53] Affixed to an entire culture, *aki miijim* begins from collective and individual strategizing and preparation, through the transport home, to consumption and proper disposal.[54] Cultural protocols associated with food have to be transmitted, and Ken argues that "young people need to know. Yup, they gotta know this stuff. They gotta have respect. They need to know what to do out there, how to look after those, those gifts and those animals, to put down tobacco. How to eat that food."[55]

Since the Asatiwisipe food system is dependent on harvesting in an often-demanding environment, collaboration and a shared workload is necessary. Harvesting *manoomin*,[56] wild rice, for example, is an activity that requires numerous individuals. Elders interviewed for the Pimachiowin Aki nomination share that the local Anishinaabeg sow *manoomin* by "carefully selecting a location with the correct water depth, clarity and bottom conditions, and then either pre-soak specially selected seeds, or place them in mud balls so they sink to the bottom of the water."[57] Putting boats in the water, tapping the tall grass, cleaning the grains from the husks, and drying them requires time and many hands. Fishing, too, requires multiple individuals to pull in heavy gill nets and to fillet, especially in the winter. And hunting needs at least a small group to skin, cut, and carry the meat home—especially if it is a big bull moose. To sustain this aggregate food system, a collective of people is needed to carry out prescribed burning, community gardening, selective harvesting, and creation of blueberry patches.[58] The community greenhouse in Poplar River is a testament to a devoted team.

Working cooperatively involves "good governance and effective management to get things done."[59] This kinship politics extends to the animals that are harvested. With *asemaa*, tobacco, a relationship is created between the animal and the harvester. In this reciprocal exchange, sometimes the hunter controls the success of the hunt, and sometimes it is the animal (or animal spirit) who controls it.[60] In this understanding, only the animal who has decided to give up its life to the hunter will be killed. As Abel shared, "Those animals know if the hunter is respectful [and] if he carries himself [well]."[61] Only then will a hunter be successful. This unique understanding arises from the belief that an animal "boss" can send humans "catch" by guiding them through dreams or prayers. Irving Hallowell, an anthropologist working with the Berens River people, describes one Anishinaabe hunter who dreamed of a beautiful girl approaching him. The man took this dream to mean that an animal had been caught in his deadfalls, and when he checked his trap the next day, he found a female fisher. Hallowell interpreted this story to mean that the success of a hunt in Anishinaabe society depends as much on the hunter's relationship with the animals or animal spirit as on their hunting skills.[62] The animal "bosses," as Hallowell puts it, were "among the great 'givers' who bestowed extraordinary powers upon men, who acted as their 'guardian spirits,' and without whose 'blessings' and assistance a satisfactory human life was thought to be impossible."[63] The *akiwenziyag* I spoke with also tended to "follow their dreams and visions" when making decisions, but many also credit Creator, God, luck, or their own skills with their fortune. Dreams are still important for many *akiwenziyag*, and when both my spouse and I dreamt of snakes the same night while at *asatiwisping akiing*, Abel informed us that Gichi-Ginebig was looking after us and we needed to listen to his message and be careful. The conversation between Abel and John about the dream brought forth the interpretation that the Poplar River is a powerful body of water, and that the Beings in the river need to be gifted tobacco. In return, they would keep us safe.

As we sit across the table from each other, Abel tells me that young people must know the *gikinoo'amaagoowinan*, teachings, so that the animals will not disappear. According to this *akiwenzi*, animals withdraw from humans because they have been disrespected. Climate change destroys their homes, development kills their young, and even several hunters here have been known to disregard codes of conduct toward the animals and the meat. Animals know when someone is disrespectful, cruel, or boastful, and they punish humans by abandoning them. To illustrate his point, Abel shares a story about the Mean Old Man who treated animals cruelly:

> Mewinzha, inigaa' yaad Gete-ininish. A'gii a'we Gete-ininish yaad wanii'igewinini. Gwa biboon, nakwebizh awesiinh niibana. A'gii zhangweshiwag, amikwag, miinawaa waboosag dasoozhag. Niibana noodwaaboosag. A'gii amikwag gijiigibizhag, a'gii zhangweshiwag gijiigibizhag, a'gii waaboosag gijiigibizhag. A'pii dash waabooz gijiigibizh, a'gii gaawizi. Idash gwa waabooz gijiigibizh, gezika a'gii a'we waabooz ozhimaa. Gaawiin a'gii biizikansii waabooz waaboozwaayaan. Gaawiin a'gii daasozhsii awesiinhyag daso-giizis. A'gii naadasoonaagane endaso-gigizheb miinawaa endaaso-naagosh. Gaawiin gegoo a'da mikige. Wiinwaa

a'wii daa Anishinaabeg kidok: "Gichi-neniibowag waaboosag nangwa biboong."

Gaawiin a'gii nakwebidoonsiiwag waaboosag Gete-Ininish idash. Miinawaa, gaawiin a'gii nakwebidoonsiiwag wazhashkwag. Miinawaa, gaawiin a'gii nakwebidoonsiiwag amikwag gaye wiinawaa Gete-Ininish. A'gii baa danege Mukawedaziibing gaye Ojijaakziibing.

A'gii bakade Gitaadizi-Ininish, miinawaa a'gii nishkaadizi Gete-Ininish. Gaawin gegoo a'do biinji-wanii'igan yaa. Indawaaj a'gii gawanaandam.[64]

The animal punished the Mean Old Man for his lack of respect toward the animals who gave up their lives for him.[65] Abel's *gikinoo'amaagoowin* teaches that respecting animals secures food. But when animals are offended, they will make their presence harder to find.[66] What is more, Abel's teaching and Hallowell's description both illustrate that *aki miijim* is a relationship; an alliance less about control or the *taking* of life and more about the *giving up* of life. The animal's point of view is central to this teaching.

Protocols around food distribution and proper disposal of one's leftovers complete this unique food system. A *nitaa-andawenjige inini*, good/respectful/proficient hunter/harvester, is one who shares their harvest with the rest of the community. Elders Norman Bruce and Abel Bruce elaborate on local protocols around access and the ethic of food distribution:

> **Norman:** In the winter we travelled together . . . to our traditional trapping area which is called Mukwastigwaan [Bear Head]. There is a lake there shaped like a bear's head. We almost always see caribou along the way.
> **Abel:** We shared that area, me and my brothers and Norman's family. It was good to work together like that when you wanted

to [harvest] something. To get to the Mukwastigwaan area we have to travel through two other traplines. Out of respect for those guys, we ask them or let them know we are going through their traplines. We don't trap there, but they don't mind if we hunt as we travel. If we kill a caribou or moose there, we will bring them some meat if we can.[67]

The pattern of sharing and gift giving has been identified to be one of the most fundamental cultural structures in numerous Indigenous hunting societies.[68] *Aki miijim* nourishes individuals as well as community cohesion. Many Elders welcomed the fish or the meat the young hunters offered to them, and I participated in this system by exchanging Polish sausages, fruits, or cheese for some filleted *ogaawag*, pickerel, or the occasional moose tongue. Harvesters also gave meat and fish to the Elder's Lodge and shared it at community events. During those times, the Elders' watchful eyes made sure that no wild food was scattered on the floor. Specific protocols around disposal ensure that the animal was not killed in vain and that no meat or bones are thrown away like garbage. The *akiwenziyag* treat foetuses respectfully and say a prayer for each animal consumed. Duck or moose leftovers are put back on the land or sometimes placed on a special fire.[69] And, although from another community, Richard Morrison stressed the importance of the "spirit plate," where a collection of small pieces of all the food from the table is put out on the land to feed the spirits of animals and of deceased family members. Both Richard and Abel were intrigued to learn that "feeding the spirits/little people" is also an old Slavic ritual faintly practised in more remote regions of Poland.

Aki miijim is an example of ICH tied to a familiar landscape, serving as an important link between ecology and specific cultural customs, traditions, and practices. While several Elders in Poplar River bemoaned instances of disrespect toward the animals by some young hunters who no longer view hunting through this lens, or who sell moose meat rather

Figure 19. Abel Bruce and John Mainville exchanging tobacco harvesting knowledge.

than share it with the community, both generations of land users recognized that cultural protocols must guide local harvesting, and that more opportunities for knowledge transmission are needed. ICH safeguarding best occurs through living experience, and cultural food systems can both teach and feed a young harvester. As they educate about animal populations and their migration patterns, for example, the *akiwenziyag* instruct about taking down a moose or pulling out an undesirable fish from a net without causing it harm. The combination of knowledge and skill is important because to ensure a successful catch, one must first go into the bush—and survive. As examples from the *akiwenziyag* illustrate, survival includes land, water, ice, trap, and weather safety, as well as knowledge of natural resources. Whereas everything in a grocery store is usually eatable, cultural knowledge related to particular berries or plants or animals—and which of their parts are edible—is essential in harvested food systems. Bush skills are also needed to ascertain which animal will not eat the harvester first. This expertise is encoded and decoded according to contemporary contexts and represents the richness of education that extends from early childhood to the moment a person leaves the earth. Thus, as young people spend time on the land, they gain experience and build their own stories about *aki miijim*, affirming the reciprocal and lived nature of ICH pedagogies.

One winter, Abel, my husband, John, and I collect and process *miskwaabiimag*, red willow, so that we can make tobacco for Abel. I also wanted to make tobacco for Inninu trapper and my friend Noah Massan, so he can have some to go with the pipe that Richard helped make for him. As we are out by the Poplar River rapids in knee-high snow, each of us takes a few branches, leaving *asemaa* in exchange. Abel usually makes tobacco from *kinnikinnick*, bearberry, so it is John's opportunity to share how his father taught him the technique of peeling the outer layer so that the inner bark can be dried. While peeling the sticks, Abel and I listen to John explain that once the tobacco layer has been peeled, the branches can be put back on the land because deer chew on the twigs (Figure 19). The small branches not only attract the deer but also work as a laxative, meaning that the properties of the medicine regulate the deers' intestines and cause them to leave their distinctive scat pellets. As in Abel's story of the healthy beaver, *miskwaabiimag* is not only used to prepare tobacco, but it also nourishes and keeps the deer healthy. In this cyclical food system, tobacco is placed for the deer that has given up its life for human consumption, and the distributed meat is gifted to the person who provided the deer with the exposed *miskwaabiimag* twigs in the first place. Preparing *miskwaabiimag* is therefore connected to tobacco, to the Creator/Spirit(s), to the deer, to the food, and ultimately to everyone's well-being. Nodding in agreement, Abel concurs that we can always pick medicines from where the good animals are because "they know best [and] we can learn from them."[70] ICH teaches us that knowledge transmission can also go from the young to the Elders.

ICH Transmission

In between jumping into the fast-moving river and warming up in the sun on Church Rock near the Catholic Mission, I listen to Abel's concern over the loss of "bush knowledge" among the youth. The *akiwenzi* shares that "sometimes, when I look at this way, myself, those youths now, today they are dying. Dying of alcohol and drugs and all that. Doing nothing all day, killing their brains out. That's all their life now, eh. I really want to help them out, I really want to help them be good. You have to teach them, that's all you have to do, teach them and tell them. This is time for us to do that, now. We have to do that for ourselves."[71] Abel believes that it is up to the people themselves to transmit culture and knowledge to the youth. Ken, too, worries about the disappearance of his knowledge and echoes the sentiment about teaching anyone who is willing to learn:

> The kids don't know how to survive. Not like them Old Timers. They don't know how to do that; too much in school, I guess. They don't know how to survive in the bush, how to get something to eat, how to survive, how to catch rabbits—to kill them rabbits. We used to snare them: you follow a rabbit trail and set a snare. It's work, yup, hard work. But the kids don't wanna do that anymore, I guess. How to teach them . . . I don't know. Who wants to learn, I don't know. Anyone who wants to learn, I guess.[72]

While some Elders and harvesters from the community find it painful that the youth do not want to experience the toughness of bush life nor have the required patience to learn certain skills like trapping, several young people in the community complained that they have too little time to learn, or that the knowledge holders do not teach them. One of the goals of the ICH discourse is to cultivate intergenerational cultural safeguarding; by doing so, ICH transmission directly nurtures the relationship between the "Old Timers" and the youth.

The most common concern among the *akiwenziyag* is that if the young people do not learn bush skills, there will be no one to maintain the traplines. The issue around ICH transmission is undeniably complex because on the one hand, if the youth do not want to learn elements of their own culture, safeguarding is pointless. On the other hand, if only several members of the group have an interest in ICH, the issue of transmission becomes as much about access to and control of ICH as it is about safeguarding. Only ICH custodians and/or the community can address the issue around transmission, but, as we will see shortly, their views may be at odds with each other. In instances where there are no interested learners, individuals who may not typically be considered "community ICH holders" or members (i.e., "outsiders") give prominence to the debate about transmission norms and rights.

Access to and participation in specific activities is determined by the ICH holder. Some ICH practices involve a single group separated by age, status, ethnicity, and gender; some gender complementarity or gender constellations may have an inherent logic that is not always easily understood by outsiders.[73] ICH practices shape these roles through ceremonies, division of labour, or holders of specific knowledge, and point to distinct roles that gender plays in a community. Certain social practices have led to inequalities, prejudices against, or even mistreatment of groups, women, and other gendered identities. Colonialism also impacts culturally constructed gender roles, identities, and practices. Human and gender rights become an issue, however, when the dignity and well-being of certain individuals is threatened and when their involvement in ICH performance and transmission of practices is denied, particularly with heritage that is at-risk. This raises the thorny question about who determines roles, gender-based practices, and traditions in cultural transmission.

Although UNESCO leaves individual cases of ICH transmission to communities, the ICH Convention makes the promotion of gender equality and human rights a priority. Values and norms related to "traditional" roles vary among societies and communities; exploring gender norms and equality permits ICH custodians to consider new possibilities for safeguarding. Living heritage manifests in practices determined by gender such as male camel breeding in Oman and floral decorations of wooden toys by Croatian women in Hrvatsko Zagorje. Among the Górale in Poland, sheepherding is a male-dominated activity and cow grazing is a female activity. In the same way, UNESCO notes that while woodcarving and silversmithing are generally done by men, women tend to make most woven and textile items.[74]

Acknowledging that an aspect of a practice, although serving an important social function, may violate human rights, the ICH Convention prompts nations and communities to exercise extreme caution when it comes to creating ICH policies on transmission.[75] National constitutions and legal frameworks that formally prohibit gender discrimination "may provide exemptions from compliance on the grounds of 'traditions' or 'custom' in customary practices or religious laws."[76] Referring to UNESCO's stance on the issues of cultural diversity,[77] human rights,[78] as well as on the elimination of discrimination against women,[79] the organization emphasizes the need to incorporate non-discriminatory provisions into ICH-related policies. ICH elements denying human rights, dignity, and well-being are not supported by the ICH Convention, and each member state is encouraged to deal with the issue appropriately.

To illustrate, UNESCO views the practice of female genital mutilation to be contrary to human rights, and educational assistance about alternatives to this rite of passage is provided by a local Kenyan community.[80] Similarly, witchcraft and sorcery accusations related to violence are being addressed through unique modifications and codifications of customary laws in Papua New Guinean communities.[81] Traditional practices that contradict the United Nation's vision of human and gender rights also include son preference, female infanticide, early and forced marriage, violence or murder related to dowry, honour crimes, and certain practices related to child delivery.[82] UNESCO affirms its commitment to human rights in stating that only ICH that is compatible with existing international human rights instruments and standards can be considered within its scope.[83]

The intersection of multiple cultural epistemologies and legal systems brings additional challenges to ICH safeguarding. UNESCO identifies a range of traditions and cultural practices that are socially accepted in many areas of the world but have drastic and harmful effects on women, children, and other members of society.[84] "Culture," "customs," and "traditions" in the Pacific Islands, for example, are frequently cited as justification for discrimination and abusive treatment of local women and girls, including bride price and fathers offering daughters to transient logging and mining workers in exchange for cash.[85] In a (post)colonial milieu like the Pacific, the mix of male violence, alcohol, and predatory sexuality continues to serve as an excuse or is tolerated as "tradition," while women and girls are blamed for the sexual violence inflicted upon them. The modern idea of individual rights, women's rights, and children's rights can come into conflict with customary norms based on collective interests.

In examining traditional "culturally appropriate" justice models in Canada, Cree-Métis scholar Emma LaRocque elaborates on the misuse of "tradition," stating that some Indigenous traditions raise ethical issues. Questioning the idea of cultural and social norms in mediation programs, LaRocque writes that it is important to "provoke thought and re-examination of popular premises concerning notions of culture, healing, and sexual offender–victim mediation programs; and to open up discussion on freedom of expression and contemporary human rights within the Aboriginal community, especially on issues of concern to women and on culturally appropriate programs/governance."[86] Recognizing that

Indigenous people have had to fight long and hard for cultural recognition, LaRocque notes that certain "traditions," such as the eye-for-an-eye dictum, public banishment, ridicule, repayment, and the "culturalization" of rape or sexual assault, may pose new challenges to the debate on cultural collective versus individual rights.[87] Sápmi scholar Rauna Kuokkanen concurs that violence in the name of tradition emphasizes inherent tensions between universal human rights standards and local cultural practices. The position of Indigenous women in Canada illustrates this, falling under a legislative contradiction that both affirms their individual human rights and freedoms and simultaneously protects collective Aboriginal rights under Section 35 of the Canadian Constitution.[88] Certain practices and norms (including those respecting women) do not always protect women's individual rights or advance women's leadership. Systematic oppression caused the devaluation of Indigenous cultures and a particular "degradation of Indian [Indigenous] women by men, Indian [Indigenous] and otherwise."[89] But, Kuokkanen argues, it is not always culture that lies at the root of violence against women; rather, some cultural practices and norms have been "employed to re-inscribe domination and patriarchal structures."[90] International human rights standards play a central role in the ICH Convention, hence all policy making that deals with intangible cultural heritage must consider multiple perspectives and exercise extreme caution.[91]

Careful deliberation, however, is needed to avoid an overly simplistic view that discounts activities simply on the basis that one gender group practises them. It is a reality in many societies worldwide that a "significant number of social and cultural practices are segregated (on the basis of age, gender and other criteria) and this alone should not be taken as a sign that discrimination is taking place."[92] UNESCO notes that gender and ICH "interact in complex and, to a degree, mutual ways" through enactment, practice, transmission, and so on.[93] Thus, gender may determine access to and participation in specific expressions of heritage. When considering gender equality and living heritage, a human rights perspective concentrates not on the differences between gender roles but whether the roles deny the well-being and dignity of those involved.[94] Interpreting practices themselves, or even differentiated roles assigned to men and women, should not be the focus. Rather, it is the specific negative consequences, such as applying stereotypical roles to women that disempower them or otherwise harm their interests, that need considering.[95] Safeguarding approaches have the potential to impact gender relations, and ICH transmission can likewise strengthen or weaken gender relations as well as the relationship between communities and their sub-groups.

To establish ICH continuity, it is important to understand the social function of a practice and the possible gender dynamics at play. For that reason, integrating all community voices in ICH work and acting on their perspectives without discrimination against political, social, ethnic, religious, linguistic, or gender-based forms, is vital.[96] Food, dress, language, life cycle rituals, modes of socialization, and other factors remain important sites for the transmission of group identity in the domestic and public spheres.[97] The women's sphere is frequently associated with the "domestic,"[98] and ICH identification carries the risk that only certain spheres and select gendered-heritages (and genders) partake in the identification, inventorying or safeguarding process.[99] To give an example from my own experience, when I asked several women in Poplar River about "resource stewardship/management" and "land-food/harvesting" systems, many of them considered these activities as "land knowledge" and attributed that knowledge to the men. As a consequence, the women tended to refer me to the men. When I asked one recognized Poplar River female Elder who had spent much of her life on the trapline about her experiences travelling across the east side of Lake Winnipeg, she immediately said that I should talk to her "Old Man, he knows about this stuff. He knows all those stories."[100] Similarly, when I asked about *manoominekewin*, ricing, one Anishinaabe woman directed me to a male neighbour who "knows traditional knowledge [on wild] rice, I just process it."[101] Humbleness is one reason why these women did not feel confident in sharing their experiences with me. However, I also believe that Indigenous women's roles in land use and occupancy studies as well as in "resource management" are regularly overlooked because harvesting activities, as well as "the bush" in general, tend to be viewed as male.[102] As these anecdotes suggest, it is important to acknowledge the plurality of expertise and experts in a community, and to value other (even the quiet and the contradictory) viewpoints.

My time with the *akiwenziyag* reinforced my position that these men are skilled in many areas: apart from their bush skills, they can speak confidently in front of the public and can address children in a plain manner; they can tell funny jokes—and some are more than willing to share crude jokes. They can dress up for a special occasion with their lady, and they can argue effectively if they feel wronged. They can sew, cook, and write poems. Even Walter, who frequently made me cook his dinners, made pretty good canned beans. Ensuring that all voices and "norms" contribute to ICH leads not only to a plurality of perspectives around safeguarding but also helps place "traditional" roles at the forefront of policy making and diversified economic development.

Moreover, traditional divisions of culture associated with labour tend to rely on particular gender roles. Despite these "traditional gender roles," the spectrum of gender relations has, in many instances, evolved to accommodate transmission. In Cyprus, traditionally only men have performed the Tsiattista, a form of poetic duelling in which one poet-singer attempts to outdo another in improvising clever oral poetry.[103] In Iran, only men have traditionally transmitted Naqqāli storytelling, a form of dramatic performance. In both societies, women have been playing an increasing role in the transmission of these ICH elements. In Viet Nam and in Japan, specific theatrical performances where men take on women's roles (*onnagata* in Japanese) transcend gender and call into question the binary female/male roles. In China, with only several Elders speaking the Hezhen minority language, outsiders are more accepted for apprenticeship and the intensive training that the Yimakan storytelling tradition requires.[104] In Poland, one woman broke the traditional division of labour associated with the Górale culture to become the first female *baca*, main sheepherder.[105] In this case, language must catch up to the revolutionary woman, as there is no female descriptor for *baca* role in Polish. Finally, in Kenya, three Maasai male rites of passage—the Enkipaata, Eunoto, and Olng'esherr—serve to induct men into important life stages in Maasai society. As the young men learn about their future roles, the rites of passage are a means for transmitting knowledge in relation to livestock rearing, conflict management, legends, traditions, and life skills, as well as Maasai core values. With the rites rapidly declining on account of new livelihoods, land tenure reforms, and climate change affecting cattle survival, the Enkipaata, Eunoto, and Olng'esherr were inscribed in the List of Intangible Cultural Heritage in Need of Urgent Safeguarding in 2018. With the continuation of this ancient tradition, many Maasai Elders are incorporating new perspectives. This includes teaching about the harmful effects of female genital mutilation to girls and women and advocating for an end to this practice in their community.[106] In all cases, heritage elements important to the identity of the communities are transmitted in an evolving way.

The *akiwenziyag* also believe that while certain gender roles are important, strict gender and insider/outsider rules should not limit knowledge transmission. Although traditionally it was men who fasted (went on "vision quests") as rites of passage, Richard Morrison takes both men and women fasting, some of them non-Indigenous. Frances Valiquette, a Poplar River Elder, indicates that survival produced joint trapping duties: "Women needed to trap around the 'home block' [near the reserve] when the men were out [of the community] hunting or trapping, sometimes for weeks at a time. We were left behind. We did all the men's tasks and all the women's tasks [laughs]. Things just need to get done."[107] Abel Bruce also emphasizes that he needed to know "the things women [did] like sewing and mending clothes," because a lack of these skills would be a death sentence on the trapline. The *akiwenziyag* broke many boundaries and "traditions" that made several people in and outside of their communities uncomfortable (many of the men acknowledge that they were always "shit disturbers," however). I too navigated between the different roles and identities in spending time with them over fifteen years: as a Polish (Non-Indigenous/White), young (unmarried) woman, I was blessed (or lucky or priviledged) to be accepted (or tolerated?) by these men. We shaped each other not always because of a particular identity, but because of what we could do together. By showing me their lives, the *akiwenziyag* enabled me to learn about my place in the world; by sharing our lives, we became each other's vehicles for transmission.

The case studies above demonstrate that lived heritage includes the ability and willingness to negotiate change and resonance over time. The ICH framework recognizes that "traditional" relations (like class, gender expressions, insider/outsider, and status) are sometimes fluid and that different ideas of norms and roles are constantly emerging. Certain traditional norms may be necessary to pass on specific types of knowledge (like mother-to-daughter culinary skills, or trapper-to-helper knowledge). Fixed roles may serve a social function in a community or group, but the application of stereotypical or "purist" roles may prove to be intricate in the modern age. Understanding the complexity of human rights, Indigenous governance, and gender equality and equity, for example, with ICH transmission and policy making will require being open to challenges. Transmission must also consider the ways in which living heritage can stay relevant in rapidly changing times and global values. Identifying grey areas in which a degree of role differentiation is acceptable requires communities to articulate their own understanding of signifiers associated with gender, traditions, culture, community member, and heritage.

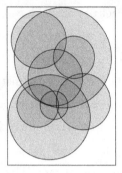

Generation A: Strong community ICH. Collective and individual knowledges overlap, interact, and transmit.

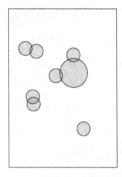

Generation B: Begins to lose ICH custodians from migration, policies, dispossession, choice, etc.

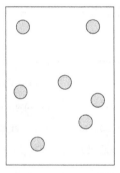

Generation C: Subsequent generations are separated from their ICH custodians, and transmission of living heritage can be challenging and/or strained. This is also a space for desire to reconnect.

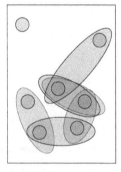

Generation B and/or C: Generations begin to reconnect with ICH custodians. ICH is rebuilt and transmitted, and also creates new communities.

Figure 20. The process of ICH culture loss and rebuilding across generations. While community ICH in Generation A is strong because of social interactions and intergenerational transmission, members of Generation B separate due to migration, land dispossession, or other forms of community disintegration. These external factors leave Generation C with individual ICH custodians separated from each other and their inheritors. Transmission can take place in Generation B and/or C. In Generation B, transmission may occur but there are few social connections. In Generation C individuals can heal, reconnect, and revitalize their ICH. New communities and "outsider" ICH knowledge holders are created for the purpose of transmission. Note that Generations A through C may not necessarily represent three generations; the processes occurring in Generation B, C, and Generations B and/or C may take multiple generations in real time.

In instances where an ICH is endangered, vitality may mean renegotiating the idea of community or tradition, and ICH custodians must determine for themselves their understanding of identity and continuity. Determined to safeguard their living heritage, communities will have to find ways to adapt to a demographic shift, not just across generations but across geographies and communities. Figure 19 shows the process of ICH loss and rebuilding. For communities with strong social interactions (Generation A), intergenerational transmission occurs. With community disintegration (Generation B), transmission to the next generation (Generation C) is disrupted, leaving the two generations with few social connections or limited abilities to pass on cultural elements (due to migration, dispossession, political situation, or other disruptions). Members of Generations C and onwards begin to rebuild elements of heritage but do so by recreating cultural heritage maintained by ICH custodians under current circumstances (such as diaspora or existing language). These generations not only reconnect with those who share kinship and heritage lineage but also engage the participation of individuals who become a part of the community based on affinity (such as individuals of diverse cultural and ethnic backgrounds forming an Indigenous student association or a Canadian-Latino organization or a Francophone club).[108] While adoptions and intercultural families have been commonplace across the world for generations, Figure 19 shows that after disruption, families of very diverse cultural backgrounds often create unique communities that may differ significantly from the traditional cultural identity of Generation A.

As communities and generations heal, revitalize, or strengthen their ICH, new ICH communities form, potentially breaking away from tradition. Richard recollects women who had powerful visions during their fasts, and Abel identifies a head trapper who was a woman during one of our routine discussions without skipping a beat. Indigenous experiences of identity politics are particularly embedded in imperialist state formations,[109] and the ICH framework simultaneously broadens and complicates the discourse. Questions of who is an accepted ICH custodian, who can learn a cultural skill, what a tradition looks like, and where urban and migrant identities as well as mixed-heritage custodians fit in—and how the state or communities recognize them—muddle the seemingly clear characterization of ICH and linear intergenerational transmission.[110] The complexities around identity and recognition need to be decided by ICH custodians and examined by legal scholars, particularly in the case of commercialization. The ICH Convention stresses that it is communities who must define their heritage identity on their own terms. While gender norms and identity politics may divide cultural practices in specialized ways, safeguarding of ICH reveals that flexible transmission also diversifies skills and cultural knowledges.

Special Things

A reader may ask the question, are ICH elements "special things for special people"? The answer is both yes and no. Humans have always celebrated special events like births, successes, faith celebrations, and life endings. Today, the crafts, skills, and languages at risk of disappearing are indeed special features of humanity's diversity and should be protected. However, as some critical heritage scholars point out, all heritage is at risk, and proclaiming heritage to be "at risk" makes the concept globally and locally discursive. The "at risk" proclamation acts as a rationalizing vehicle for other agendas that go unchecked.[111] As Chapter 1 highlighted, the survival and support of some heritage places, elements, and languages is not entirely accidental. Identity politics, political agendas, and historical or ongoing colonial factors all play a role in decisions around cultural heritage. ICH custodians, notably language speakers whose linguistic expressions are diminishing, would benefit immensely from policy and financial support that ensures survivability—this is evident through the abundant nominations UNESCO receives each year to place on its Representative, in Need of Urgent Safeguarding, and Best Practices lists. The question about "special people" accents the sheer fact of rarity and hence makes some ICH holders truly special.

At the same time, effective ICH policy, one that provides consistent and competent transmission, contradicts the notion of specialness. When ICH is thriving, it is not a "special" thing reserved for unique individuals. To illustrate, it is highly doubtful that Canadians are concerned about the state of the English language; with time, many immigrants switch to English as their dominant language, and most countries around the world use English as their language of day-to-day administration. Very few individuals worry about this language disappearing.[112]

Born of informal social interactions, ICH draws its strength from a coherent body of people whose "habitus" is held in living memory, stories, and relationships. It is an array of experiences and "techniques of the body,"[113] sourced from heritage but constantly shaped by history and contrasting circumstances.[114] For the *akiwenziyag*, the symbolic connection between culture and the past is tied to their intellectual traditions, individual experiences, and wisdom in the present. These unique ways must be embedded within the daily life of future generations. One Poplar River Elder, Albert Bittern, shared: "I just do what I was taught [to do]. I was born in 1948. I have lived here for most of my life. I went to residential school for seven years. What the Elders taught us was to respect Nature, that if you take anything, always thank the Creator for giving you that. That's why I always remember to do that. And we have to make sure our youth do that too."[115] The Elder continued, arguing that cultural knowledge is not "natural" anymore because residential schools disrupted that organic process of learning: "My grandpa taught me that when you cut wood, you just don't go cutting anywhere and that you don't hunt every animal you see. . . . The old ones taught me that. I have a pretty good teaching from my grandpa. I went to go pick wild rice with [him]. I still hunt. I still gather medicines. We get a lot of that, the medicines from the earth. I didn't get a lot of that [because] I was gone [to] residential school but the youth must know those [values and practices] again."[116] For Albert, in order for the land to nourish local people, cultural practices must once again become a part of youth development. Frances Valiquette likewise shared that "everyone lived from trapping and fishing."[117] Until the welfare system came in the 1950s, trapping was not considered special by anyone in the community; it was daily life. Noah, the *kitayatis* currently residing in Gillam, also pointed to the fact that if there are no more Inninuwak trappers, Manitoba Hydro will just "do what they want" on the land.

Today, instead of going for eight months out of the year, many trappers now go to the trapline on the weekends only. Less extensive time on the trapline caused trapping to become a part-time activity rather than a full-time occupation. In our conversations, *akiwenziyag* and the *kitayatisuk* insisted that this cultural mode of production deserves "special" attention. So perhaps the ultimate goal of the ICH framework is to "transiently exist" until individuals "navigate their social environments 'like a fish in water': it does not feel the weight of the water, and it takes the world about itself for granted."[118] In that sense, because living cultures and thriving languages do not need safeguarding, only at-risk and endangered cultures require special attention. The ICH discourse teaches us that living heritages exist through permanence.

Most of the *akiwenziyag* are also aware that their diminishing cultural livelihood has brought significant interest in cultural programming and Elder workshops. Recognizing their unique role in society, these men likewise point to the fact that an ICH custodian today possesses a level of social capital. A few decades ago, traditional bearers may have been seen as old-fashioned or looked down on socially for being out of touch with the present; being associated with a family member who lived in a traditional way or wore traditional clothing could also have been considered embarrassing (which is why historically Indigenous people and immigrants were forced to or chose to anglicize their names; this "Canadianizing" still occurs today).[119] Being a tradition holder or harvester could even be dangerous as one could be arrested for breaking the law. Ironically, although popular culture hints that it is more acceptable or desirable to pursue a modern life with a disposable income to buy new electronics, to travel, to attain an education, and to move to big cities that offer "opportunities," the rising interest in traditions and heritage also illustrates that a cultural and social shift is occurring. There is a strong desire to carry on traditions.

This new phenomenon extends to recognizing tradition bearers and including them in formal education. Chuckling, Richard said that while knowledge holders or Elders should be recognized for their wealth of knowledge, he also differentiated between *akiwenziyag* and individuals who rely on titles for self-advertising and recognition: "Back in the day, everyone just lived. They just lived like this. They all spoke Ojibwe. No one was special. Everyone was just busy [on the land]. Today, people don't do the work, but they all want to be Elders. Too many Elders and not enough 'Nish, I guess."[120] For Richard, there is a difference between knowing and understanding cultural teachings. Familiarity with many different teachings does not equal a deep understanding and application of the teachings: "If you are gonna talk your walk, you better walk the talk," Richard maintained. For Richard, the cultural lifestyle was not something to be worn but something to be lived, which is why he refused all Indigenous signifiers associated with his identity. He never wanted "fluffs and feathers" to represent his Anishinaabe-ness,[121] and he rarely put on the "Wise Old Man voice," as his family called it. But he knew how to play the game and when to put on a show that met expectations of his "Indianness." He was aware of the cultural and social cachet of carrying on traditions and displaying them to specific audiences.

Privately (and sometimes openly), Richard was also critical of individuals whose teachings were not wholly genuine, such as outsiders pretending to be Indigenous so they can become ceremonial knowledge holders or Indigenous community members bearing the epithet of "Elder" without having earned it. Like the other *akiwenziyag*, Richard was a believer in investing significant time and energy to understand the teachings. No matter who it was (Indigenous or non-Indigenous, male or female), if the individual was willing to help cut and load wood, handpick rocks for a sweatlodge, travel for hours to help perform a healing ceremony, or learn the language, he shared his teachings with them. Aware of the rising popularity of "traditional men of the land," all the *akiwenziyag* whose voices inform this book placed a high value on a lifestyle that left them with wearied, timeworn hands and too busy for accolades.

A number of thematic currents emerge from the question of whether or not ICH elements are special and unique to certain people only. First, unless conditions for transmission, whether formal or informal, collective or individual occur, *any* cultural element may disappear. This can happen because the element is no longer in use or desired by the community, because it has been naturalized or assimilated, or subject to political factors (such as outlawing a practice). The ICH discourse shows us that *all* heritages can be at risk, and all deserve to be considered for protection and transmission. Correspondingly, the framework also points out that being of a certain cultural heritage does not always guarantee knowledge of that culture. The *akiwenziyag* narratives demonstrate that explicitly: not everyone from a particular cultural group has ICH elements or the same forms of ICH; anyone can learn a cultural element. The fact that cultural elements can be learned calls attention to politics of identity, where the complexities of navigating insider/outsider dynamics of tradition can—and often do—collide with the perceived (and somewhat romanticized) idea of intergenerational transmission.[122] Not every parent or family member is a good teacher and not every community interprets transmission in a harmonious way. Not every group possesses "traditional" knowledge or can access practices with ease. In my work, I have encountered ICH custodians who share knowledge with anyone but only for a very expensive fee, and I have met Elders who exclusively teach their select apprentices for free. I have likewise come across knowledgeable individuals who take their expertise to the grave, and I have met "regular" young people (i.e., not publicly recognized as Elders) who are not only culture keepers but also excellent teachers. Sometimes individuals and communities do not know they have cultural knowledge, and it takes special questions to get them to see that they are rich with heritage-sourced expertise.

As I have suggested here, ICH transmission comes with an array of intricate conundrums. The process brings forth questions around who ICH inheritors are, who is a knowledge holder, and who has the power to make the decisions around cultural heritage transmission. Currently, there are communities in Canada that hold gender-diverse powwows, that debate over the need for women to wear skirts in a ceremony, and that dissent over hereditary lineages and responsibilities. Communities may approach these convoluted issues in completely different ways; clearly, there is no one way. I have presented these divergent and contradicting perspectives without coming down on the debate. It is not my place to say if these are right or wrong. But the discussion deserves exploration in greater depth, particularly in terms of policy making and community engagement. ICH conveyance is immensely personal, and I have attempted to introduce the complexities around the ICH framework on gender, tradition, and insider/outsider transmission, and intergenerational learning by introducing stories of my own experience with living heritages.

An anecdote about Richard merits the last word on passing down ICH elements. During a breakfast discussion at Smitty's restaurant in Winnipeg, Richard brought my attention back to the teachings he learned from his Elders about the Four Directions, focusing on the bond that is created when humans learn from one another. Revealing a particular Midewewin teaching, Richard recounted that we are all connected to that *ishkode*, that fire, that energy. And it comes from all of us. Every one of us. When I was talking about those four stars, the four directions, there is the fifth star [too]. The fifth star is every human being in this world. There is five stars on a Mide[wewin] drum. And those five stars have very significant meaning. There's five fingers and five toes, and the drum is half blue and half red. The red is the people of the world; the blue is the spirit of all, of everything. And there's a yellow line that separates the red and the blue. And that yellow line is the walk of life. All the lights and energies of the whole universe, they connect us as human beings, that yellow like, is like every molecule in every atom.[123]

Illustrating that the role of Anishinaabe culture and knowledge is to energize and teach, Richard emphasized that everyone can learn something from Anishinaabe *gikino'amaagoowinan*. Although he maintained that there are traditional "preventative" measures set in place to prevent gender crossing in some circumstances, like women not stepping over guns (so they do not take the lead hunting role), he also pushed a lot of boundaries, such as permitting women to go into the *madoodoo*, a sweatlodge ceremony, on their menses and allowing homeless people under the influence of drugs and alcohol to join some of his healing ceremonies (he was a believer in the here-and-now as a start to healing). While Richard's protocol-breaking attitude angered many of his peers, he was also very careful about which teachings he shared and with whom. This man believed that many Anishinaabe teachings can be relevant to contemporary societal problems. During our discussion about "authentic traditional" teachings, Richard referred to a "purity" in *mino-bimaadiziwin*, declaring that "all these vibrations in this world, we, we feel them. So, there is no ugliness and there is no beauty. It's all balance. It's all learning from both the beauty and the ugliness of everything. About the good and bad in humans, in other people.

[. . .] You remember those Four Directions, those stars I told you about? All those stars gathered in the universe. . . . It's those vibrations that keep them [together]. The culture is like that. The culture, it's about *ishkode*, it's keeping that fire, that heart beat alive, like *ishkaabewis* [fire-keeper]. It's like being like *ishkaabewis*."[124] Merging the *gikino'amaagoowinan*, teachings of his Elders, with his own lived experience, Richard chose to teach *for* and *through* heritage. He attempted to keep *ishkode*, that fire, that heartbeat alive in his work as *mashkiki inini*, father, brother, and teacher. Before passing away in July 2020, Richard adamantly expressed that he did not want to be the last person to know what he knows.[125]

Chapter Four

"Clean energy, they say"

In 2013, I was at the Manitoba Clean Environment Commission (CEC) hearings for the Keeyask Generating Station, sitting next to my friend Noah Massan. Holding a pouch of tobacco that I had made for him in Poplar River, Noah attentively listened to the hearings. The CEC is an arms-length provincial government agency providing advice, recommendations, and opportunities for the public to get involved in decisions about the environment in Manitoba. At the time, the commission was conducting public hearings on the proposed Keeyask dam, a 695-megawatt hydroelectric generating station located approximately 725 kilometres north of Winnipeg on the Kichi Sipi, Nelson River—and on Noah's trapline. Noah and I were observing the expert testimonies that were made on behalf of the proponent, Keeyask Hydropower Limited Partnership (Manitoba Hydro and partners). As the experts shared their views on the potential effects of the dam on heritage resources, they pointed to a map of some heritage sites projected behind them and described the archeological finds they had discovered on the project site. Noah and I followed the discussion by looking at the printed copy of the map in front of us (Figure 21), examining each red dot that indicated a heritage site. As the proponents discussed the archeological particulars and small excavations in the area, as numbers were gauged and comparisons made of the red dots scattered around the project site, Noah leaned over to me and whispered, "So how come we don't have any in our area?"[1]

Referring to the fact that no red heritage "dots" were present in his community area, Noah perceived, as did I, that indeed much of the

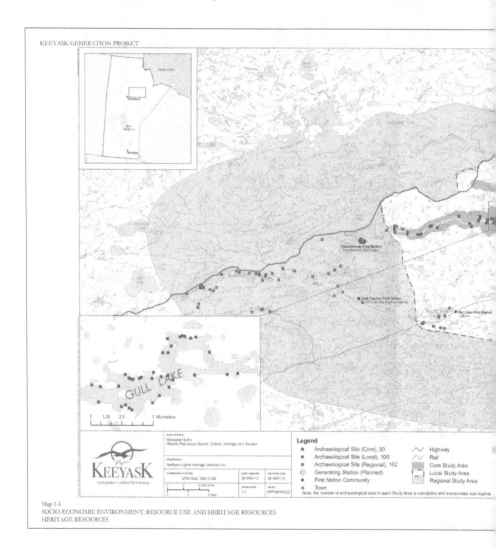

Map 1-1
SOCIO-ECONOMIC ENVIRONMENT, RESOURCE USE AND HERITAGE RESOURCES
HERITAGE RESOURCES

Inninuwak traditional territory around Gillam and the Fox Lake Cree Nation community of Bird lacked any identification of heritage. The study area map shows registered archeological sites as well as potentially affected archeological sites.[2] Created by the proponent, the map uses little red, yellow, and orange squares to indicate all the places that could be affected in the Keeyask Generating Station study area. But Noah's understanding of heritage is not limited to a few dots on a map. He sees his whole territory imbued with living heritage.

June 2012

N

Heritage Resources
Study Areas
with Registered Archaeological Sites

Figure 21. Map of the Keeyask EIS project area and heritage sites within Makeso Sakahican territory. As Noah Massan pointed out, very few dots marking a heritage site are present on the Fox Lake Cree Nation territory and on his trapline.

Source: Map 1-1, "Heritage Resources and Study Areas with Registered Archeological Sites," in *Keeyask Generation Project: Environmental Impact Statement*, supporting volume, *Socio-Economic Environment, Resource Use and Heritage Resources*, part 3 "Heritage Resources" (Keeyask Hydropower Limited Partnership, 2012), 1–42. Accessed from https://keeyask.com/wp-content/uploads/2012/07/KeeyaskGP_HR_SV_1of1.pdf.

ICH and Environmental Impacts

As mandated by the Canadian Environmental Assessment Agency (2012), the proposed Keeyask Generating Station underwent an environmental assessment review and licensing process in 2014. Named after the Keeyaskopawistik (*keeyask*, meaning gull, and *pawistik*, rapids, because a lot of gulls lay their eggs near the rapids), the Keeyask project is a partnership between Manitoba Hydro and Tataskweyak Cree Nation, War Lake First Nation, York Factory First Nation, and Fox Lake Cree Nation (called the Keeyask Cree Nations by Manitoba Hydro), together forming the Keeyask Hydropower Limited Partnership (KHLP). At the CEC hearings in 2013–14, the Cree First Nations were present to articulate their support for the Keeyask project through the licensing process. The process in Manitoba is open to the public and groups and individuals may apply as intervenors. Noah and I applied for participant/intervenor status at the hearings to present some of Fox Lake Elders' concerns over the hydroelectric project. We received funding from the CEC and established a group composed of Elders, Indigenous community members, and a few academics.[3] Called the Concerned Fox Lake Grassroots Citizens (CFLGC), we were one of the six intervenors at the CEC hearings who hoped for a more thorough examination of the project and who joined in the deluge of voices demanding a comprehensive review of cumulative impacts from all hydroelectric development in Northern Manitoba before building the fourth dam on the lower Kichi Sipi, Nelson River. At the heart of our participation in this process was our hope that the generating station would not be built because it would further negatively impact the Makeso Sakahican Inninuwak and other Indigenous communities.

The Makeso Sakahican Inninuwak, or Fox Lake Cree, call Northern Manitoba their home; Gillam is the nearest town and the place where Noah resides. Gillam is often called "Hydro Town" by the locals because three dams are already present in the area, and the land is criss-crossed with powerlines, generating stations, access roads, equipment sites, and other hydroelectric infrastructure. Also near the town is Noah's trapline, which has borne the brunt of the province's hydroelectric development and resulting environmental devastation since the 1960s. In 1971, the Kettle Dam flooded Noah's cabin and large tracts of his traditional trapline for the Stephen's Lake reservoir on Kichi Sipi. Since then, Noah's trapline has seen roads, quarries, transmission towers, reservoirs, foreign workers, and an influx of automobile traffic, as well as the growth of the Town of Gillam and its resident population. The community of Fox Lake Cree Nation, to which Noah belongs, has been heavily impacted by the three dams, and despite the ongoing construction of the Keeyask Generating Station, more dams are proposed for the river.

Keeyask is an expansion of an integrated system, not an isolated, standalone project, and CFLGC's Makeso Sakahican members have expressed their apprehensions over the impacts another project will have on the already fragile social, cultural, and economic fabric of the Inninuwak landscape.[4] Even though Fox Lake Cree Nation has made the decision to partner on the project with a heavy heart, there were many Makeso Sakahican Inninuwak who opposed the project and were eager to share their experiences of Hydro misconduct. Many Inninuwak in our group were Elders, trappers, hunters, and fishermen—*kitayatisuk* in Inninumowin, who felt that their voices, views, and knowledges were not listened to by Manitoba Hydro and their consultants. They also wanted to directly respond to the proponent, KHLP, and to the findings articulated in the 2012 Environmental Impact Statement (EIS). The Keeyask EIS is a multi-volume document outlining the environmental impacts and benefits of the project. The project promoted sustainable growth, with power exported to the U.S. markets, and Keeyask was framed as the "clean and green" solution to the growing energy needs of Manitobans.[5]

Having reviewed the Keeyask EIS, our group determined that many short- and long-term adverse effects from another dam and its infrastructure would be detrimental to the well-being of the Inninuwak. Other intervenors, including families from Split Lake, Pimicikamak, York Factory, and Shamattawa Cree Nations, presented their concerns about Keeyask as well. The intervenors argued that the information presented both in the EIS as well as in the hearings did not reflect the true nature and interpretation of the negative effects or its substantive consequences on the harvesters. For many *kitayatisuk* in Northern Manitoba, Hydro development continues to represent the destruction of the values, the way of life, and community *mino-pimatisiwin*. In Fox Lake, where development started more than fifty years ago, Hydro is still seen as the initial destructive force that has led to the loss of countless cultural and natural heritage elements of the Inninuwak. Although colonial policies and the residential school system also contributed to the loss of *mino-pimatisiwin*, the large-scale physical destruction of their homeland led to a significant rupture between the past and the present. Referring to the effects Hydro has had on his trapline, Noah states that the community lived *mino-pimatisiwin*, "but then Hydro came in. They destroyed everything."[6]

For Noah, *mino-pimatisiwin* serves as a reference point that separates life before and after hydroelectric development in the 1960s. Because hydro infrastructure resulted in land loss, factions in the community, poverty, and a disruption of the traditional way of life, the Inninumowin expression also alludes to the peoples' struggles to find ways to return to that balanced way of life. Before the first flooding in Fox Lake, community cohesiveness was strong, and many combined the hunting and trapping economy with wage labour from the rail company. Many activities and practices associated with a land-based livelihood were lost with the land, and diverse social issues developed. Noah explains that after Manitoba Hydro came in "people stopped beading, stopped making things because the drinking started. With the caribou gone, the people were gone. A lot of those skills are gone. It's as if they lost something, like a piece of something in them."[7] In a conversation between Noah and Ivan, another community member in our grassroots group, the destruction that followed the utility's arrival in the area was enormous:

Noah: "Everybody in my community used to be . . . We weren't poor, everybody was okay. I don't think we were poor, eh?"
Ivan: "No."
Noah: "Everybody helped each other, we lived off the land."
Ivan: "I liked it better before Hydro came in."
Noah: "Yeah, we lived better before, before Hydro destroyed everything. You know, everything was nice, and the river and fish was good. Now it's everything back to swamp, I guess. They, they flooded it lots. Look at all that water, some of these trappers [line], like Jack's [Massan], there was [trap]lines in the water too."[8]

With the traplines under water and entire livelihoods gone, a sense of purposelessness and hopelessness was felt within the community. The Elders and harvesters used the Inninumowin term *oohcinowe* as a teaching about "doing things right on the land" or else there will be consequences.[9] This sense of loss and *oohcinowe* deepened with each subsequent hydro-electric project. The Inninuwak experienced tangible losses as well as "loss of self-determination, loss of control, loss of relationships, loss of self-sufficiency [. . .] loss at an emotional level."[10] Rampant sexual abuse, rape, racism, and children abandoned by transient Hydro workers are further allegations northern communities continue to make against the Crown Corporation.[11]

The depletion of lands and animals, the destruction of culturally important places and spaces of memory, and the disappearance of concepts associated with significant sites caused immense cultural detriment. Resource development changed the narrative in the community: "In the past, many people talked about everything, now, it seems like the community just talks about Hydro: the development, the loss, the flooding, the impacts, the Hydro workers, the Hydro dads [Hydro men who fathered children with local women and left after the project was completed]. All that changed and Hydro is all we ever talk about."[12] Hydro development significantly impacted the elements associated with Inninu knowledge as well as other ICH manifestations. Beginning with the first dam and advancing with each subsequent one, hydro development caused a loss of social cohesion. One couple, Christine and Jack Massan from Fox Lake, stated that "the elder Elders, the ones who are older than us and have lived through all those years, say the other dams did a real, did a lot of damage on the Cree here. And they're afraid that if they go through one more, that'll be the end of them. And I think they're speaking not, just, lives, but also culturally. Our environment is, is not very clean anymore. You know, a number of our Elders still use plants for medicinal uses. [...] you used to go in a place and pick. And now you gotta go further and further."[13] Noah echoes that having to go further and further away from the community to obtain a livelihood is hard on the *kitayatisuk*: "Our people, they go hunting, [...] they have a camp there they go hunting, spring hunting. And, look at those kids that come now, look how far you got to go now for trout. And the trout used to be right in our community before Kettle [dam]. Before Kettle, we could go fishing here. Look how far we['ve] got to go now. We got to take a train, Gillam is [mile marker] 326, we have to take a train to 374. That's forty-eight miles away."[14] Social cohesion, cultural knowledge, and *mino-pimatisiwin* are some of the Inninuwak ICH elements this resource-exhaustive industry has affected.

Hydroelectric development in Northern Manitoba significantly impacted local food systems as well. Changes to caribou migrations and hunting areas and the destruction of *nameo*, sturgeon, populations deprived people of their food sources as well as diminishing local knowledges and skills related to the activities involved. Noah discloses that after hydro development "there was no caribou in our area. They were all gone. Hydro destroyed that land. They destroyed that life. That's my [trap]line there. The old people used to tell stories about lots of caribou crossing the river. But after hydro came, there was no caribou. Hunting, trapping, that was gone. We used to eat caribou all the time. It's good meat, that caribou. . . . What will happen to the caribou on my [trap] line after Keeyask? Where will all the caribou go?"[15] Caribou knowledge associated with herd movements is profoundly guided by cultural values, familiarity with the herds, and Inninu relationship to the animals. Since the Inninuwak were largely dependent on caribou prior to the incoming of hydroelectric development in the 1960s, the building of the first dam was a highly destructive force on the traditional diet,[16] forcing the Inninuwak to rely on moose for meat instead.[17] Many of the oral expressions about caribou and skills associated with caribou hunts diminished as well. Noah shares one teaching about caribou that can lead to death if it is not passed down: "You can't just chase them. You have to be ready [for them]. They go far those caribou and can take you out far. You can't just chase them."[18] Like the loss of heritage associated with caribou, each hydroelectric project, construction phase, influx of workforce, brings with it losses to cultural heritage and profoundly alters Inninuwak *achimowinan*, stories/narratives.

Hydro's Metanarrative and Inninuwak Achimowinan

Within the framework of sustainable development, the Impact Assessment Agency of Canada (formerly the Canadian Environmental Assessment Agency) conducts reviews of projects and their impacts to help Canadians make informed decisions, and each new generating station must undergo a review and licensing process. The agency handles the licensing of resource-exhaustive projects, and the Impact Assessment Act (IAA) of 2019 guides the process (for Keeyask, the 2012 Canadian Environmental Assessment Act was in place). The IAA provides opportunities for public and Indigenous consultation, influences mitigation measures, and helps to limit or reduce a project's potential environmental effects. The IAA encourages cooperation and communication with Indigenous peoples as well as the use of Indigenous knowledge. Yet the 2019 Act continues to rely on the same definitions and perspectives present in the 2012 Act. Lumping together "Indigenous governing bodies" and environmental impacts,[19] consideration of a project's impact on "Indigenous cultures" is limited to "any changes in the environment—on (i) physical and cultural heritage [and] (ii) the current use of lands and resources for traditional purposes."[20] While the notion of cultural heritage now includes considerations of tangible and intangible elements, the IAA continues to interpret heritage as "any structure, site or thing that is of historical, archaeological, paleontological or architectural significance."[21] The conceptual ICH framework of UNESCO's 2003 ICH Convention does not play a role, hence the IAA limits "heritage" to tangible manifestations and narrows consideration of Indigenous cultures to "traditional environmental use."

At the CEC hearings and in the Environmental Assessment on Keeyask, "cultural effects" were grouped together with "social effects" of the proposed dam rather than considered a feature impacted by the multiplicity of infrastructure associated with each hydro project. The proponents interpreted historic cultural configurations solely through tangible artifacts requiring conservation, and traditional knowledge was presented at the hearings as something antithetical to contemporary cultural transformations, necessitating "validation" through Manitoba Hydro's preservation programs. The focus on traditional *ecological* knowledge extracted local people's experience and made it a singular and clichéd feature of their identity, thereby limiting the larger comprehensive Inninuwak knowledge system. This led one Fox Lake Cree Nation member of our group to state that "Hydro never sees us as a people."[22] Cumulative factors associated with cultural heritage, such as well-being, linguistic retention, and cultural transmission, appeared mainly as unrelated irritations to be dealt with by Hydro officials.[23]

The Keeyask EIA statement presented a limited view of lived reality. In responding to questions about impacts at the CEC hearings, Noah shared: "Well, look at all of the gravel pits and the quarry, you know, there will be a lot of—like there is going to be a quarry some place for rock to be blasting and all of that. And they are going to knock down all of the trees to get to these gravel pits. [...] that's what I got to see, that is all going to be disturbed too."[24] After his testimony, Noah said to me that "of course, there's going to be a lot of stuff going on in my trapline. They are going to be blasting, there is going to be lots of noise there. How can Hydro say there is no disturbance in my trapline?"[25] For Noah and other Inninuwak, the most devastating aspect of hydroelectric development was their inability to change what was happening to them and to their world: "I know the disastrous impact of what Hydro has done. He has destroyed so much land here. We used to make a living from the land [...] We had a good life long ago, before Hydro. He wrecked everything."[26] People's sense of powerlessness and their increasing distance from *mino-pimatisiwin* are impacts that repeat and extend exponentially with each subsequent project. While the proponents associated such narratives with something antecedent—a past project, or the residential school experience—these narratives reveal that environmental regulations, impact assessments, and impact statements rarely, if ever, reflect lived experiences. Since ICH is articulated through daily life, Canada's resource-exhaustive policies, including impact assessments, need to integrate the ICH framework.

As part of the assessment process, Manitoba Hydro relied on the category of Valued Environmental Components to evaluate and mitigate impacts on the Inninuwak and the environment. Valued Environmental (or Ecological) Components (VECs) are a science-based selection of flora and fauna (like moose, caribou, and sturgeon) taken into exclusive consideration. As ecological factors, VECs help decision makers assess the impacts projects will have on the environment. The Keeyask project's Environmental Assessment Report defines VECs as "fundamental elements of the physical, biological or socio-economic environment, including the air, water, soil, terrain, vegetation, wildlife, fish, birds and land use that may be affected by a proposed project."[27] Broad socio-economic VECs such as culture, spirituality, and domestic harvesting are also mentioned in the Keeyask Environmental Impact Statement, but the few elaborations on mitigating cultural effects did not satisfy the Inninuwak. Fox Lake Cree Nation participated in identifying VECs but continuously asserted that categorizing species creates significant problems: "By its very nature, the VEC approach tends to ignore interrelatedness of people, animals, water, landscape, and plants. . . . Our people do not place greater importance on certain species and all are valued equally. The entire Kischi Sipi [Nelson River] including the Inninuwak [the Cree people], fish, birds, plants, and wildlife, all of whom use, inhabit, and benefit from the river would constitute a VEC."[28] The compartmentalization of VECs and other impacts was problematic for the Inninuwak because it not only essentialized Indigenous land use around several "sexy" species but also disregarded the interconnectedness of ecological systems.[29] Noah's question about non-VEC animals during a break at the CEC hearings illustrated the challenge of merging the Inninu world view with the scientific process of Manitoba Hydro consultants: "And what about the squirrels, why doesn't anyone ask about the squirrel? He's important."[30] In response, the Hydro panel member stated that squirrels flourish profusely outside of the project area and in other areas of Manitoba, and as such, they are not scarce enough to be placed on the VEC list.[31] The Inninuwak *kitayatisuk* in our group outlined detailed information about the local world and the relationships between all beings in that space, attributing hydro impacts to every element of their life. The Keeyask VEC framework, however, included species considered significant to Inninuwak life but failed to recognize their associated ICH elements such as local food structures, resource stewardship systems, caribou knowledge and caribou-hunting skills, for example, as a direct part of the totality of cultural heritage.

Nuu-chah-nulth scholar Richard Atleo writes that separation of experience assumes that some parts have no relationship to other parts.[32] I have found this to be the case with environmental assessments, where specialized expertise and impacts are sequestered into moose, caribou, sturgeon, or "Aboriginal/Indigenous traditional knowledge" realms. This was evident both at the Keeyask hearings and during community consultations, where diverse specialists presented information on impacts of hydroelectric development but could not answer many of the Elders' concerns about Hydro employees overfishing or why all the construction workers are from Quebec rather than from Inninu communities. There are biologists, caribou experts, hydrological experts, workforce experts, Indigenous traditional knowledge experts, none of whom rarely, if ever, overlap, collaborate or exchange information. The fragmented view exists in tables and graphs, indicating differences in respective areas of expertise, and any analytic arguments based on the idea that everything is related, overlapping, and cumulative for local people is not part of that understanding. As the Keeyask project progressed and their questions remained unanswered, the Inninuwak found the process frustrating, illustrating how Canada's environmental assessments feature data disconnected from more complex realities of local people.

Appealing maps featuring blue reservoirs and green landscapes shown at the CEC hearings made Noah chuckle. The maps camouflage the actual effects of hydroelectric projects on the water. In reality, generating stations create murky, grey-coloured, algae-filled lakes. They flood water basins and fill the shorelines with debris and floating bodies of animals. Raw sewage from leaky lagoons causes oddly shaded slime to form along the shorelines. In 2013, as I sat in a boat with Makeso Sakahican Elders looking at the damage to their traplines, we struggled to navigate around floating logs but were unable to access some of the usual riverbanks. For Noah, who relies on a cane, unstable ground at the traditional gathering spot near Butnau River means he can only look at these important places from a distance (Figure 22). Local narratives point to the inability of the Inninuwak to have traditional shore lunches and overnight camping along the Kichi Sipi because of inaccessible shorelines (Figures 23 and 24). The sense of loss associated with the failure to access heritage spaces because of the release of raw sewage from the work camps was also not discussed at the CEC hearings. As we sat in the boat, Noah shared other impacts he experiences from hydro infrastructure. The sadness in Noah's voice when he described how the migrating caribou try to access their calving grounds only to drown in the engorged river was rivalled only by his anger at Hydro's insistence that he could not be seeing the endangered woodland caribou because they do not exist in these parts. "Hydro. Clean energy, they say. Yup, there's nothing clean about the shorelines here," he says.[33]

Figure 22. Noah Massan on the Kichi Sipi, pointing to an old campsite.

Figures 23 and 24. Erosion of the shorelines prevents local people from accessing traditional campgrounds or even going on shore, rendering water travel nearly impossible for Noah and others.

To compensate the Inninuwak, the Keeyask Impact Benefits Agreements was put forward as a replacement for the loss of harvesting associated with the flooding for the dam. The alternative was to ensure that Aboriginal and treaty hunting and trapping rights were not infringed on. According to the *kitayatisuk* in our group, the project's proponents had a very limited understanding of Inninu land epistemes. Manitoba Hydro's solution to the land loss was to fly out or temporarily relocate the harvesters to other areas so they could access resources (i.e., do their "Indigenous thing"). No details were made available to us about this three-year program during the CEC hearings, and many Inninuwak Elders and harvesters were confused: Whose territory would they harvest from and how had these arrangements been made with the local harvesters? How many resources could they take for food and how many for fur? How would they get there—by plane in the morning and return in the evening or would the harvesters be "left" there for a week? And how often would this take place? While the Off-Setting Program has value, it suggests that the *kitayatisuk* can be moved to another (seemingly empty) area of Crown land and put in a position where they take resources from someone else's territory.

Several knowledge holders in our CFLGC group, including Jack and Christine Massan from Fox Lake Cree Nation, laughed at the idea and the inappropriateness of relocating trappers and hunters from their traditional territory to "let" them hunt in someone else's land:

> **CFLGC:** [Manitoba Hydro] said we could move, we could move your trap, trappers to a different area.
> **Christine:** Elsewhere (laughs).
> **Jack:** Elsewhere. And I said no way (laughs).
> **Christine:** Why should we move? Why don't they move? [...]
> **Jack:** See, that's another thing, what we're saying. What are we gonna do to help the animals? Like, gotta help the caribou. How can we help them? Well, the best way to help them is, don't do anymore damage to the bush.
> **Christine:** Yep.
> **Jack:** You know, just, just leave everything, what's, how it looked before, eh. You can't; that's the best way to help the animals.

Yeah, don't, [do] uh, just forget about all the construction that's going on in the bush.[34]

The words above illustrate how the *kitayatisuk* tie their identity to a heritage space. Jack and Christine also highlight the irony of Hydro's attempt to "save" the wildlife and Inninuwak trapping rights by flooding another trapline area and by relocating the harvesters elsewhere. This is particularly odd, given the fact that relocation has shown to be ineffective and traumatic for Indigenous people.[35] Speaking to the inappropriateness of relocation, two Split Lake Cree Nation harvesters spoke at the public portion of the Keeyask hearings:

> When [Keeyask Generating Station] is built, our lives, our heritage, our ancestral lands will be altered and destroyed forever. [...] This is what the damage will be to our family and homeland alone, displacing our way of life, flooding us out, disconnecting the integrity of our connection of our past, ruining our relationship to our land. Destroying the way of the hunting and fishing [...] Traditional land uses [have] been passed on from generation to generation in our culture. Each family has their own territory [...] That's what Hydro is trying to do to us, is to find another trapline for us. First of all, we find another— if we find another suitable trapline area, it will never substitute for our homeland, where we have always been. It will be like forced location. Anyone who understands Cree culture would never say to a Cree person, just pack up and move on. That would degrade who we are because we are about the relation to our land. The land the Creator gave to us to live on and take care of it.[36]

For Inninuwak harvesters, sovereignty and heritage are intertwined with a particular landscape. Brushing aside Inninuwak customary governance, the Off-Setting Program deepens the displacement already felt by the *kitayatisuk* and circumscribes the vitality of ICH elements. As recently as the summer of 2020, Noah and some other Elders still had no idea how this program could be accessed.

One of the most common complaints community members made was that Manitoba Hydro ignored their knowledge and lived experience with on-the-ground effects. For example, *nameo*, sturgeon, a fish Manitoba Hydro claimed was no longer spawning in the Nelson River, continues to be seen by local land users. The argument frustrated the *kitayatisuk* because the endangered status of the fish means that First Nations cannot fish for it, yet Hydro can build more dams. Agreeing that special measures to maintain fish populations such as fish ladders are better than nothing, Noah shared that

> North-South [consultants] told us there were no fish, no sturgeon, maybe one or two, between Long Spruce and Limestone. As a core group we wanted to go set a net ourselves to see if we find sturgeon. So, we went ahead, three of us, Johnny Beardy, and Jack [two other Elders] were in a boat. We caught sturgeon. But, then I asked Smokey, or that other guy, I asked him, how come you never caught sturgeon? We caught sturgeon. Where did you catch sturgeon, he said. I'm not telling you. And we measure one there, about 32 inches I think. We caught [it]. Jack [Massan] got a picture of it. And Johnny [Beardy] and everything. We took pictures [. . .] And then there's one sturgeon there. . . . We caught one, I give it a kiss and I let it go. And later on, he jump right out of the water, that sturgeon. That's how happy he is that I let him go [laughs].[37]

Sturgeon is endangered in the Gillam region but because of their size and taste, they are very prized and often fished by Hydro workers. In addition to illegal fishing, massive caribou poaching, increased localized hunting and fishing, destruction of trails and traps, chasing after the animals with their snowmobiles, and using moose and bears for target practice are some disrespectful behaviours Noah and the other Elders have seen from Hydro employees.[38] Observing that the conduct of Hydro workers did not reflect the theoretical promises of "controlled work camps" presented at the hearings and in the EIS, Noah exclaimed that "those big Hydro guys up there [in Winnipeg offices], they don't know what their guys [on the ground] are doing."[39] This harvester recounted stories of equipment and other construction garbage buried rather than properly disposed, trailers flipped upside-down so First Nations people do not move into them, and workers taking advantage of Inninuwak women.[40] While working for Hydro once, Noah witnessed animals left to die in the drained pools of water prior to a dam's operation, and fish purposely captured so Hydro employees could harvest the most prized species and leave the "leftovers" to perish.[41] Disrespectful conduct toward the Inninuwak and the animals (Figure 24) occurs regularly, but the proponents never act upon these grievances. Stating the fact that "Hydro people, they have no respect for First Nations," Noah's anger at the little control Hydro has over employees directly engaged with the Inninuwak was evident. In that conversation, Noah's anger turned to tears welling up in his eyes as he discussed "job opportunities" for local people and reflected upon his own employment history on past generating stations. With his voice breaking up, Noah disclosed: "It was a job. There was nothing else. I destroyed my community. I helped destroy my community."[42]

The issue of caribou was one of the biggest disagreements between Manitoba Hydro and the Inninuwak. Arguing that the endangered woodland caribou are not in the Keeyask project area, Hydro sidestepped the controversy by classifying the woodland caribou as only "summer residents" of the Barren Land Caribou herd, which warrants extra precautions but does not address the possibility of extirpation of the species. This claim challenged the testimonies of the Inninuwak, who

Figure 25. Photo of a fox dismembered by a Hydro worker, found by Noah near his trap.

maintained that woodland caribou were routinely seen by community members and that they had always hunted them in their territory. This is a sensitive and frustrating issue for *kitayatisuk* like Noah, who identified *noschimik atikuk*, woodland caribou, as present in the Keeyask area. This harvester's keen eye should not be underestimated, and after the proponent's presentation on caribou, Noah became visibly more and more annoyed over the issue. During the break, he told me that he can tell a woodland caribou from other caribou: "They are dark, and big. I know that caribou. I've killed them. I know what is on my land. Manitoba Hydro, they are telling me bullshit."[43] In an interesting turn of events, when our team, the CFLGC, was later cross-examined at the CEC hearings, Noah made a compelling and powerful argument about the woodland caribou on his trapline. Claiming that his nephew had killed a woodland caribou just prior to the hearings and in a state of agitation at his knowledge being challenged, Noah burst into a powerful outcry and proclaimed that he would kill a caribou and place it at the examining lawyer's door as proof: "Because as a user, I get to see stuff there, you know. So you can't prove, you have to be there to see these things. But next time I kill a caribou, I'm going to bring it to you [Hydro's cross-examining lawyer], if you are around. I will take pictures of it."[44] This caused the entire room to fill with applause and laughter, especially from the Inninuwak watching the hearings at the back of the room. The moment still resonates with many community members, and Noah became a hero for publicly talking back to Hydro "higher-ups."

As the Inninuwak narratives show, resource development and its immense infrastructure impact the daily life of *kitayatisuk* as much as they limit the continuity and transmission of ICH elements. Knowledge of the land, waters, and wildlife, the responsibility to care for traplines in accordance with *mino-pimatisiwin*, and teaching cultural skills to future generations are several elements impacted by development. Under current environmental regulations in Canada, not only is the notion of intangible cultural heritage nonexistent, but the broader understanding of heritage as "alive" is generally absent. However, an ICH lens helps recontextualize the nature/culture dichotomy to better construe Inninuwak traditional territories as values based on explicit performativity on the land rather than as material artifacts to be assessed. The Makeso Sakahican community members in our group identified the following elements and their locations as features of their intangible cultural heritage impacted by hydro development: games, experiential learning, art, craft, dancing, music, *kiskinohamakaywina*, teaching(s), *aska achimowin*, tradition(s), *aski kanawicikiwin*, keeping or looking after the territories, *atunogawina*, stories and legends, including events occurring prior to human occupation of the earth, *atchimowina*, accounts of past events as remembered by speakers and considered factual, *aski atchimowina*, land stories/narratives, Inninumowin, the language the people speak as well as *mitewewin*, traditional and spiritual ways of life, *kosahpahchikkun*, shaking tent, Christian jamborees, and sweatlodges. More could have been identified, but time limitations and the objectives of the CEC hearings restricted our exploration of Makeso Sakahican Inninuwak living heritage.

ICH inventories need to be a mandatory component of impact assessments. Since ICH represents "invisible data" generated from very tangible adverse effects local people experience from a project, inventories gathered during the review stage, amid the lifespan of any approved project, and through to decommissioning can serve as indicators of on-the-ground impacts. ICH inventories provide communities and resource developers with a new vocabulary with which to enhance existing traditional knowledge, land use, and archaeological studies. Whereas traditional knowledge and land use studies ground specific activities of knowledge holders in the landscape through maps, ICH inventories strengthen these documentations to show processes of transmission and social interactions between and across generations. In resource development contexts, inventories show the link between humans and the land as well as demonstrate how that land constructs specialized cultural manifestations. For example, Inuit-made igloos or Maghreb Arabic music played on the *'ūd* with a wooden *plectrum* (stick) are both testaments to Indigenous knowledges, skills, and practices. The soundscape of Tuvan throat singing, where the male herders ride horses against the open mountainous steppes of Mongolia, or the process of sculpting images of the goddess Durga using clay pulled from the Ganga River for the Durga Puja annual festival in Kolkata, India, likewise demonstrate that explicit landscapes create cultural processes (and often products) directly tied to that landscape. When incorporated into environmental assessments, an ICH inventory of cultural manifestations can reinforce existing studies to protect the means of transmission from being disrupted. Combined with other mapping and archaeological methods, community-led ICH inventories offer communities, the Impact Assessment Agency of Canada, *and proponents* an expanded view of the totality of impacts.

In evaluating costs and benefits, losses and opportunities, inventories can not only help Indigenous people take a stronger stance when negotiating economic benefits but may even contribute to a development project not going through. Unfortunately, this was not the case with Keeyask. When I spotlighted a few ICH elements at the CEC hearings, Noah said to me, "That's good you told them we do those things."[45] A number of individuals later approached me to ask me how I "found" these elements, to which I replied that the *kitayatisuk* told me about them. It occurred to me later that the examples I shared at the hearings were only a few of the elements I had in my notebook; no one who was at the hearings learned about the other ICH elements the *kitayatisuk* identified because I never had the chance to speak about them (for the purpose of time, I was told to move on with my questioning of the proponents). I subsequently asked myself: Does Manitoba Hydro know that so many more elements have *already* been identified by the *kitayatisuk* as being vulnerable to further hydroelectric development? Did they even take into account the few items I mentioned or where these ICH elements "too cultural" for an environmental assessment? And, more importantly, was I effective in articulating the urgency of inventorying Inninuwak and *kitayatisuk* living heritage *before* the Keeyask dam floods the landscape?

ICH documentation offers Indigenous people a new perspective with which to assess impacts on their communities; it may also catalogue elements which a resource-exhaustive project will extinguish.[46] In recognizing and mitigating effects, the ICH discourse offers the public a comprehensive view of eco-cultural impacts, and it is disappointing that this important framework was not included in the 2019 Impact Assessment Act.[47] Explicit valuation and valuation methods are gaining momentum across the world, and impact assessments are a technical policy design that *must* include an ICH framework in public decision making at local, regional, and national levels.[48] The ICH framework can oblige industry and the Canadian government to observe Indigenous and treaty rights and to enhance their environmental obligations and commitments to climate change.[49] Including documentation as part of impact assessments would show that Canada's commitment to UNDRIP and to the TRC is more than lip service.

No Access

Between the Keeyask CEC hearings, Noah and I shop at the big box stores: he has the truck, I have the Costco card, and we both enjoy browsing up and down the aisles for hours. We also go to the hardware store because Noah is looking for new materials to build a trap. Noah has an innovative idea for building traps that will keep the poachers out; he examines some materials, pulling and tugging on some wire nets. Even though Hydro flooded his trapping cabin—twice!—and Keeyask infrastructure is further destroying his trapline, Noah hopes to set his traps anyway. Despite all the destruction to his way of life, Noah continues to be in good spirits and very determined. Joking that he will invest in snorkels or in a submarine so he can see how his cabin looks after all those years of being submerged, he then informs me that he will fight Hydro and hold them responsible until his death. "One time, there," he tells me again, "I found a monkey or teddy bear in my trap. I took a picture. Some guy, he drove on my land and put a [stuffed] bear or monkey in my trap. They do that, those Hydro guys. They got no respect for my line."[50] Noah pulls out a photo from his wallet and shows me a photo of a white stuffed toy that a Hydro worker put in his trap (Figure 26). Noah worries about the animals on his trapline, and his affection and concern for their well-being is evident:

> I don't want to see that land be flooded. These other dams. Those beavers that make their houses already and everything, they don't have time to go move out. Like that old lady I was telling you about whose house was knocked down [by Hydro for a project].

Figure 26. Photo of the stuffed animal that was put in Noah's trap by Hydro employees.

Beaver must have a same feeling [laughs]. I can't speak to animals.
Whoever lives in the [bush], like the bears, they have a den in the
back, you know. I seen lots of it in Kettle [Dam] there, dead, like
dead beaver, dead bears. It hurts me, you know. I worry about
those animals.[51]

Several years after the Keeyask CEC hearings, I travel to Gillam to visit
Noah. We are driving around Gillam in his truck and catching up. Forced
to rely on a wheelchair for much of the time now, Noah still goes into the
bush (he attached skis to his walker so he can walk from his ski-doo and
check his traps!). It is the summer of 2018, and we stop to say hi to a few
people, which gives us all the chance to reunite and get updated. Noah is
taking me to some familiar places around town but also wants to show
me the changes that are happening with Hydro here: new quarries, bigger
worker camps, old dams deteriorating, and new signs put up. As we are
overlooking one reservoir, our discussion turns to caribou and their calving

Figure 27. Photos of the construction of the Keeyask Generating Station (Figures 27–33), show the impacts to Noah's trapline, before flooding and the building of the dam. Note that in this image of a quarry, there are spruce trees in the background, and the sign that says "Danger: Sudden Drop." The quarries are built alongside the road on the way to Keeyask.

Figure 28. Transmission lines from previous dams tower over the trees and the local landscape.

Figure 29. Construction work: new facilities, loud trucks, and other vehicles replace the boreal forest landscape. Note the dense spruce in the background, as well as the dug-up and torn trees ripped from the soil, commonly known as a slash pile.

Figure 30. Construction cranes and permanently damaged shorelines at the Keeyask rapids. This will be the site of the Keeyask Generating Station. It is probably one of the last photos of the *Keeyasko* (gull) rapids in their natural state. After the dam blocks the river, they will forever disappear.

Figure 31. An army of trucks stand like soldiers to construct the dam. Note the ground: the pounded rocks and gravel replace the swamps of the northern landscape.

Figure 32. Construction alters the landscape, exposing rock and filling the air with dust, noise, and machinery.

Figure 33. Not too far down this main road to the Keeyasko rapids, Noah points to a place on the right, stating that the beaver have built their own dam and flooded a large space of the forest adjacent to this road. Laughing, Noah says that "the beaver are fighting back."

grounds, one of which is an island that was to remain protected for the pregnant caribou. "Oh, I'll tell ya what happen[ed] to that island," Noah reports, pointing to an area across the water. "They'll put rocks all around the island, they say. How they gonna do that? They['re] not even doing it anymore. They['re] not doing it right now. I don't think they protected the caribou, look at that caribou over there, they got nowhere to go."[52] Frustrated that Manitoba Hydro does not keep its promises, he starts his truck and we drive to our next "station." A few minutes later, a half-ton truck with the familiar blue company symbol speeds by in a 30-kilometre zone and we are shrouded in a cloud of dust. This time it bothers Noah. As we turn to a side road, Noah complains that Hydro does not have control over its workers and says, "Those guys, they just go under all the power lines with their ski-doos into my trapline. They just take everything." His irritation is valid, as few Hydro workers seem to possess knowledge of Inninuwak culture and of their land tenure systems.

We approach the gate of the Keeyask dam construction. Noah is showing my family and me the landscape that will forever alter the Keeyasko rapids. Noah wants us to see and take pictures of all the destruction that is occurring on his trapline so we "can tell people" (Figures 27–33). We drive deeper into the "project site," as Noah's line is now called, and capture videos of the traffic, the multiple work camps, the large amount of equipment that is brought in to cut, grind, chop, shred, tear, and blast areas of his line. Finally, we see the skeleton of the dam in the distance. It is a huge concrete wall, right above the last of the rapids in the area. The noise from all the activities does not allow us to talk. I am simultaneously saddened by the view and enraged at the unfairness of it all. Given our shared unsuccessful and oh-so-time-consuming fights against more hydroelectric development in Noah's territory, I feel defeated and tears come to my eyes.

Later, I ask Noah if he ever gets tired of fighting Manitoba Hydro. He replies, "No, I don't get tired, no. Ah, I just talk to you, I don't care about

Figure 34. Noah's trapline is scattered with different types of signs, many of which insist on authorization or no access/no trespassing to the area.

'em. I like fighting them. Even my trapline. I almost beat up a security guy," and he proceeds to tell me about the time Manitoba Hydro put up a No Trespassing sign at the Keeyask project site. A security guard stopped Noah a few kilometres past the sign and proceeded to question him about who he was and what he was doing, informing him that he was on private property. "He kept telling me," recounts Noah, "that there is no access here" (Figure 34). As Noah gave the security guy only curt answers (on principle he never provides explanations to Manitoba Hydro), the guard became frustrated. "Oh boy, he kept telling me that this is private property," recounts Noah, "that there is no access here. And when I asked him, 'So how come you're putting No Trespassing signs on my trapline?' the guy, that's just a monkey suit he [was] wearing, he said to me, [that] I had no right to come over there. And then he threw in a 'buddy, you need to leave' comment and starts shaking his finger at me." By now very annoyed, Noah asked the man, "Listen buddy, listen buddy. Where are you from?" The security guard, surprised at the question, answered, "Toronto—why, where are you from?" Noah responded: "I am born and raised here, and you are on my trapline. And if you don't stop waving your finger at me, I'll put it where you no like it."

Then, at over seventy years old and with a debilitating muscular disease that causes him to rely on a mobility aid, Noah drove further past that No Trespassing sign to set some traps.

Chapter Five

"The land will stand for you"

As a well-known *mashkiki inini*, Richard Morrison is employed to conduct ceremonies for prisons, universities, and health centres. In Canada and in the United States, organizations have hired Richard to teach their members about Anishinaabe *bimaadiziwin* and to conduct Anishinaabe ceremonies, drumming, and building *madoodoswaan* for health and healing. Richard is paid for the three-hour-long sweatlodge ceremony, yet there is an entire process that precedes the ceremony. Two days before, Richard cuts down specific trees and forms them into the frame of the lodge. To put up the sweatlodge itself, he uses a shovel, a wheelbarrow, a crowbar, and five or six tarps to make the lodge completely dark. Richard brings in cedar boughs to cover the floor but sometimes he uses rugs or blankets; he carries the firewood and the *omishoomisaabigoog*, grandfathers (rocks), to the site shortly after. To get the wood, Richard cuts down a tree with a chainsaw and hauls the wood to the truck by hand. To ensure the safety of the participants, Richard picks the rocks by hand, inspecting each "grandfather" scrupulously as a faulty hot rock can explode and kill a person. On the day of the ceremony, Richard brings in buckets of water and food; it is customary to feed the spirits and the participants. The red-hot grandfathers are put in the lodge in an explicit order with a pitchfork. *Ishkaabewis*, a firekeeper/helper, often assists him with keeping an eye on the fire outside the lodge. For the ceremony, Richard always brings in a large pouch of *asemaa*, tobacco, which he makes himself, though he also likes using the tobacco I bring him from Poland. The sage, bear grease, eucalyptus oil, sweetgrass, and many other *mashkikiwan*, medicines, are used up during the ceremony. These arduous activities take a lot out of Richard, and he tends to rest before and after a sweat. As the reader can envision, an expanse of behind-the-scenes cultural knowledge and hard work demands one *madoodoo'iwe*. The ICH discourse pushes these invisible economies to the forefront of policy work.

Sustaining Livelihoods

Akiwenziyag like Richard illustrate the double economy that exists in many communities—a formal and an informal one. The first is material—the visible economy where formal wage is noted, calculated, and paid to members for their labour. This labour consists of jobs with schools, administrative bodies, businesses, or other community infrastructure. The other, invisible economy exists in addition to the formal employment sector and aligns more closely with a land-based ICH economy, where individual and collective livelihoods garnered from the land serve as surplus wealth. An *akiwenzi*'s livelihood is not employment in the formal sense because there is no hourly wage or annual salary; it is not formally written or bureaucratized within national statistics either.[1] This mode of production often extends beyond the regular work hours of an *akiwenzi*.

Akiwenziyag livelihoods include going inland to cut wood or mowing the lawn at the local church in the summer, or shovelling snow off the roof at the Elder's Lodge in the winter. Driving Elders to health appointments, drumming, running a sweatlodge, or going to the trapline enhance social relations and contribute to ICH transmission. Abel Bruce, the Poplar River *akiwenzi*, describes the hard work that goes into trapping:

> I don't have a job. I go hunt what I want, when I need to. Sometimes I go set traps. I set about twenty-five traps a day, twenty-five traps a day. Maybe I go over thirty. And, there is nothing here. First trap you go, there is nothing here. If you go to five, six traps, there is nothing there. Maybe you go to about twenty traps a day, you go to see about twenty traps a day. Next day you go and [see] twenty again and all that. Then, you know, there is nothing there. [Then], there is only one I got for today. And it sort of makes me happy when I get that one. That one for a day. Sometimes I get one marten a day; maybe I get one fox a day. That's what it is, to hunt, just to make your life. Just like you make up your life [. . .] but you have to try hard, the more fur you get, the more money you get. That's what it is now. Sometimes I get one rabbit a day, set snares, rabbit snares and you can just get all the fur that you want. It takes long time. We never used be in Poplar [River, the community], when growing up. We used to go trap. Used to go every spring, fall, when we do it. Trapping, it's our life. And now, you can't even, you can't even go trap nowadays, you're busy doing something else.[2]

Harvesting is very labour intensive and demands a lot of time. Before going out on the land, it is important to maintain equipment, obtain enough bullets and snares, and ensure enough gas is in the snowmobile or the boat. "These days," shares Abel, "getting good trapping partners, that's a job."[3] Many land users take time off from (paid) work or take vacations in early fall to go geese or moose hunting, to set snares or to pick blueberries. On the West Coast of Canada, communities take time off collectively to process salmon during its run.[4]

At present, many *akiwenziyag* merge wage labour with ICH work, illustrating that ICH safeguarding can be amalgamated with economic development. UNESCO recognizes that ICH-inclusive economic development can "encompass not just income generation but also the development of sustainable livelihoods, productive employment and decent work."[5] While only community members can identify their ICH priorities and economic ventures, opportunities exist for living heritage to play a role in capacity building and sustainable livelihoods. Whether for local purposes or commercial use, tangible economic value through direct revenues can benefit ICH custodians, especially when considering the economic losses arising from non-intervention. Losing trapping skills, for example, may lead to a loss of income in some isolated communities; depriving young people of moosehide tanning expertise will likewise force them to buy expensive commercially tanned hides. Inadequate *manoomin* (wild rice) safeguarding measures can cause a cultural food system to disappear and increase food insecurity.[6] ICH restitution, revitalization, and transmission benefit livelihoods.

Living heritage strengthens local economies by encompassing "a diversity of productive activities, with both monetary and non-monetary value, and [. . .] it can also constitute an important source of innovation in the face of change to help achieve inclusive economic development at the local and international levels."[7] Enhanced through intergenerational transmission, this driving force can also contribute to ground-breaking solutions to global issues like climate change, food security, and peacekeeping. Traditional skills held by craftspeople can also have immense practical applications. For example, in France, twenty-first-century prosthetics are made using the artisanal skills of porcelain workers. Dayak *ikat* weaving, a symbol of culture and identity of the Kallimantan people in Indonesian Borneo, has become a significant economic resource to raise the standard of living for local women.[8] In a like manner, Samoan fine-woven mats blend ecological knowledge of pandanus plant cultivation with traditional weaving, and local people use these mats as currency and in ceremonies.[9] The Polish and Belarussian tree beekeepers too rely on cultural knowledge and their special relationship with bees to attain a livelihood. These "guardians of ways of living in accord with nature and respecting its laws [by] respecting bees" placed tree beekeeping on the UNESCO ICH list in 2020 to employ intergenerational knowledge transmission as a tool for biodiversity protection and economic diversification.[10] Based on cultural values, these examples show how culture custodians use innovative strategies to ensure ICH sustainability in a global context.

Southeast Asia is making the most headway in blending sustainability with ICH-based economic development. Japan, for example, has been actively engaging in policies related to the transmission of living expressions. Japan's post-1945 destruction led the nation to rely on local Elders and knowledge holders to teach young people cultural skills, crafts, and traditions in a way that the country could join the global economy. Some of the country's registered ICH elements include music, drama, and art, as well as craft techniques like metalworking, woodworking, doll making, textiles, and pottery. Japan gives recognition not only to the immaterial features of ICH but also to the individual or collective "owners" of an element to encourage transmission and restitution of heritage. ICH custodians can obtain funding, in some cases more than $25,000 USD ($34,000 CDN), to help protect their craftsmanship, their employment, and its continuity.[11] Since Japan views its Elders and their knowledge as "living national treasures" (*Ningen Kokubō*), the country funds and promotes activities to encourage and train young people in cultural skills, to disseminate creativity, and to enable their learning and production as a viable form of participation in the contemporary economy.[12]

China's approach, on the other hand, is much more comprehensive because it pushes the commodification of ICH through tourism and the cultural industry. Since many officially recognized ICH elements in China are facing a crisis of losing young inheritors, the country is disseminating the values of ICH to larger audiences with the intent to generate new social and economic development. Ethnic minorities in the Dali Prefecture of the Yunnan Province, for example, use ICH associated with tie-dying as a popular tourist attraction. Recognized as an ICH element in 2006, the handicraft uses natural herbs to dye cloth by needleworking unique patterns, such as plants, insects, and geometric patterns in the material.[13] To help sell artisanal products from Dali and other regions, China launched an online ICH Shopping Festival in 2020. Along with e-commerce platforms and the promotion of ICH through digital media (such as video and social media), the country found an effective way not only for young audiences to be exposed to ICH but also for producers and consumers to interact digitally and generate an income. Because ICH commodification in China includes governments, businesses, listed ICH inheritors, non-listed ICH practitioners, and the public, it yields both economic and social effects, which together contribute to inheriting, creating, and disseminating ICH.[14]

ICH custodians have proven to be a driving global force for mobilization, innovation, and revenue for many communities. Through program administration and diversified pathways to capital projects, ICH fosters cultural revitalization at the same time as capacity building. Communities can enhance their local economies in ways that merge skills, practices, and ICH-related customs with the larger market economy. In Canada, Indigenous heritage already drives local community development in art (carving, painting, fashion, moccasin making),[15] food (wild rice, medicines, seafood),' and knowledge systems (governance, education, societies). Through the Pimachiowin Aki World Heritage Site, the community of Poplar River is investing in their living cultural and natural heritage to foster community economic development. The Anishinaabeg Cultural Interpretative/Visitor Reception Centre serves as the hub for cultural heritage interpretation and language preservation. Many young people are learning and deepening their heritage interests and combining them with skills geared toward eco-cultural tourism. Some are getting trained in information technology, wilderness survival, First Aid, tourism, and other entrepreneurial initiatives; local restaurants and small businesses are involving more people career in management and trades.[16] Elders like Jean Nanawin are eager to market their beautiful moccasins, mukluks, gloves, and new crafts to visitors; others too are creating art and jewellery as well as joining the fishing industry as economic opportunities arise. By incorporating contemporary and traditional materials, methods, and designs into new ideas, young people are finding inspiration in heritage to create their own livelihoods.

Over the past fifteen years visiting Poplar River, I have heard many young community members claim that they could never imagine leaving the community (many of them are grown up now!). They love the freedom the vast natural space offers. But they also enjoy "escaping" to Winnipeg and other big cities to experience urban life, shop in the malls, pursue higher education, and drink at night clubs and bars, while intending to come back to Poplar River. One community member, Byron Mitchell, said that he loves the space and the quiet that help him "reflect and pray" as much as he hopes to take advantage of the opportunities that the World Heritage Site offers.[17] Another member, Freddie Bruce, shared that he loves being on the land and hopes to make his livelihood from *asatiwisipe akiing*:

> I do a lot of hunting. I do a lot of hunting, and fishing. I've been here all my life and whenever I leave, I miss it. Just the sense of being in a wilderness; it's nice and quiet. A place you can relax and let everything go. I went up north, all the flooding that

happens with Hydro, and then I come back here, like the land is untouched. Up there, it's so messed up, and just to see that land being destroyed like that. That doesn't have to be. We're pretty lucky where we are, we're not flooded and the animals here, they are not running away from all the flooding. I mean, we are lucky the way we are, the location. [...] Like I was saying, to leave the land the way it is, and everything will be okay. I don't want to leave this place; I am going to die here. That's how much I love it here. This is my home.[18]

Emphasizing that he is "tired of being *bookoshkaa* [broke]," Freddie is happy that the First Nation is relying on the leadership of "those that grew up here and have lots of knowledge about the area."[19] The community already offers "nature" trips, where tourists can learn about the medicinal, cultural, and technological uses of plants, and can experience wilderness survival adventures. "The attraction," explains Ernest Bruce, the community's policy and economic development advisor, "would be not only [to] be living as our people have [done] for generations, but also just seeing the land." Visitors who come to the community are "surprised to find many different birds, poplar, and pine in one area," Ernest points out, and argues that others are likely to be impressed with the "thousand-year-old ecosystem that has been sustained" by local *akiwenziyag*.[20] Eco-cultural tourism in this Anishinaabe community allows visitors to experience the cultural and natural landscape and contribute to ICH transmission.

Living Culture

The year 2012 was good for Abel because he caught about thirty lynx and "a whole bunch" of marten.[21] We are checking some conibear traps; it is a beautiful sunny day but immensely cold, and the camera keeps shutting down when I face the wind. We are at *asatiwisiping akiing*, near Marchand's Creek, in absolute silence of the bush, except for the crunching of the snow under our feet. Explaining intermittent harvesting, Abel tells me that

> you can't just go ahead and trap every animal. Like a couple of years ago, like five years ago, I had seventy-eight martens, a whole winter, seventy-eight martens. Sometimes I used to get four a day; sometimes I used to get two a day and I'd come home with that. That [northern] part of the area [points with hand] I used to trap marten, not the other ones. I tried to save the other ones for next winter. I never set a snare for the lynk. Forget it, I save that one for next year. Even fox are good. For the trapper, for the fox, for the fisher, I save that for next year. I'll just go after marten for this year. I'll just go for marten this year.[22]

Elaborating on his responsibilities as head trapper, the *akiwenzi* reminds me that *ji-ganawendamang Gidakiiminaan* is in fact "everything you do on the land in the right way" so that the land can provide for humans: "Say me, I always pick the right thing. Sometimes I'd get five or ten or fifteen lynk a day you know. [...] They are smart animals; it wants to keep his life. You can't just go there—like marten, you can't just get it in the trap, [like] the fisher [...] that's how animals are. That's why I have been a trapper all these years; I know what it's like. You can't just trap every animal."[23] For Abel, *ji-ganawendamang Gidakiiminaan* determines harvesting. Abel never went to high school and like many of his contemporaries, he attended a residential school that changed the dynamics of *aki onaaji'idizowin* and *aki gikendamowin*, land-based practices and knowledges. Despite the break with his culture that happened when he went to school, Abel acknowledges that caring for the land is his whole life: "That's what I've been doing, in my hometown. I have been trapping all my life, like my father did, and his dad before him. That's my way of life, doing it; no job, nothing. That's a job for you. If you do things right, the land will stand for you."[24]

For generations, the *akiwenziyag* have been stewards of their respective traplines. Abel monitors the wildlife in the area, knows how much fish to catch from a river or lake, and how many fur-bearers to take. Because knowledge about the landscape is gained by going out on the land for much of the year, many experienced *akiwenziyag* have the best and most detailed knowledge of black bear and beaver populations, of locations to kill moose, and of the places to pick blueberries. These *akiwenziyag* know the best time to hunt geese or moose, which traps catch marten better, and where the fattest fish are; they are also familiar with fire occurrences and offering sites. The body of knowledge behind protocols such as not killing pregnant cows in the spring (so that they reproduce) or why bears are not consumed in this area (because of the Bear Lodge ceremony), is gained from experience and from having been taught by experts of previous generations. Having spent most of his life as a head trapper, Abel has been travelling the Mukatewasipe for over sixty years. "This is what I am doing," he says, "my uncle gave me his trapline. His name was Philip Bruce. Now I use it the way he was using it. It was in the 1980s that he gave me his trapline. He said: keep it clean, use it. It is beautiful, take care of it like it's your life. Your life is important to you, take care of it. Ancestors are over there; they were there taking care of it. They took care, now we are doing it for them like they did [for us]."[25] Abel emphasizes that the responsibility to care for his trapline was passed down to him from his family and that the obligation to "take care of it like it's your life" extends to future generations.

From my time spent with the *akiwenziyag* and with *kitayatisuk* like Noah Massan, I learned that their presence is important for on-the-ground checks and balances; any imbalance in the local ecosystem is carefully targeted and handled over time. These experts are not only skilled at skinning, butchering, and/or processing furs and meat, they also make sure important sites and family cabins are not desecrated or forgotten about. These men (and women) are aware of the trends of the ecosystem and record them in their memory (or in little notepads, like Frances Valiquette did); they also confer with others and compare their information with previous years. A trapper considers the well-being of the overall environmental system: through careful actions and practices, the knowledge holder monitors, manages, selectively harvests, and permits (or refuses) others access to the area. The *akiwenziyag* and the *kitayatisuk* interpret their role as the exclusionary right to determine land sustainability.

A brief discussion on traplines is needed. As shared in the Introduction, much of the information about trapping in this book comes from the *akiwenziyag* and the *kitayatisuk*. These knowledge holders (not all Elders) contribute to the larger conversation on natural and cultural resource management by challenging the typical way Indigenous "hunters and gatherers" are perceived. Trapping is generally interpreted as an economic activity arising out of the fur trade rather than as a cultural way of life. A significant portion of land-based research focuses on hunting and gathering or on historical trapping in the fur trade era, leaving little room to consider contemporary trapping and snaring.[26] However, trappers are not merely hunters or gatherers; sometimes they are both. The *akiwenziyag* and *kitayatisuk* with whom I spoke all expressed that their identity, their pride, and their way of being reside in being culture-and-land keepers: trappers. Many of them believe that trapping does not get the recognition it deserves. They see outside opposition to the fur industry as an obstacle to their way of life and livelihood. And because there is more esteem in hunting large animals, several expressed regret that young men prefer to go hunting rather than become trappers.[27] Acknowledging that small game activity is too time-consuming, two young hunters in Poplar River shared their view that trapping is not a "traditional activity" because "it's not about food."[28] This point of view is vehemently opposed by the *akiwenziyag* and the *kitayatisuk* who assert that Indigenous people have always depended on the fur of animals for clothing, shelter, bedding, and a livelihood.[29] The fur is still used today for moccasins, gloves, mukluks, artisanal crafts, and ceremonies; some trappers still eat the fur-bearers' meat. Reinforcing pride in the activity and in the bush skills it entails, the *akiwenziyag* and *kitayatisuk* illustrate that ICH knowledge and performativity within the trapping way of life continue to be viable forms of livelihood.

The *kitayatisuk* and *akiwenziyag* reveal that the life of a trapper is not easy. The work is physically demanding and ends only when people go to sleep. Noel Bruce, a retired education counsellor, Elder, trapper, and university graduate (who also once won the lottery!), recalls his days on the trapline, where the daily challenge was to end the day safely: "Trappers used to take their families to their traplines in the fall and came home after the spring trapping season has ended. The trappers would sell their furs to the HBC [Hudson's Bay Company]. Many of the trappers came back to Poplar River to sell their furs during the winter—mostly by walking or some used dog teams. And most trappers would take dogs to traplines and make wooden toboggans and snowshoes to use for all purposes, but especially to haul all the furs."[30] Since trapping is so hands-on and close to the animals, there is also always a danger of getting hurt, which is why the term "surviving in the bush" is part of the common narrative. Ken recalls his incident with wolves while out trapping:

> I used to trap beaver, muskrat, otters, on Rice Lake. I miss it once in a while 'cause I used to go in the spring and every fall with my old man. My grandparent, Tom Douglas, he used to go with the Valiquettes, Marcel and his brothers there, Jim Valiquette. He used to go there. He used to have his trapline there. That's [trapline number four] where the Bruces go in, Abel and his dad; they use to go trapping there. Mukatewa Lake, in the spring and winter and the fall. In the fall, we used to go Mukatewa River [Mukatewasipe], we used to trap there in the fall. One time when

I was trapping in Black River, there, in the tall grass, I'd jump over it and all of a sudden, a wolf came out, all five of them. They just were there, and I couldn't move because then they would attack me. Wolf, it's a pretty big animal, sometimes they take moose. There can be ten of them, and they take a moose. . . . You're just supposed to survive; that's hard work. There's a lot of stories [and] I am sure we did our best, how we survived way back then.[31]

Trapping requires extensive travels across the land for long periods of time. As a result, the trappers know their territory intimately. Walter Nanawin illustrates the extent of travels made by trappers on the traplines: "I've travelled on foot north of Poplar River, north and east into this protected land. I've travelled and waded in the muskeg. We waded through here with Willie Bruce, it was 1948, I guess. There [through] all this water and bog and portages here [shows on map]. All those guys who go up to Weaver Lake to trap, know where all the portages are."[32]

Pointing with his finger to the *aki mazina'igan*, map, Walter shows me the large area of land that he regularly crossed. Given the immensity of boreal forest landscape on this side of Lake Winnipeg, travelling on foot or on a snowmobile requires the perseverance, strength, and bush knowledge of an *akiwenzi*. Abel echoes that to be a *nitaa-wanii'ige inini*, good trapper, one must experience the hardship of the muskeg and the incessant insects. A good trapper, shares Noah, the Inninu *kitayatis*, must also have the strength to open a sharp, heavy metal trap and the finesse to take out a small fur-bearer's limp body delicately and respectfully. Sometimes the traps "have finnicky springs," he says, and so "it is easy [for someone] to lose a hand."[33] Trappers also face the challenge of prey being not quite dead and thus having to take its life by twisting its neck—only to be surprised by its ferocity to live. Abel shares one *dibaajimowin*, story, about the time his trapping partner "caught" a lynx:

One time I had a lynk there, it was in '72 or '76, with Sophia's brother there, Gordy, Gordy Bittern. In the wintertime, me and my brother [Albert] went; I went to Gordie that time, I took Gordie that time. Sometimes we took turns driving a ski-doo, and one time there, Albert told me, "You go to that creek over there, and me, I'll go there on that south side." There used to be creeks in that lake, you know. Now you got [beaver] dam after dam after dam on that river. And you get to the last one there, and there used to be little rapids over there, small ones, over there. Every time you go to a dam like this, and there is lots of water, you have to go cut it down. After we pass that river, coming home, we set snares, we drove and set snare after snare, snare after snare. The last trap we went to over there, I told Gordie, "Gordie," I said to him, "don't bother lynk if you get a lynk, don't bother." All of a sudden, I hear him yelling, "Abel," he says, "I got a lynk, he's alive!" I look there and, after I took that lynk from my snare and it was frozen; it was small enough, not too big, but medium size, and I come to [Gordie's] snare there, and I see a lynk there. And I say, "Gordie, you're too close to him, he'll jump on you right away." Gordie, I was looking at him, got a stick, [I said] "Don't touch him." And all of a sudden, that lynk jumped up, and jumped up like this [articulates with his arms], you know, and I guess he just took an axe or something, and he took an axe and tried to hit him. And instead of hitting him, he hit the snare and just cut off that snare. And that lynk went running away, you know. And Gordie was running right behind him, and that lynk was running away. And I see him, that lynk, jumping like this growling, jumping like this, you know [animates the story with his hands]. And I told Gordie, "Gordie, why did you have to do that?" And then I see his jacket, his jacket was all torn up in the back here [laughs]. I guess that lynk must have gotten his back there, you know. I couldn't laugh, you know. I didn't want to laugh hard. . . . "Well, you can laugh now, Abel," he says. I didn't want to laugh. I says, "I am not laughing at you." So, after that there, we had a fire and made some tea; good to make some tea before we leave.[34]

While the story illustrates that the lynx earned its freedom, the *akiwenziyag* narratives also substantiate the reality that trapping is hard work and requires a wealth of knowledge and skills—and a good teacher, to pass these on. During one of our travels to Mukatewasipe, Abel and I had an exceptionally tough time. Our snowmobile kept getting stuck in the deep snow. We were forced to excavate the trailer from the fresh snow by digging trenches around the snowmobile and packing the snow into a path. I was panting and sweating from the work and utterly amazed at Abel's strength to do the heavy lifting. Our excavating needed to be done four times—and we were barely thirty minutes inland from the reserve! That incident taught me that the expression "living off the land" has become imbued with romanticized images existing only in film montages. In reality, ICH transmission consists of intense, repetitive labour—but, as the *akiwenziyag* and *kitayatisuk* frequently show, it is also "good to keep a sense of humour about things."[35]

Having trapped his whole life, Abel is eager to pass down the knowledge he gained from his Elders to his grandson and his nephew Willie. He shares that

even my grandson there, he knows everything already. Just by talking to him, all those things, you know, teaching what to do. He never used to know how to set a snare, a rabbit snare. So, I am here to teach him how to do it; how you do it and all that. A stick there, with a wire and all that. Right. Even wood. I showed him how this winter. All winter, I been showing him how to do it. Trying to get some wood: "Look at that tree. No, uh, don't cut that down, ahhh, don't cut down a green tree. Dry wood, not green tree," I said to him. "Look at the branches. That thing's dry, that's dry wood." Every time I go with him too, I offer tobacco before I cut down this tree, so everything will be good. So, I ask the Creator, I ask [for the] dry wood to try and keep nice, warm, for the kids, you know. What, what, I always do that when I go for wood. I offer tobacco, I always do. They used to do that a long time ago, the Old Ancestors you know; used to offer tobacco. When you go out trapping, there's a place there, they call an offering place, you know, where Memegwesiwag are. And those are the ones that you're offering to, so everything will be good when you go trapping. I tell him all that.[36]

The *akiwenziyag* and the *kitayatisuk* are recognized by their respective communities as much for their harvesting skills as for their role as keepers of traditions. They are experts in the field: they know the best paths, rivers, and streams to follow, and where the best camping sites are. They are aware of the places and times to offer tobacco, and to whom. Noah Massan, who has a trapline near Gillam, is always monitoring how Hydro workers treat the animals and makes sure that the animals who stay in the area are treated respectfully. These knowledge holders are constantly aware of the changes to their local environment and to animal populations. For example, they are cognizant of birth, age, and sex ratios in the moose population, and they distinguish the size of colonies and litters as well as new families in beavers. "I learned early on from my Elders, that when there are too many beaver," explains Ernest Bruce, "taking only older male beavers, in specific seasons, is important, [otherwise] they kill each other."[37]

Skilled in long-term and continuous empirical observations, pattern recognition, and repetitive behaviour evident through predicting ecosystem relationship and forecasting, Inninuwak *kitayatisuk* and Anishinaabeg *akiwenziyag* can "easily discuss these trends with an outsider, comparing present conditions with those of last year, the year before, or five years ago."[38] Some of the observations are the same ones used by ecologists to monitor wildlife populations.[39] Frequent visits to the trapline (long-term observation, experimentation, and methodical application), discussions with other harvesters (peer review process), ensuring intergenerational transmission (dissemination of knowledge), and "data-collection" of the natural resources (analysis) is similar to the work of a full-time researcher. No other scientist or federally/provincially instituted conservation officer could have more in-depth and long-term knowledge of wildlife populations, fire history, and even sacred sites on a provincial Registered Trapline Management Area (that is also the trapline of an *akiwenzi* or *kitayatis*). ICH illuminates the fact that outside authority does not have as detailed knowledge to look after a trapline territory as a local land user.[40] Like other professionals in their field, trapline holders need to be compensated for their work as stewards and teachers.

The *kitayatisuk* and the *akiwenziyag* are the best caretakers of their territories. To obtain the intricate and long-term knowledge about an area that Abel or Walter or Noah or Richard have, a state-sanctioned conservation officer would have to live there. Most of the time conservation officers periodically fly in to collect data, gather specimens, or do tagging. Considerable time and money could be saved by using local harvesters already present in the area to do the fieldwork or to lead data management. The benefits of a wage-based monthly supplement for such stewards (head trappers, *keyoh* holders, clan chiefs, etc.) would signify investment in community economics and decolonization of natural resource management. Precisely because the recognition of ICH is about decentralizing "authorized heritage," natural resource management likewise requires change. Founded on values articulated by people themselves, the ICH lens merges natural/cultural and tangible/intangible heritages. It also places "heritage management" in the hands of experienced ICH custodians. These stewards already ensure sustainability on a volunteer basis, and they are performing an ecosystem service that needs remuneration. A funded program for stewards as a component of payments for ecosystem services,[41] for example, would be an opportunity for reconciliation "between Indigenous and settler societies, and between broader Canadian society and the land and waters."[42] It would also be an honouring of Indigenous knowledges arising out of living heritage.

The idea of conservation officer–like powers for stewards is not a novel idea. In fact, it has been on the minds of the *akiwenziyag*, the *kitayatisuk*, and other Indigenous people for some time. Albert Bittern, a Poplar River Elder, was thinking of such a policy back in the 1970s. He tells me that "in 1975, there was an Indian Agent or something coming around here. He would look at everything, and I'd think, I don't need you! I can speak for myself. That's why [now] we want people to train, like conservation officers, to look after the land or something like that."[43] Rose Klippenstein also argues that in spite of the challenges Poplar River youth face today, getting them involved in land use would be meaningful: "We want them to go and explore [outside the community] but come back. A lot of us still suffer from residential school and stuff. And now you also have the drugs. I think some of that knowledge is lost. Some of the young parents don't wanna get into the land, you know, be the land. A lot of things put us back, like TV, you know, internet, cell phones, iPads, and videogames. So, getting the youth involved like, making sure there's something like game wardens around would be good."[44] Another community member, Noel Bruce, expresses that *asatiwisipe aki* can be a source of livelihood as well as an opportunity for future generations to learn from their Elders. Claiming that this was precisely the goal of the Pimachiowin Aki World Heritage Site, Noel elaborates: "We're doing this for the young people [. . .] We are hoping for young people [to become] conservation officers, someone to look after the land and to look after tourism. There will be a lot of activities and lots of opportunities in the future on the land. We teach them that [our land] is for future generations, we saw what happened down south [resource development and hydro infrastructure], and we don't want that. These young people can watch over the land even if the leadership makes bad decisions or choices"[45]

Infusion of funds into Indigenous resource management systems can offer young people a culturally relevant and feasible career choice. With already established Indigenous-led monitoring programs,[46] Indigenous Community Conserved Areas (ICCAs),[47] Indigenous Protected and Conserved Areas,[48] Tribal Parks,[49] and other stewardship initiatives embedded in land use plans and governance structures, the youth, as paid stewards, can explore career opportunities that align with cultural transmission.[50] Using modern technology like computer modelling, Lidar sensors, satellite imaging, GIS software, drones, and DNA sampling to monitor species and to look after their own watersheds, communities are already implementing innovative ways to create capacity-building opportunities within cultural traditions. Training to go out on the land and waters, to take notes, to report, and to effectively communicate issues to their communities places young stewards in capacity-building positions. Adhering to their own cultural protocols and land use plans reinforces accountability and customary governance structures. Because it is local people who directly face the consequences of any negative effects or bad judgements, there is an obligation to make the best decisions.

ICH-based livelihoods permit young apprentices to obtain education from their knowledge holders and to sustain cultural transmission.[51] Providing land users with financial means to ensure that the next head trapper or steward is well prepared to have a trapline signifies that cultural heritage—knowledges, skills, practices, oral expressions and traditions associated with a specific customary governance system—are transmitted. To attain the position of a respected steward (an *akiwenzi* or a *kitayatis*), other members of the community must recognize competency; therefore, imparting ICH is as much about cultural revival as it is about building expertise. Abel reiterates how experience and good teachers gave him the skills to be a head trapper: "Those young people. If they want to learn. I say to them, 'If you want to learn, I'll teach you. Come and go work with me. I wasn't born knowing this. I go [out] there every year. I know Mukatewa[sipe]. I know that land. [...] The Old People, they taught me everything. They taught me all I know. I can teach you all I know, too."[52]

The painful fact is that not every person carries this knowledge and not every hunter can lead the life of an *akiwezi*. The intricate knowledge of the *akiwenziyag* and *kitayatisuk* is learned and perfected over a lifetime of experience. An acquaintance from the Amah Mutsun Tribal Council from California once tearfully expressed in a class that it is "embarrassing to admit that we don't have the 'traditional knowledge' people expect community members to have." Mindful of the fact that they must now relearn traditions and cultural elements from books and archives, the Amah Mutsun are also working with scientists by co-teaching local knowledge to the community.[53] The ICH discourse reinforces what many land users know: unless the conditions for intergenerational transmission of heritage are present, elements of culture diminish or disappear. But the ICH lens also teaches us that with determination and supportive avenues, proficiency of cultural elements can be revived, learned, and mastered.

ICH-based livelihoods can also prove to be very important monitoring baselines, particularly in the face of climate change or unethical leadership practices. If trapline holders were asked to find solutions to low marten populations or to relay the ecological history of the area, they would not only make use of local knowledge but also account for far-reaching global impacts. The time and labour spent obtaining information from state-funded conservation officers and scientists to figure out knowledge that local land users already hold would be saved. Wage-based compensation for land users, as the most qualified individuals for the job, represents a financially viable economic strategy, especially for northern and remote Indigenous communities as well as for communities dominated by industrial development. Provided with conservation officer–like powers to monitor resource-exhaustive projects, *kitayatisuk* like Noah could hold industry accountable to environmental and ecological threshold points. Already taking the role of "Hydro watchdog," Noah does his job by telling Hydro workers to do theirs: "Yeah that, that's another thing. I complain to Hydro all the time to do what I say and to [be] careful. It's my [trap] line. Those guys don't care [so] someone's gotta do the job."[54] Addressing the need for better surveillance over the workers and the insulting way they treat the caribou, for example, Noah exclaims: "You know, sometimes you see caribou in the dump, there. People have seen the caribou there. Those Hydro people just throw away the caribou and all those animals. Us people, we never disrespect the animals like that. Hydro doesn't know what these guys are doing. Someone needs to watch over them all."[55]

The unethical (and sometimes illegal) behaviour of Hydro employees toward the "free" resources in Canada's North shows that current regulatory frameworks perpetuate unequal powers relations between Indigenous people and the natural resources sector, especially on the ground.[56] The *akiwenziyag* and *kitayatisuk*, on the other hand, demonstrate that the ICH framework can create economic opportunities for custodians while they monitor their lands and transmit their knowledges and skills to future generations.

Current approaches to honouring customary systems and recognizing the work of living heritage limit the ways that stewards experience and *do* "natural resource management." Recognition of ICH, therefore, brings customary governance to the forefront of community territorialization and Indigenous rights. Noah's experiences with Hydro development tells us that if Indigenous stewards like him had recognizable powers, then perhaps outsiders would not be as inclined to "cut corners," as he says.[57]

"Keeping that little fire going"

It is my position that Indigenous customary governance systems are an Aboriginal right. Indigenous customary governance, specifically, the diverse ICH-sourced resource stewardship structures like *ji-ganawenda-mang Gidakiiminaan* and sovereign foodways such as *aki miijim*, has never been extinguished and thus continues to exist as a right performed through living heritage.[58] The rights approach I take below provides a framework through which ICH and its recognition can influence policy making.

My position is inspired by the *akiwenziyag* and the *kitayatisuk*. Their stories of limited and seized harvests, convoluted history with conservation officers, imposed projects, destroyed livelihoods, and frustrations with diverse boards, teams, policies, and governments who overrode their knowledge of and authority over what happens to the resources drive this philosophical framework. The numerous Anishinaabeg *dibaajimowinan* and Inninuwak *achimowinan* presented me with another way to interpret customary governance. In consolidating a rights approach to the ICH lens, Indigenous models of food production and resource management have been (and continue to be) "legally" circumscribed in Canada. Historic land and resource policies, often created without adequate consultation, insufficient subsidies for proper food and funds for harvesting equipment or tools have restricted customary governance.[59] Historic policies like the Natural Resources Transfer Agreement of 1930, the Indian Act, and welfare programs[60] have caused many Indigenous people to shift to a Western diet, resulting in disproportionate experiences of ill health, a shorter life expectancy, poverty, and food insecurity.[61] Unfulfilled treaty promises,[62] forced relocations, dispossession, and numerous extractive resource development projects significantly affect Indigenous food procurement and resource management today. Sovereign stewardship and food systems are all too often overlooked in environmental policies, only to be sometimes lumped together under the buzzword of "Aboriginal/ Indigenous traditional knowledge."

"All I can say," Richard shares with me, "is that stewardship, that, that looking after our lands that you talk about . . . it's a natural law." He continues, "it's the feel of the natural law, the feel of the tree, the feel of the water, feel of the wind, feel of the sun, all of that is natural evolution. The ones that feel the evolution of, of that life, they know it. We're inclusive of that, we're not exclusive, we're part of it, we grow [with] it, we're not the masters, we're not God . . . *Ganawaabamwaad* [to look after it]. That's what it is. *Ganawendaaman gidakii*[*minaan*]. To take care. To watch over that land. It's law."[63] Looking after the land and the animals is part of law and good governance for Richard. In his view, these laws recognize that we are a part of the ecology and that individuals who "touch and feel the land" are the ones to govern it. He likens *inaakonigewin*, law, to a helper at a sweatlodge ceremony. But he tests me first, asking, "How do we, what do we call a helper at a sweatlodge ceremony?" I stammer and answer uncertainly, "Uh, *ishkaabewis*?" "Yes," Richard says, "*ishkaabewis*, firekeeper, from *ishkodens*, a little fire, a little bit of fire." He continues, explaining that the little flame must be nurtured and passed on, like a teacher who passes Anishinaabe knowledge to a sweatlodge helper: "*Ishkaabewis* is what keeps the fire going. *Ishkaabewis* [. . .] is a man who takes care of this energy and this fire [he creates a circle with his hands]. So, that's how we teach to stay connected to the land. That firekeeper is like, they're like a doctor taking on a student, teaching another person to be a doctor. It's the same thing. The only thing is, it's more intense. [By] being *ishkaabewis*, you stay connected to the power and energy of life."[64]

For Richard, *ishkode* is the fire we all carry within us. The *-ode* part of *ishkode* is the heart, the essence of our being, and it is also the fire that drives Anishinaabe laws and our collective responsibility to take care of the lands and waters. To fuel that fire, we need food; food the Creator gifted to us. We must take care of the land that feeds us, that keeps our "little fires" going. "*Mino-ayaa* [feeling good]," Richard tells me,

> means your little fire is going. *Ji-ganawendam[an] Gidakii[minaan]*. We have to use our body and our spirit, *ishkodens,* to make sure all the other, those *ishkodens* keep going. *Inaakonigaade* [law is made that way]. *Bimaadiziwin* [to live]. It means, I live, I live the way I am supposed to. I live according to that law. *Bimaadiziwin* meaning that I'm using my energy at its greatest and I'm not going to abuse the land. *Ji-ganawendam[an] Gidakii[minaan]*. I'm not going to take more than what I need. It's about working together, caring, and doing things together. It's about keeping *ishkodens*, keeping that little fire going.[65]

Laws that guide customary stewardship are vital drivers for *akiwenziyag* land use. For Richard, the set of relations that govern "taking what I need" are a part of Anishinaabe *inaakonigewin*, law, and underscore its *sui generis* or unique form of governance (Figure 35).

Figure 35. Richard Morrison putting out tobacco prior to harvesting sweetgrass to show respect and appreciation for the plant.

Recognition of ICH highlights the fact that Indigenous customary systems are processes (not products) and are founded on critical and intellectual frameworks, cultural practices, and heritage-sourced political arrangements.[66] Passed down from generation to generation, many of these systems have been configured into written formats such as land use plans, conventions, constitutions, and map biographies. Inclusive of knowledge and performativity, *akiwenziyag* and *kitayatisuk* narratives show that their governance systems are anchored to lands through social relations and cannot be separated into ecological/natural and human/cultural spheres. As these men point out, the connection between people and the land is based on valued interactions with the land, with other-than-human Beings, and hinges on relationships with other people.

Complex decision making within food and resource management systems takes all these relationships into account because those who cannot demonstrate responsible use and knowledge of an area do not have rights in it.[67] Indigenous land-tenure systems are already upheld by various international conventions, such as UNDRIP (2007),[68] the United Nations Convention on Biological Diversity (1992), and the International Labour Organization's Indigenous and Tribal Peoples Convention (1989).[69] The ICH Convention, however, emphasizes the need to understand customary regimes of communities as central to the protection of the "rights of communities and bearers [. . .] about ownership and access to and use of the ICH."[70] Manifested through the culturally diverse values that guide them, Indigenous *sui generis* resource stewardship and foodways are ICH elements that broaden the current understanding of Indigenous and treaty rights.

Sipping our coffees after Sunday mass, Abel explains that the Asatiwisipe Anishinaabeg could never give up the land because the land is a gift from the Creator; it was never theirs to give up.[71] Other *akiwenziyag* maintain that the land is a responsibility that cannot be abdicated. While there are processes such as dispossession or migration that can diminish food sovereignty or resource stewardship systems, these ICH elements continue to exist until the custodian no longer transmits them. ICH elements are heavily intertwined with intergenerational transmission, so intangible features are "given up" only when an individual or community abandons the practice(s). The late Stanley Bittern went so far as to joke that the government can "never take what's in his mind,"[72] and Abel similarly expresses the sentiment that "no one is gonna tell me what I can do on my [trap]line. They would have to put me in jail. [. . .] They can't stop me from thinking about my land."[73] These *akiwenziyag* stress that the intellectual approaches and ICH practices that make up the entirety of a customary governance system cannot be ceded. As signatories of the "cede, release, surrender" clause to the Treaty 5 adhesion in 1905, the *akiwenziyag* believe they never relinquished their rights to look after their traplines. If treaty rights were interpreted in the sense that they would naturally have been understood by Indigenous peoples,[74] they would allow for the *akiwenziyag* understanding that their resource stewardship and food sovereignty are unextinguished intangible elements integral to the totality of *Anishinaabediziwin*, the Anishinaabe way of life.

Abel's understanding of "land rights" is comparable to Richard's aforementioned belief that knowledge of local ecology and history are essential to governance. Although separated by three hundred kilometres of boreal forest, Abel and Richard both emphasize the importance of decision making by land users. Putting his hands together over the table and leaning forward, Abel asks: "Ever hear that song, 'Oh Canada'? 'Our home and native land,' yeah? That's what I often say about that. Our own native land. People think I'm dumb, no? And I tell them: 'What do you know about the bugs, what do you know about the trees and all that, you know? The animals and all those things? What do you know about them?' I [say] to them. 'You don't know 'cause you never come to my land.'"[75]

For Abel as for Richard (and Noah), having rights to the land means not just knowing it or talking about it, but also acting on the responsibilities toward it and using it. For these men, having rights to the land implies experiencing the good and the bad of it: one "can't just talk about the land and [not] go to the bush. You gotta go out there. You gotta be there like I am there, me."[76] Another Poplar River Elder, Walter Nanawin, agrees, expressing that a "man's land" is where his stories and his food are:

> So that's why I got to write "Tales from a Trapper's Cabin." [...] That's how they were, the old fellas I write about. See there's stories all over this lake [points to map]. [...] When they [the trappers] are lonesome, by themselves, and they go out into the bush up to the rivers, back in the bush after the caribou. [...] Then they go over here [near Ojijaak Creek] and get after these caribou here. These [points to map] are sections of land. This, this is Crane Muskeg here. And this is the Poplar River muskeg. And then the Berens River muskeg. And then the *atikaki*. *Atikaki* means the caribou land, eh. [...] So, when a man's talking about where he, he's been trapping, where he comes from. He knows snow, he knows the deep snow, you see, and all the moose meat. [He] come[s] from *atikaki* with caribou meat. And that's how stories are done. In the bush. Where there's no roads. That's a man's land, eh.[77]

For the *akiwenziyag*, understanding rights to and legitimacy over the land and resources is interpreted in multiple ways. The right to be a keeper of cultural traditions requires using that knowledge of stories and having a set of skills. Harvesting from the land is important because, through use of the resources, it is tied to good governance and affirms social relationships with fellow harvesters and other-than-human Beings. Life in the bush also affirms identity: it provides knowledge and authority to speak about the bush. Ernest Bruce, the political advisor to Poplar River, concurs with Walter that "the Anishinaabeg are the rightful caretakers of the traplines because that's what we were told to do by our Elders. We were taught to take care of that land. We still do take care of it."[78]

These accounts show that Indigenous land rights include the "right to engage in practices reasonably incidental to hunting, trapping, and fishing [. . .] and the right to expect that hunting, trapping, and fishing will continue to be successful, measured by reference to the fruits of past practice."[79] More deliberate than "incidental," however, resource stewardship and food systems "shape how people make use of the land [and] how people gain access to the land."[80] These harvesting activities are central to the maintenance of land tenure and stewardship practices, which in turn are the foundations for *akiwenziyak* and the *kitayetisuk* cultural heritage transmission. Having existed since time immemorial, customary governance systems are *direct* drivers of existing Aboriginal and treaty hunting, trapping, and fishing rights.

From long-standing diplomatic relationships that prepared them for treaties with Canada to the dearth of Indigenous legal constructs in modern circumstances,[81] Indigenous communities reveal the dynamic nature of Section 35 of the Constitution Act of 1982. Section 35 is the part of the Constitution Act that recognizes and affirms (not creates) "existing aboriginal and treaty rights of the [A]boriginal people in Canada."[82] In 1996, the Supreme Court of Canada explored the political legitimacy rooted in Indigenous peoples' *sui generis* "practices, customs and traditions" through the *R. v. Van der Peet* case.[83] In this landmark case, the appellant, Dorothy Van der Peet, a member of the Stó:lō Nation in British Columbia, was charged with selling ten salmon out of her car to a friend. A First Nations fishing licence permitted Aboriginal people to fish solely for the purposes of sustenance and ceremonial use but prohibited the sale of fish to non-Aboriginal people. Van der Peet challenged the charges, arguing that as an Aboriginal person, Section 35 of the Constitution Act protected her right to sell fish. Underscoring the need for the reconciliation of Aboriginal rights with Crown sovereignty, the Supreme Court argued that "the practices, customs and traditions which constitute aboriginal rights are those which have *continuity* with the practices, customs and traditions that existed prior to contact with European society. Conclusive evidence from pre-contact times about the practices, customs, and traditions of the community in question need not be produced. The evidence simply needs to be directed at demonstrating which aspects of the aboriginal community and society have their origins pre-contact."[84]

Because selling fish did not constitute an "existing" Aboriginal right, the Supreme Court ruled that Van der Peet's right to sell fish was not protected by Section 35 of the Constitution Act (while fishing constitutes an Aboriginal right, the sale of such fish does not). The ruling resulted in the "Van der Peet Test," which determines how an Aboriginal right is distinctive and/or integral to the culture of the claimant. The court's ruling emphasized that "practices, customs and traditions" must be of central and independent significance to the Indigenous culture in which they exist. Highlighting the idea of continuity, the court decided that an activity "does not require an unbroken chain between current practices, customs and traditions and those existing prior to contact [because] the practice existing prior to contact can be resumed after an interruption."[85] Although the notion of a pre-contact right was employed, the court stipulated the avoidance of the "frozen rights" approach to understanding Section 35.

Emphasizing that the right in question needs to be a "defining feature" of a society, the court in *Van der Peet* argued that the distinctive practice, custom or tradition must be of "central and significant part of the society's distinctive culture" and one that without which the community is fundamentally altered.[86] The time-centred approach generated much criticism from scholars advocating for flexibility in the *Van der Peet* analysis,[87] including Anishinaabe legal scholar John Borrows, who argued that specific practices are not important to the definition of Aboriginal rights: "What counts is whether these practices contribute to the survival of the group."[88] While critics also point out that the ruling ignores the dynamic and adaptive nature of Indigenous cultures, *Van der Peet* also demonstrates that Aboriginal "practices, customs and traditions" such as resource stewardship systems and foodways bring these elements into the discussion on rights. The voices of the *akiwenziyag* and the *kitayatisuk* tell us that resource stewardship and sovereign food system are defining features of their respective cultures. For the Poplar River *akiwenziyag*, *ji-ganawendamang Gidakiiminaan* and *aki miijim* reflect *specific* laws (Anishinaabe *inaakonigewin*) driven by customs (such as placing *asemaa*), skills (such as *wanii'igewin*, trapping), resources (such as *atikag*, caribou, and *manoomin*, wild rice), and the landscape (*asatiwisipe aki*). Together, these are a "significant part of the society's distinctive culture," to paraphrase the *Van der Peet* ruling. The Stó:lō viewed fishing for food and exchange of salmon as a significant and defining feature of Stó:lō society; similarly, *akiwenziyag* narratives construe Anishinaabe *ji-ganawendamang Gidakiiminaan* and *aki miijim* as "significant" elements of their living heritage. Intrinsically rooted to a local ecology through Anishinaabe values, these ICH elements highlight the obligation and fundamental right of the *akiwenziyag* to look after that landscape.

Unlike the proprietary arguments framing Aboriginal rights, *R. v. Van der Peet* alludes to the fact that Aboriginal "practices, customs and traditions" are processes; these intangible elements, much like the ICH discourse, strengthen the interpretation of Aboriginal rights. Since the judges in *Van der Peet* deduced "practices" as being part of an Aboriginal right, then ICH elements associated with "managing" resources (for food or for sustainability or cultural transmission) should also be considered a practice and a right. If stewardship systems and foodways are recognizable expressions enacted by a specific people so that future generations can also attain a livelihood, then the ICH custodians who employ *deliberate* "practices, customs and traditions" to ensure integrity of their territories are carrying out their Indigenous[89] rights. For the *akiwenziyag, ji-ganawendamang Gidakiiminaan* and *aki miijim* are systems (again, processes, not products) consisting of specific knowledge anchored to an explicit geographical area and consciously acted upon. Whereas *knowledge* about blueberry bushes growing in an especially sunny place in the forest may be a part of community harvest, resource stewardship dictates the *deliberate act* of burning trees to make space for the berries in the first place. Consequently, both "the knowing" and "the doing" interpret the defining features of ICH "practices, customs and traditions" as a significant part of a distinctive Indigenous cultural heritage.

ICH has the potential to influence legal frameworks and policy making. I recognize the limits of my proficiency in Canadian judicial structures, but my position is that Indigenous customary governance structures such as *ji-ganawendamang Gidakiiminaan* and *aki miijim* are meant to explore the potential of the ICH lens. The 2003 UNESCO ICH Convention asserts that State Parties must take "necessary measures" to safeguard ICH, and it is possible that ICH can offer alternative pathways to examining the Indigenous rights discourses.[90] Global ICH policy making has been immensely diverse, and several examples offer striking points of departure for Canada. For instance, both Brazil and Venezuela have included ICH in their constitutions. While Brazil provides its own definition of ICH and some safeguarding suggestions, Venezuela's constitution interprets ICH as a "fundamental right to be encouraged and guaranteed by the State."[91] The Bolivian constitution acknowledges Indigenous rights by stating that nations and rural native Indigenous peoples have the right to have their ICH "valued, respected and promoted," including that any "collective ownership of the[ir] intellectual property" be recognized.[92] Additionally, countries like Burkina Faso and Belize have created cultural policies that use ICH as the main driver in community economic development.[93] In 2016, attesting to the distinctiveness and diversity of the culture of Latvia, the republic created the Intangible Cultural Heritage Law to facilitate the understanding of values around ICH, to improve the quality of life, and to initiate public dialogue and programming through the Latvian National Centre for Culture.[94]

In a similar way, Indigenous peoples in Canada can use the ICH framework to enlarge Indigenous rights and to influence natural and cultural heritage policy making. Until that change happens—and especially if it does not—the *akiwenziyag* and the *kitayatisuk* will continue to live the life that is "stored in their bones."

Conclusion

Indigenous cultural heritages involve a dazzling variety of elements ranging from specific social practices and cultural expressions to oral traditions and cultural landscapes. The boundaries between intangible and tangible heritage are malleable and may vary from community to community. Combined with the overarching understanding that heritage is something valued and passed down from generation to generation, the concept of intangible cultural heritage has grown in the past several decades on an international scale. Arising from the 2003 UNESCO Convention for the Safeguarding of Intangible Cultural Heritage, the discourse of ICH can assist Indigenous communities in Canada in self-determination over natural and cultural heritage. The Convention's multi-sighted conceptualizations of heritage place an emphasis on *living* heritage and the idea that people enact and transmit culture in their everyday being and performativity. The focus on processes of culture rather than on cultural products has led 181 states to embrace this conceptual approach and ratify the ICH Convention.

ICH comprises the living heritage of communities, groups, and individuals. The recognition of ICH and ICH work illustrates what a community values and helps establish measures for transmission to future generations. ICH is a community's identity, springing from the context where people live or have lived: the food, tools, languages, creativity, and skills that stem from their heritage. ICH also informs cosmological explanations and belief systems, giving "spirit" to natural landscapes and jurisprudence. Adapted as the environment and context changes, knowledges, practices, and skills shift to form and forge diversified economies, social beliefs, and soundscapes. Without participation from the state, communities can rely on the ICH discourse to document as well as create safeguarding measures to ensure cultural and linguistic transmission at their own pace and convenience. An inventory built into the already lived repertoire of community members can reconnect people and restore specific practices in innovative ways. The point of this book is to raise awareness about ICH and provide a conceptual tool for communities and policy makers to use when advocating for cultural and linguistic revitalization and transmission.

My exploration of one community in the boreal forest, of one Clean Environment Commission hearing, and the living knowledge of one culture custodian illustrates how the ICH discourse is applicable to Indigenous contexts. By providing clear principles and strategies for ICH safeguarding, the 2003 Convention can help Canada respond to the TRC's Calls to Action on culture and education and to address several UNDRIP principles, an agreement Canada signed in 2016. Acknowledging that nature/culture and tangible/intangible heritages are woven together, the ICH discourse offers a unique way of thinking about cultural heritage transmission. Because safeguarding of ICH is community-led, it offers communities a way to truly have control of cultural heritage in accordance with their laws, protocols, internal structures, and priorities.[1] Living heritage has a role to play in human ingenuity, environmental concerns, economies, and our relationships with each other. Taking into consideration the vulnerability of heritage-inspired livelihoods, endangered languages, and irreplaceable ways of living on a particular geography, I argue that Canada needs to re-evaluate its understanding and policy making around heritage. The *akiwenziyag* and *kitayatisuk* illustrate that aside from the beautiful-yet-silent tangible archives and museum-held objects, art pieces, and traditional tools, culture transmits "bone to bone" through living heritage.

The ICH discourse and praxis can be a fruitful mechanism in contextualizing self-determination outside of colonial framings. The combination of multifarious effects like environmental degradation, competing harvesters, and overriding values have caused foodways and culturally diverse stewardship systems to become fragile in many Indigenous communities. Colonial policies disrupted intergenerational knowledge transmission, and communities are revitalizing the epistemic elements within these customary governance systems. The plurality of overlapping documents and methodological approaches dealing with heritage and ecological sustainability separately underscores how Canadian environmental and cultural policies need to be more inclusive of each other. While my goal is to bring the ICH lens into the conversation, scholars must pull the strings of the legal arguments further.

For the *akiwenziyag* and *kitayatisuk*, respecting Others in the landscape is manifested by the transmission of stories of Sasquatch, Thunderbirds, and Muskrat, as well as those of uncles, grandmothers, and nephews. By putting out tobacco, the *akiwenziyag* and the *kitayatisuk* affirm the Beings' and their own existence and ongoing presence on the landscape. By transmitting their *aadizookaanag*, *dibaajimowinan*, and *achimowinak*, by giving life to other Beings in that landscape, they are bringing their cultural landscapes and territoriality to life. In this understanding, *akiwenziyag* and *kitayatisuk* trapline territories are spaces that are co-created, experienced, and occupied. As the Anishinaabeg and Inninuwak land user experience shows, living heritage can empower sustainable livelihoods, improve resource development negotiations, and bolster self-determination. Reconceptualizing rigid categories of heritage and culture as more than products can improve environmental regulatory frameworks and expand on Indigenous rights. When the "practices, customs, and traditions" that are valued by the communities themselves are at the nexus of interpretation,[2] the discourse of Indigenous and treaty rights better serve ICH custodians. Indigenous customary governance systems are a combination of tangible and intangible elements arising out of heritage and *directly* steer socio-ecological activities and decision making on a particular landscape. The stewardship activities the *akiwenziyag* and *kitayatisuk* know of and perform *in addition* to their hunting, trapping, fishing activities help maintain those harvesting rights.

Living heritage carriers, like the *akiwenziyag* and *kitayatisuk*, are the libraries of their communities and landscapes; they are our human heritage. ICH custodians play a leading role in representing their living heritage, and they determine the extent of transmission, safeguarding, and management of their natural and cultural heritage. While Indigenous people are increasingly in control their own cultural productions and self-representations and can proceed with their own ICH safeguarding and inventorying strategies, legal and legislative frameworks are crucial in the protection of cultural knowledges, practices, and languages.[3] Recognition of ICH needs to be located in a variety of legal places in Canada; this can take place within legislative, constitutional, and policy making contexts, and is urgently pressing in [environmental] impact assessments. Canada—rather, every one of us—needs to put more value on language and cultural transmission. Together, we can make linguistic plurality and living heritages of communities a fundamental part of the public good and humanity's diversity.

To safeguard ICH in Canada, I have only one recommendation for Indigenous communities: *document your own heritage elements and establish your own conditions for ICH transmission*. The ICH framework can help provide the initial safeguarding steps over your natural and cultural heritage elements. You control the process, the data, and who has access to it. This is more critical for communities impacted by resource development. Expecting assistance from governments may come at a loss of your cultural elements.

Do not wait for policy to change.

I am also responding to the TRC's calls with my own three Calls for Action. I urge the Government of Canada to do the following:

1. Re-evaluate its position on the 2003 UNESCO Convention for the Safeguarding of Intangible Cultural Heritage and especially the ICH discourse. There is a need to examine current national and regional policies to determine the goals of ICH policy making and to assess its relevant mandates, including stakeholders, intellectual property regimes, funding, and especially community obligations. This requires an analysis of the historical, political, and socio-economic situation to determine the trends and range of relationships between different cultural spheres and legislations in the country. Engage with communities and the public, do the research, and take an active step to strengthen the living heritage of communities and families in Canada. Make ICH a public good.

2. Create a Canadian Centre for Intangible Cultural Heritage and invest in ICH carriers.[4] In collaboration with other stakeholders (communities, ICH custodians, museums, and researchers, as well as provinces and municipalities), governments should allocate funding for ICH in a way that ensures capacity building, community engagement, collaborative partnerships, language revitalization, acquisition, and retention, and sustainable livelihoods. Have a free and accessible library of language materials, videos, workshops, and online classes; create opportunities for promotion of ICH. Work with communities,

organizations, and families on the best practices of cultural and linguistic transmission; they know their needs best. While making these suggestions, I stress the importance of *meaningful* engagement with communities on any safeguarding and inventorying processes.

3. Amend the 2019 Impact Assessment Act to include the recognition of ICH and the principles outlined in the ICH Convention. Urging communities to examine the impacts of resource-exhaustive industry on their ICH and obliging proponents to assess the impacts a project will have on ICH will provide the public and Indigenous communities with a more comprehensive view of the losses and gains of economic development.

This "compilation of demonstrations of ICH work" is my support for the land users who are determined to pass down their cultural traditions to future generations. It is also my attempt at promoting ICH and creating ways to better value cultural heritage elements and linguistic diversity. Safeguarding ICH can become a lasting grassroots solution for maintenance of cultural and linguistic wealth, and governments need to support communities and families in their efforts at transmission. I hope the narratives of the *akiwenziyag* and *kitayatisuk* in this book inspire Indigenous and non-Indigenous communities, families, and organizations in Canada to use this universalist framework for cultural mobilization in the twenty-first century.

———

It's dawn and I am standing outside overlooking the Poplar River. It's grey, and the November drizzle is cold. This early in the morning, I have the world to myself, and in the quiet I begin to notice the details of the shore-line. I look at the houses in the distance, lined up along the river, some with smoke already coming out of their homes. Abel Bruce's house is directly across the river from the Mission, where I am staying. I love it that when he sees my lights on in the evenings, he calls me up on the phone to chat.

I see that he is already up and about too. He is getting into his canoe to cross the river and go to the Northern Store or elsewhere. As usual, he parks his canoe near the Mission and comes over to say hello. He smiles at me, and I see the warmth of his eyes. Abel stands beside me and we make small talk. He tells me who lives, and used to live, in all the houses along the river, and how he has just a few more days, maybe just under two weeks to use his canoe before the river begins to freeze over. He reminisces that he started trapping at seventeen years old, and after inheriting the line from his uncle, he wants his nephew to "use it like he uses it now." After a brief silence, Abel tells me that the values of the past should be carried forward, like the wind that carries leaves around, "same thing as us, we are alive. Even the trees that you see there, the trees are alive. The tree talks and all that, you know. The wind carries around, the wind carries the message around. That's what it is. It carries your message, and so you have to take what I am telling you," Abel waves his hand out to the river, "out there."

———

Abel died during the COVID-19 pandemic, as did Richard and Walter, and I could not attend their funerals. Noah died right before this book's publication. I never had the chance to show these men the final version of this work. But like the wind that Abel talked about, his and the other *akiwenziwag* and *kitayatisuk* voices are carried "out there" through this book. Now, encouraged by their experiences, I am going to spend time with my children and make sure my heritages are stored in their bones.

Acknowledgements

N'donji Zaagadikiing, Poland. A'apii niin a'gii oshki-ikwezens, n'gii bimaadizid naami Russiano inaakonigewin. Russiano a'gii gimoodimaan akiing-Zaagadikiing. Niin a'da zhangaso-biboon. Niin a'gii Anishinaabeak-iing biijigoz niibana boon naagatch. Gegapii, niin a'gii wiiji-anokiimaa akiwenziyag. A'gii donjiwag Gojijing miinawaa Anishinaabe'aadazi Aza-tiizibing miinawaa Nigigoonsiminikaaning. N'nii diibaajim iw apii wiiji-akiwenziba, a'gii Abelba izhinikaazoba. Naaningim, ngii zhaa ko kapii. N'gii daa wiiji-wani'igemaa niibana n'sa zhaangaso-boon. Noongom a'niboba Abelba. Niinawind a'da daa miikaasing bimi-ayaad endaso-boon. Niinawind a'da daa giiwedinong biinish Gichi-Mukawewaziibing. A'gii naadamowaa ozhibii' diibajomowinan miinawaa aadizokaanag. A'gii noonde-minjimendaan bimaadizijig a'do ji-izhichigewin. A'gii nenda-gik-enimanaa Anishinaabewing wanii'igewin a'giiw. A Niinawind a'da daa ni'maada'ookid dibaajimod inaadiziwin. Abiding, niinwe a'kii namadabid nopiming, a'gii gaakaapiagane'aakwaadin. Niinwe a'kii boodawaazod miinawaa aniibiishaabooked. A'gii pimeyii madabit, gezika gagwejimaa Abelba: "Dibaadodan a'do babaa-akiing." A'da maajii-dibaajim. "A'gii beshaa biitoowaabawi" a'gii naa.

Nomak, niin a'da mikwendan biitowaa bimaadizijig niigaan aadawe amigong. "Maampi omaa niibawin', ni maa-maa a'gii yik. A'mii dash a'gii daa maajaa nimaamaa. A'da daa zhaa anokiiwin. A'gii daa mi'onji-naganigod niigaan aadawe-gamgong maajaa anokiiwin. N'gii daa niibaw daso-diga'igan biinish azhenan nimaamaa aadawe-gamgong anokiiwin baanimaa. Aaniin danaa a'gii omaa niibaw ina? N'gii bii ashandiwin dibishkoo wiiyaas miinawaa ziinzibaakwaad gaye mukademashkikiaaboo. Gakinaa misawendang agwanewenjiizabaakadoons o'biidaamawag oniijaanisanag! Amanji igo, gakina geyiinwaa ninda giziindime'onan adaawen. Gegapii, a'da aadawe gamgomg niigaanigaabawing ishkwandem, niin a'da biinji-dapaabi gamgong. Akina a'da bishishigwaag desaabaanan. Giji eta desaanaan zhiiwaaboo yaa. Ingwana, niin a'dayaan ashange-ataadowegan naajimiijime. Akina gegoo niin a'da naajinzha'ige onji-ginowaakobiigewin. A' danege aadaweshii-ikwe biinji zagakanige-makak. A'gii nimiinig ziinzibaakwaad dash a'we giji doopwinining yaa. "Gaawiin yaadsii wiiyaas. Niin a'da jaakasenan ninda. Maanda anama'e-giizhigong," a'gii go. A'pii dash nigiiwe, a'gii o'gishkegwanaan a'do mashkimod-ziinzibaakwaad. Gaawiin ganabaj a'wii a'we aawanzinoon gabeya'ii. A'gii ni'naap nimaamaa giiwe endaayin. A'gii ayegozi. A'gii zhoomiingwetawishin apii a'gii ombinan mashkimod-ziinzibaakwaad. "Niinwe a'nii wiishkobipogwad-aniibiishaabookeme," a'gii yik nimaamaa.

Baaanimaa apii, Abelba a'gii dibaajimoba Maji-Ininish. Ganabach a'do dibaajimowin dibishkoo a'nii dibaajimowin: mii go eyiizh maji-gidoodawnan gichi-ogimaag miinawaa inaakonigewinan akiing.

I would like to say *gichi-miigwech* to Poplar River First Nation for welcoming me into their community, for the friendships I made there, and for enduring my numerous questions and academic expectations. Listening to the *dibajiimowinan* of and about your members helped me to better understand your living heritage. A special *gichi miigwech* to Abel Bruce, Ernest C. Bruce, Albert Bittern, Stanley Bittern, Willard Bittern, Colin Bruce, Willie Bruce, Noel Bruce, Freddie Bruce, Rose Bittern Klippenstein, Kate Douglas, Guy Douglas, Ken Douglas, Russell Lambert, Langford Mason, Emile Mason, John McDonald, Byron Mitchell, Jean, Walter, and Bill Nanawin, Ray and Sophia Rabliauskas, Marcel, Frances, and Byron Valiquette. I also thank Casey and all the ladies at the Band Office for assisting me with different administrative things. To the *kitayatisuk* and Elders from the CFLGC and the Gillam area, thank you for trusting me with your *achimowinan*. To the members of these communities: your willingness to share your experiences and perspectives has enriched the content and made this work possible. It is your voices and cultural heritage elements that have given this work its depth and authenticity, and for that, *gakina gegoo nimiigwechiwendaan*. To my CFLGC colleagues, Peter Kulchyski and Stephane MacLachlan, I learned so much from you through our CEC work, thank you. This publication and much of the continuous visits with the people in this book would not be possible without the support from the Manitoba Research Alliance, the Social Sciences and Humanities Research Council, UNBC General Research Fund, and the Northern Scientific Training Program. Some of the knowledge found in this work was part of the project No. Polonez Bis1 2021/43/P/HS2/01350 Exchanging Knowledges on Best-Practices in Folklore and Intangible Cultural Heritage Safeguarding, co-funded by the National Science Centre in Poland and the European Union's Horizon 2020 research and innovation program under the Marie Skłodowska-Curie grant agreement no. 945339.

Dziękuję mojej rodzinie: mamie i tacie, moim ciociom i babciom, wujkom i dziadkom, siostrze i wszystkim moim przodkom za wsparcie i cierpliwość, za wartości i wychowanie, za naukę i za wspólny wkład w moje życie kuturowe i osobiste. *Miigwech* to my Momma Mainville, Donna, and to James, Bill, and Toni for the extraordinary examples of life lessons and experiences. To my Anishinaabemowin teachers, Lloyd Swampy, Pat Ningewance, Roger Roulette: miigwechiwendam a'do gikinoo'amaagoowinan. Gichi-miigwetch Stewart Roy o'gikinoo'aamaw Anishinaabenowe miinawaa daadibaajimod. Aapijii ozaagi'aan Anishinaabewibii'igan minaawaa Anishinaabemo. Merci à mes collègues du Cercle des Canadiens Français de m'avoir montré le patrimoine vivant culturel et linguistique de la francophonie - et de m'avoir accepté dans la lutte. Immense thank you to my UNESCO co-chair, Kristin Catherwood, for providing thoughtful comments on this book, and for all the amazing conversations on ICH. Thank you to UMP, particularly to Jill McConkey, who believed in me and worked on this project with me so patiently, and to Glenn Bergen, Barbara Romanik, and Maureen Epp who helped finalize the book. I am grateful to my reviewers whose constructive feedback made this work stronger. I take full responsibility for any errors in what is written as they are my own reflections and experiences. I also take full ownership for the clumsy and grammatically silly Anishinaabemowin translations: once away from Anishinaabewi akiing and with some of my Anishinaabemo friends-and-teachers deceased, I find it hard to keep up with my learning.

Noah, Abel, Walter, Richard: your strength and determination, your sense of humour and positive attitude, despite everything, were always so inspiring. You had a profound impact on my life, and I will miss you very much, my friends. Rest.

My colleagues, friends, and mentors have been instrumental in getting me to this moment. I am extending a warm and humble thank you firstly to my professors who taught me how to think critically and look beyond what is presented: Peter Kulchyski, Chris Trott, Emma LaRocque, Rodney Clifton, Colin Scott, Norman Gull, Iain Davidson-Hunt, and Renate Eigenbrod. Your passion for knowledge and justice as well as your unwavering commitment to education have been invaluable sources of inspiration throughout my journey. Your guidance has shaped not only my knowledge but also my love for learning, and I am deeply thankful for the impact you've had on my intellectual growth. To my friends and colleagues Heather Schach, Sidney Ballantyne, Leslie Agger, Liz Cooper, Rosa Sanchez, Byron Mitchell, Mike Lawrenchuk, Antonia Mills, Katharine Turvey, Barbara Filion, Yvonne and Ron Pierreroy, and Mildred Martin, I am very grateful for the role each of you has played in shaping my learning.

Bardzo serdecznie dziękuję kochana Mamo i Ciociu za ogromną pomoc i wsparcie w opiece nad moimi dziećmi kiedy byłam zajęta swoją pracą zawodową i tym bardziej podczas pisania tej książki. Wasza bezinteresowna troska i poświęcenie sprawiły, że mogłam skoncentrować się na tworzeniu z pasją, wiedząc, że moje dzieci są w najlepszych rękach i że maja prawdziwą edukacje kulturową i językową—taką z pokolenia na pokolenie. To dla mnie niezastąpione wsparcie i dar, za które jestem niezmiernie wdzięczna.

Dla Johna, Nelusi i Edwarda: dziękuję że bez przerwy wybaczacie mi te długie dni i weekendy spędzone nad pracą i nad tą książką. Ironia w tym że praca i czas poświęcone na przekazywaniu dziedzictwa kulturowego z pokolenia na pokolenie odbywa się dla naukowca jakiego jak ja, w samotności i podczas kiedy Wy, kochani bawicie się na dworze beze mnie. Ale to nad czym pracuję, to dla Was.

Appendix 1

Intangible Cultural Heritage Inventory Card

This card can be printed out and completed and/or adapted for your own purposes. This card is for guidance purposes and should be used as a starting point to a larger, more comprehensive documentation process. Each ICH element should have very detailed information, almost like a small research project, and will likely be very long. A downloadable copy of this ICH Inventory Card and other helpful resources are available on the UNESCO Chair in Living Heritage and Sustainable Livelihoods website: www.livingheritage.ca.

(Name of Community/Cultural Group) ICH Inventory Card	
Date and place where the ICH element is identified and ICH custodian	*Image of element (optional)*
Community/peoples/First Nations/institutions associated with the element	
Short summary of the description and characteristics of the element	

State of the element and general safeguarding measures

Current:

Future actions & mechanisms:

References & research data associated with the element

Data gathering, accessibility: (laws & protocols governing management & protection of the data)

For community members:

For others, with permission:

Not accessible to _____(describe principles):

ICH element recorded and reference number to complete documentation

Audio:

Audio-visual:

Other:

Written description:

Located:

Contact information of person recording this inventory

Appendix 2

Inventory Guidelines

Guidelines adapted from UNESCO Infokit "Identifying and Inventorying Intangible Cultural Heritage" (2011), by the author, specifically for the use of Indigenous communities.

1. **Identification of the element:** Name of the element within the community and any existing features associated with the element: locality (place), the culture (group or community), corresponding language, ICH custodians through which this element is transmitted and understood.

2. **Short description and characteristics of the element:** This includes any associated tangible or intangible elements, perceived origins (stories associated with it, evolving nature, narratives), and meanings. Through the description, it is best to articulate why the element is important, what it signifies to the community, the culture, and/or family. It is important to be as detailed and thorough as possible. It may be helpful to the community to describe how the element is "integral to the distinct culture" and "essential to cultural survival" as per the *R v. Van der Peet* ruling.

3. **Persons and institutions involved with the element:** Here, practitioner details such as age, gender, family name can be included. Any participants, holders, or custodians of the specific ICH can also be indicated. For multiple custodians, record how each works with the element.

4. **Customary law:** Describe the local law, protocols, and practices governing access to and protection of the element. Identify any words or concepts associated within the elements that may be found in the local legal order. Describe modes of transmission and customs. Any inherent legal traditions governing the elements should be indicated here.

5. **State of the element:** Threats to the enactment or transmission of the element are named here, as is the availability and viability of the associated tangible and intangible resources. A brief mention of the specific cause of the loss can clarify the rupture and necessary protection and revitalization of the element. The safeguarding and revival measures in place or in development are also noted here.

6. **Data gathering and inventorying:** Consent from and involvement of the community in data gathering and collection are noted; restrictions, if any, on the use of inventoried data and identification of the resource persons, date, and place. Measures for the protection of intellectual and cultural capital, the inventory, and any digital, written, or recorded data should be established. It may be helpful to articulate archiving of the inventory through the principles of Ownership, Control, Access, Possession (OCAP) or other methods most appropriate to the community.

7. **References:** Any literature, discography, audiovisuals, archives, research, etc., affiliated with the element or the inventory are identified here.

Appendix 3
Useful Resources

Information about ICH from UNESCO
- UNESCO website on everything related to intangible cultural heritage: https://ich.unesco.org/
- 2003 Convention for the Safeguarding of the Intangible Cultural Heritage: https://ich.unesco.org/en/convention
- Ethical Principles for Safeguarding Intangible Cultural Heritage: https://ich.unesco.org/en/ethics-and-ich-00866
- Examples of ICH elements put on the UNESCO Lists: https://ich.unesco.org/en/lists.

Information about Intellectual Property (IP)
- Heritage-Sensitive Intellectual Property and Marketing Strategies (HIPAMS): https://hipamsindia.org/
- Intellectual Property Issues in Cultural Heritage: https://www.sfu.ca/ipinch/
- World Intellectual Property Organization (WIPO): https://www.wipo.int/portal/en/index.html.

Organizations doing ICH work in Canada, in alphabetical order:
- Conseil québécois du patrimoine vivant (the Quebec Council for Living Heritage, in French only) : https://www.patrimoinevivant.qc.ca/
- Heritage BC: https://heritagebc.ca/resources/first-peoples-heritage/
- Heritage NL (Heritage Foundation of Newfoundland and Labrador): https://heritagenl.ca/
- Heritage Saskatchewan: https://heritagesask.ca/
- First Peoples' Cultural Council: https://fpcc.ca/
- Indigenous Heritage: https://indigenousheritage.ca/
- UNESCO Chair in Living Heritage and Sustainable Livelihoods: www.livingheritage.ca.

Notes

INTRODUCTION

1   Richard Morrison, personal communication, 5 August 2018.

2   Ibid.

3   Ibid., 30 July 2016.

4   Ibid.

5   Ibid.

6   I use the term "Indigenous" to refer to First Nations, Inuit, and Métis people in Canada who are recognized as Aboriginal Peoples of Canada in the Canadian Constitution Act of 1982. "Indigenous people" is also the term used in the United Nations Declaration of the Rights of Indigenous Peoples (UNDRIP).

7   I use the Anishinaabemowin (Ojibwe) term *akiwenzi* (singular) interchangeably with other terms, including land user, harvester, (trap)line holder, steward, resource user, etc. Although not all *akiwenziyag* (plural) are harvesters or trappers, Richard Morrison argues that the term implies extensive knowledge and use of the lands and waters, including making a living from that way of life.

8   While the term implies that the man is old, my conversations with *akiwenziyag*, including Richard Morrison (personal conversation, 2007), Abel Bruce (personal conversation, 2009), and Walter Nanawin (personal conversation, 2007), suggested that the term and the use of "old" can also mean "experienced" or "having a lifetime of experience" and does not refer to age.

9   Noah Massan and Ivan Moose, personal conversation, 2013.

10 Schechner and Brady, *Performance Studies*.

11 Lenzerini, "Intangible Cultural Heritage," 102.

12 Ibid., 102–3.

13 Stefano, Davis, and Corsane, "Touching the Intangible: An Introduction," in *Safeguarding Intangible Cultural Heritage*, 1–8.

14 Some works discussing this issue include Doxtator, *Fluffs and Feathers*; LaRocque, *Defeathering the Indian*; and Cole, *Captured Heritage*.

15 Cole, *Captured Heritage*; and Asch, "Concluding Thoughts and Fundamental Questions."

16 Lenzerini, "Intangible Cultural Heritage," 103.

17 Halbwachs, "The Collective Memory."

18 UNESCO, "Text of the Convention," Article 2.

19 Ibid., "Drawing Up Inventories." In Appendices 1 and 2, I have adapted the summary of the inventorying steps with examples relevant to Indigenous peoples in Canada.

20 Ibid., "Purpose of the Lists."

21 Ibid., "Browse the Lists."

22 Ibid., "Craftsmanship of Alençon Needle Lace-Making," inscribed in 2010.

23 Ibid., "Places of Memory and Living Traditions of the Otomí-Chichimecas People of Tolimán," inscribed in 2009.

24 The twenty-four countries are Germany, Saudi Arabia, Australia, Belgium, Croatia, United Arab Emirates, Spain, France, Hungary, Ireland, Italy, Kazakhstan, Kyrgyzstan, Morocco, Mongolia, Pakistan, Netherlands, Poland, Portugal, Qatar, Syrian Arab Republic, Republic of Korea, Slovakia, and Czechia.

25 UNESCO, "Text of the Convention," Article 2.3.

26 Ibid., Information Sheet: "Culture Policy," 2.

27 Ibid., "Ethics and Intangible Cultural Heritage," Principle 8.

28 Ibid., "Safeguarding without Freezing."

29 Ibid.

30 UNESCO, "Ethical Principles for Safeguarding Intangible Cultural Heritage," Principles 1, 2, 6.

31 Pawłowska-Mainville, Roque, and Filion, *Conversations on Intangible Cultural Heritage*.

32 Bourdieu, *Outline of a Theory of Practice*, 52–65.

33 Mauss, *Sociologie et anthropologie*, 364–86.

34 Since food must be consumed daily, it is often one of the last cultural elements to disappear; language is often the first element that perishes.

35 Smith, "Discourses of Heritage." I also discuss the difference between heritage 'experts' and 'professionals' in community-based contexts in Pawlowska-Mainville "Experts and Professionals," 2385–87.

36 Royal Commission on Aboriginal Peoples, Report of the Royal Commission on Aboriginal Peoples, Volume 5: Renewal, Appendix A: Summary of Recommendations Volumes 1–5, 2.4.61 & 3.6.1.

37 TRC, Calls to Action, Calls 6–16.

38 Pawłowska-Mainville, Roque, and Filion, *Conversations on Intangible Cultural Heritage*, 2.

39 Ibid., 5.

40 Please see Nicholas, Pawlowska-Mainville, and Turvey, "Intangible Cultural Heritage." Here, I use the term Living Heritage as a form of the highest esteem for the *akiwenziyag* and *kitayatisuk* I collaborated with.

41 Japan uses the term "Living National Treasures" to describe their ICH custodians or creative persons. I am also very careful to avoid a misconstrued understanding of "living heritage." The term Living Heritage (capitalized) is not meant to be a title that I give to knowledge holders and it should not serve as a form of granting status. Dialogue with communities across different sectors is necessary to examine the role of ICH custodians in tandem with the technicalities associated with professional classifications or designations, taxes and equitable supports, social capital, and the capitalization of the cultural industry.

42 Lévi-Strauss, Introduction. Lévi-Strauss built on Ferdinand de Saussure's notion of the arbitrary sign to discuss a symbol with no fixed referent.

43 McLeod, *Cree Narrative Memory*.

44 Pawłowska-Mainville, "Accessing and Transmitting Living Heritage."

45 Even if families are from different cultures, the efforts to maintain linguistic and cultural viability in Canada have similar challenges. Cultural and linguistic minorities who reside in areas that are largely English-speaking are equally exposed to Hollywood/American

cultural content as to other groups, and thus caregivers require significant labour to sustain the value of and interest in their own heritage for young people.

46 In 2019, more than 26 million people took an at-home test, and even though these tests are controversial, the growing interest in culture and identity illustrates an important shift in the North American public in wanting to learn about their past. For one article examining the growth of commercial ancestry and health databases, please see Regalado, "More Than 26 Million People Have Taken an At-Home Ancestry Test."

47 Kulchyski and Pawlowska-Mainville, "The Incalculable Weight of Small Numbers."

48 *R. v. Van der Peet.*

49 Some interpretations of the term *mindimooye* are "old woman" and "my" woman (hence the pre-verb *min-*, referring to the personal). Stewart Roy, an Anishinaabemowin instructor, also shared that the term *dimooye* refers to "a lady with responsibilities" and she does not have to be old.

50 There is a vast literature on women's cultural knowledge, including Geniusz, *Plants Have So Much to Give Us*; Simpson, *Dancing on Our Turtle's Back*; Kermoal and Altamirano-Jimenes, *Living on the Land*; Turner, *Ancient Pathways, Ancestral Knowledge*; Cruickshank, *Life Lived Like a Story*; Anderson, *Life Stages and Native Women*. I also speak from personal experience and my own efforts at cultural transmission.

51 For numerous papers and information on the subject of gender-based violence and securing environmental sustainability, please see IUCN, "Gender-Based Violence and Environment Linkages."

52 See Pawlowska-Mainville and Pierreroy, "Duni zuz 'utilnilth, 'Tanning Moose-Hide.'"

53 Richard Morrison, personal communication, 21 June 2007.

54 Sartre, *Critique of Dialectical Reason*, vol. 1. Peter Kulchyski also discusses totalization in the context of Indigenous resistance in "Hunting Theories."

55 Since the term "Aboriginal" still has some relevance in legal and Constitutional contexts, I use the original term when discussing specific legal cases. I use the term "Indigenous" to refer to contemporary political contexts.

56 To make a personal comment that intersects with my ICH work: I dislike using the term "White," as it erases my entire cultural identity; so does "non-Indigenous," as it defines my existence from the point of negation [of culture and heritage]. I find it makes me "non-something," a blank slate. The term "Indigenous" in my view is also too often used as a homogenizing replacement of the cultural identity that comes with being Anishinaabe, Inninu, Dakelh, etc., which is why I prefer to use ethnonyms or the term "cultural" over "Indigenous" when discussing ICH (e.g., cultural [Anishinaabe] knowledge, [cultural] Dakelh food, Makeso Sakahican Inninu tradition).

57 Although the term "Indigenous" is used here, I do not identify as Indigenous. Polish people, Polanie/Polacy, our ethnonym, means "people of the glades/open fields, or meadows," and while Polish people view themselves as authochtonous/indigenous, the political concept of Indigenous (versus non-Indigenous) does not exist in Poland.

58 For example, my work on Dakelh ghuni language revitalization with my friend Yvonne Pierreroy has involved generating ideas for children's books and trying them out on my kids. Likewise, Polish-learning books, Anishinaabemowin books, and French dictionaries have been helpful resources in creating accessible and innovative language books for Yvonne. Please see Carrier Linguistic Society and Pawlowska-Mainville, *Nak'azdli Medical Pocket Phrasebook*, published by the Carrier Linguistic Society in 2016 as an example of a language material inspired from other language books. Dakelh ghuni is the language of the Dakelh, also known as the Carrier peoples of central British Columbia.

59 Coulthard, *Red Skin, White Masks*, 13.

60 Pawlowska-Mainville, "Engaging *Dibaajimowinan*, 'Stories,'" 127–43.

61 This notion is very much inspired by Renate Eigenbrod's book, *Travelling Knowledges*.

62 I had passively accepted Others' change of my name to "Agnes" in order to fit in to the larger anglophone society in Canada. My name "Agnieszka" still surprises people; perceived as too hard to pronounce and too "ethnic," my name is still often anglicized as Agnes.

63 *Zaagadikiing*, "we come to an open area/small meadow opening," is the literal Anishinaabemowin translation of Polanie or "people of the glades/meadows" that refers to Polish people.

64 This is the oral history of the Polish people and neighbouring Slavic peoples that I translated into Anishinaabemowin. This oral history is roughly translated as follows:

> A long time ago, a man named Lech lived in a house in the forest with his two older brothers. One afternoon, his mother said to Lech: The people are hungry. There is nothing to eat. Take your two older brothers and find something. It is spring, and Lech prepared for four days by catching and salting pike and put them in a bag. Worried about his travel, he took a bit of fish on the way to his place when he noticed his big brother to the side of the smokehouse filleting fish, and he said to him: We leave tomorrow early in the morning. They walked through forest for days and seldom stopped. One day, when they woke up, they saw a bear. One older brother, Rus, said, "I will follow that bear" and he went north. Lech and his other brother, Czech, walked about for one week when they noticed a deer. Czech said, "I will follow that deer to the mountains." He walked south over the tall mountains. Lech kept walking north until he arrived at a clearing and said, "what beautiful opening," and rested against a large oak tree. Suddenly, he noticed a white-eagle nest in the tree and the eagle flying about in the distance. And he decided to stay near the water, where he hunted and fished for pickerel, and ate up all the strawberries in the nearby woods. At night, he watched the white eagle as he worked in his garden. Finally, he said to himself, "This is the land that gives life. I am very content here. I am not hungry, and many wildflowers grow here. I will get my people to come here." So, the story goes, the people walked to the clearing and considered the white eagle their clan. This is one oral history of Poland, Russia, and the Czech Republic.

Filled with errors and irregularities in English, this story is part of my ongoing effort to learn Anishinaabemowin. I acknowledge my Anishinaabemowin instructor, Stewart Roy, for his fantastic teaching and encouragement in this area.

65 Abel Bruce, personal communication, 16 March 2013.

66 Diana Taylor discusses the idea of official archives and repertoires in performance studies in *The Archive and the Repertoire*, 22.

67 I have also placed my collection of Walter's written works on the UNESCO Chair in Living Heritage and Sustainable Livelihoods website so the public can enjoy his creativity and talent in storytelling.

68 I reside on the traditional and unceded territory of the Lheidli T'enneh, the homeland of the Dakelh people. Much of the information on Dakelh culture has been shared with me by my children's "adopted" Dakelh *'utsoo* (grandmother) and *'atsiane* (grandfather) in

Dakelh ghuni. Yvonne and Ron Pierreroy are Elders from Fort St. James and Lheidli T'enneh, respectively, and we do a lot of ICH-based work together, such as publish Dakelh language books, develop Dakelh-English children's books, and co-teach classes at the university. Yvonne and I speak about our moosehide tanning class in Pawlowska-Mainville and Pierreroy, "Dani zuz 'utilnilth, 'Tanning Moose-Hide.'"

CHAPTER 1: LIVING HERITAGE

1 Poplar River First Nation is a community composed of Anishinaabeg, Cree, and Oji-Cree members. The First Nation identifies as the Asatiwisipe Anishinaabeg, but other spellings and names can also be found: Azatiiziibe Anishinaabeg, Asatiwisipe First Nation, Asatiwisipe Aki, Azaadiwi-ziibi Nitam-Anishinaabe, and even Negginan.

2 Although Cree and Oji-Cree families and identities are present in the community, the First Nation refers to its political and collective identity as Anishinaabe.

3 Pimachiowin Aki, *Nomination for the Inscription* (2012), 12.

4 Pawlowska, "Using the Global to Support the Local."

5 UNESCO World Heritage Centre, "The Criteria for Selection."

6 As of 2023, Canada's twenty World Heritage Sites include Writing-on-Stone/Áísínai'pi, Alberta; Pimachiowin Aki, Ontario and Manitoba; Nahanni National Park Reserve, Northwest Territories; Dinosaur Provincial Park, Alberta; Kluane/Wrangler-St.Elias/ Glacier Bay/Tatshenshini-Alsek, Yukon and British Columbia; Head-Smashed-In Buffalo Jump, Alberta; SGang Gwaay, British Columbia; Wood Buffalo National Park, Northwest Territories; Canadian Rock Mountain Parks, Alberta and British Columbia; Historic District of Old Québec, Québec; Gros Morne National Park, Newfoundland and Labrador; Old Town Lunenburg, Nova Scotia; Waterton-Glacier International Peace Park, Alberta; Miguasha National Park, Québec; Rideau Canada, Ontario; Joggins Fossil Cliffs, Nova Scotia; Landscape of Grand Pré, Nova Scotia; Red Bay Basque Whaling Station, Newfoundland and Labrador; Mistaken Point, Newfoundland and Labrador; and L'Anse aux Meadows National Historic Site, Newfoundland and Labrador.

7 UNESCO, World Heritage Committee, 37th Session of the World Heritage Committee (37 COM), Decision 37 COM 8B.19, 2013:175 §b.

8 Representatives of four First Nations (Pauingassi, Poplar River, Bloodvein, and Little Grand Rapids) and from two provincial governments (Manitoba and Ontario) sit as equal partners on the Board of Directors of the Pimachiowin Aki Corporation.

9 The World Heritage Committee comprises two advisory bodies, the International Union for the Conservation of Nature (IUCN), which looks after natural sites, and the International Council of Monuments and Sites (ICOMOS), which advises on cultural sites.

10 Some of the gaps were highlighted in Pimachiowin Aki, *Nomination for the Inscription* (2016), and in Cameron and Rössler, "World Heritage and Indigenous Peoples." Te Heuheu, Kawharu, and Tuheiava also talk about the challenges of the World Heritage Site nomination process for Indigenous peoples in "World Heritage and Indigeneity." I discuss some of the challenges experienced by the Pimachiowin Aki communities in my doctoral dissertation "Escaping the 'Progress Trap,'" 70–87.

11 UNESCO groups North America and Europe together; however, I have recreated the graph to show the world heritage properties in North America separately from Europe. Figure 6 consists of State Parties to the UNESCO 1972 Convention and includes the following regions: Africa (35 State Parties), Latin America and the Caribbean (28 State Parties), Asia and the Pacific (36 State Parties), Arab States (18 State Parties), North America

(2 State Parties, which are composed of Canada and the United States of America), and Europe (48 State Parties).

12 It is interesting to note that Canada currently has 12 sites on the tentative list with the nominations placing more emphasis on cultural elements and mixed-heritage (natural and cultural). The sites currently include Gwaii Haanas (2008), Ivvavik / Vuntut / Herschel Island (Qikiqtaruk) (2004), Quttinirpaaq (2004), and Sirmilik National Park and Tallurutiup Imanga (proposed) National Marine Conservation Area (2018) —mixed-heritage nominations; Tr'ondëk-Klondike (2004), Qajartalik (2018) —cultural nominations; and Île d'Anticosti (2004), Hecate Strait and Queen Charlotte Sound Glass Sponge Reefs Marine Protected Area (2018) —natural nominations.

13 On this website, Italy is consistently ranked in the top three countries with a "history richer than most": U.S. NEWS, "10 Countries with the Richest Histories."

14 Wikipedia, "Culture of Italy."

15 UNESCO World Heritage Centre, "The Criteria for Selection."

16 McBryde, "Travellers in Storied Landscapes."

17 UNESCO: World Heritage Convention, "Pimachiowin Aki."

18 While I cannot tie this thought to any specific *akiwenzi*, during our discussions, all of them frequently interpreted themselves as "a part of" their traplines/territories and as making a living from them. The men emphasized that living close to the land, that is, in "natural environments," is simultaneously normal and healing.

19 Davidson-Hunt, Deutsch, and Miller, *Pimachiowin Aki Cultural Landscape Atlas*, 14.

20 Some of the authors who discuss the complexity around Indigeneity and [Indigenous] identities include Lawrence, *"Real" Indians and Others*; LaRocque, *When the Other Is Me*; and Cook-Lynn, "American Indian Intellectualism." Homi Bhabha elaborates on hybridity in *The Location of Culture*; Perley, "Living Traditions."

21 Besio, "Conservation Planning: The European Case of Rural Landscapes," 61.

22 te Heuheu, Kawharu, and Tuheiava, "World Heritage and Indigeneity," 17.

23 UNESCO, International Expert Workshop on Integrity and Authenticity of World Heritage Cultural Landscapes, World Heritage Committee, 2.

24 ICOMOS, "Authenticity and Outstanding Universal Value Webinar," 20 January 2021 and 10–12 March 2021.

25 Ibid., 10 March 2021.

26 Frances Valiquette, notebooks, 1981/2013.

27 Ibid., 1977/2013.

28 Pimachiowin Aki, *Nomination for the Inscription* (2012), 14.

29 Ibid.

30 Ibid.

31 Pimachiowin Aki, *Nomination for the Inscription* (2016), vi.

32 Ibid.

33 Ibid.

34 Ibid., vii.

35 Ibid., vii.

36 Ibid., 19.

37 Stanley Bittern, personal communication, 9 July 2008; Ken Douglas, personal

communication, 16 July 2008; Abel Bruce, personal communication, 16 March 2010; Noel Bruce, personal communication, 22 July 2008; Ernest C. Bruce, personal communication, 23 July 2008; Kate Douglas, personal communication, 2012.

38 Pimachiowin Aki, *Nomination for the Inscription* (2016), 19; translations in original. I interpret the cultural tradition of *ji-ganawendamang Gidakiimiinan* as a form of "resource governance/resource management" but the term also includes notions of "good governance" or "stewardship" or "looking after" the resources, waters, people, and the relationships between people, land, and other-than-human Beings. I use the terms "stewardship" interchangeably with "resource management" and "customary governance."

39 Poplar River First Nation, *Asatiwisipe Aki Management Plan* (2011) and Pimachiowin Aki, *Nomination for the Inscription* (2016) both argue that Indigenous heritage is tied to the land.

40 Abel Bruce, personal communication, 21 March 2013.

41 Ibid., 20 March 2010.

42 Pawlowska-Mainville, "Aki miijim, 'Land Food.'"

43 Cajete, *Native Science*, 205.

44 Battiste and Henderson, *Protecting Indigenous Knowledge and Heritage*, 44.

45 Cadena, *Earth Beings*, 94.

46 UNESCO, "Kihnu Cultural Space," inscribed in 2008.

47 UNESCO, "Cultural Space of the Yaaral and Degal," inscribed in 2008.

48 UNESCO, "Places of Memory and Living Traditions of the Otomí-Chichimecas People of Tolimán," inscribed in 2009.

49 Dzieje.pl: Portal Historyzny, "Muzeum Tatrzańskie chce wpisania Góralskiej kultury na listę UNESCO."

50 Tatrzański Park Narodowy, "Dziedzictwo Kulturowe w Tatrach."

51 Ceklarz, "Tradycja i Kultura."

52 The UNESCO ICH register holds numerous elements that use the term "cultural space," "cultural landscape," "socio-cultural space" or even "practices/traditions associated with _____ [name of territory or group]." In 2008, for example, the Russian Federation, Kyrgyzstan, Uzbekistan, Morocco, Colombia, Guinea, Jordan, Dominican Republic, and Viet Nam have all successfully inscribed their individual "cultural spaces" to the UNESCO Representative List of the Intangible Cultural Heritage of Humanity. These spaces may extend to other cultural expressions such as music, and Jamaica, for example, placed reggae music on the ICH Representative List as an expression of Jamaican cultural identity and space.

53 Walter specifically wanted me to record and share this story. This is a summary of the story as told by him in our personal communication, 15 March 2010.

54 Both Walter and Abel shared similar versions of this story with me, with many Anishinaabe and Cree terms in the story. This is a summary of the story I translated to Anishinaabemowin from memory. "If a person travels north along Lake Winnipeg, he will surely arrive at Poplar River. And then, he starts walking kind of to the east, as far as until a large mountain. Thunder Mountain it is called. He should look around for a bit. A nest is off the side of the path. If he searches on the bottom of the hill for a while, there he will find Thunderbird eggs in a nest, possibly before dark. So it is said, every spring, the big Thunderbird wakes up. He gets up from sitting and spreads his wings. He flies and [as] he flies, he casts a shadow on the forest. And the rain comes as a consequence. Now, the Thunderbird is flying about the land. He flies away making noise. That noise reverberates. That is, his long wings are

these things [that make noise]. As he shakes his wings, he makes thunder. Immediately the earth shakes. The Thunderbird flies about for a while. Once in a while, there is a flash of lightning. Thunderbird throws lightning from his red eyes and once in a while, a tree is struck [with lightning]. Consequently, a tree is set on fire. This fire starts to grow and grows until bush country is burned completely so there is nothing left. For a long time, there is no one in the forest. All wild animals left [are gone]. No more life. None are heard and the forest is filled with smoke for so many days/a lot in the spring. Eventually, a pinecone bursts open. A plant stand [sapling] stands up from surface. And much more [of them] appear and green the earth. New trees appear. Soon blueberries will grow in a bunch. Therefore, the forest is new; he [Thunderbird] can rest. And, he goes to sit back on his eggs."

55 Walter Nanawin, personal communication, 15 March 2010.

56 Ibid., 14 July 2008 and 15 March 2010.

57 Ibid., 14 July 2008.

58 Ibid., 17 July 2008.

59 Ibid., 14 July 2008.

60 Ibid., 15 May 2015.

61 Ibid.

62 Abel Bruce, personal communication, 16 March 2013.

63 Fixico, *That's What They Used to Say*, 6.

64 Ibid., 21.

65 Hulan and Eigenbrod, *Aboriginal Oral Traditions*, 2.

66 Henderson, *First Nations Jurisprudence and Aboriginal Rights*, 158.

67 UNESCO, "Oral Traditions and Expressions."

68 Ibid.

69 Archibald, *Indigenous Storywork*, 70.

70 Abel Bruce, personal communication, 12 March 2015.

71 Richard Morrison shared that *asemaa* literally means "offering" or "to place something down as an offering." While it can be bullets, coins, or even hair clippings, tobacco is usually put down, thus *asemaa* implies "to put [tobacco] down as an offering" (a verb) but the term has come to be used as a noun signifying "tobacco-as-offering."

72 Ken often said he is more Saulteaux than Anishinaabe, but he also identified the Saulteaux to be a part of the Anishinaabe culture and nation.

73 Ken Douglas, personal communication, 14 March 2011.

74 The name is also spelled Binesiiwapigon Zaagai'gan; however, since the community uses Pinesewapignung Sagaigan to identify the areas around Thunder Mountain [Lake] and Weaver Lake, I have used their orthography. Literally, it means "Thunder[bird] Narrows/Lake."

75 Ken Douglas, personal communication, 18 March 2015.

76 Ibid.

77 Ibid., 9 March 2013.

78 The term *aadizookewininiwag* was used by Albert Bittern in a personal communication, 12 March 2018; as well as in my discussions with Noel Bruce, personal communication 12 March 2015; and with Richard Morrison, personal communication, 16 August 2016.

79 *Negginan* has several different interpretations but Albert Bittern shared that it means "home," and it is one of the administrative names for the community, personal communication 12 March 2018

80 Pawlowska-Mainville, "Engaging *Dibaajimowinan*, 'Stories.'"

81 Walter Nanawin, personal communication, 14 July 2008.

82 Ibid.

83 Ray Point, quoted in Archibald, *Indigenous Storywork*, 70.

84 Pawłowska-Mainville, "Cannibalizing."

85 Also spelled as Mishipeshu.

86 Johnston, *Ojibway Heritage*.

87 Walter Nanawin, personal communication, 14 July 2008, 15 March 2010, and 7 March 2015.

88 Brosius, "What counts as local knowledge," 135.

89 Walter Nanawin, personal communication, 20 March 2018.

90 Ibid.

91 Pawlowska-Mainville and Massan, "'The Flooders' and 'the Cree.'"

92 Bordo, "Jack Pine."

93 Abel Bruce, personal communication, 9 March 2013.

94 Ibid.

CHAPTER TWO: INTANGIBLE CULTURAL HERITAGE

1 The old settlement of Black River is north of Poplar River First Nation on *asatiwisipe aki*. The residents of Black River were relocated to Poplar River in the 20th century. The old settlement should not be confused with the current Black River First Nation (Band) located 138 kilometres northeast from Winnipeg.

2 Frances Valiquette, notebooks, with 1982 dates.

3 Abel Bruce, personal communication, 9 March 2013.

4 Ibid.

5 In the past few years Abel has gone out on the trapline for two or three months at a time.

6 Abel Bruce, personal communication, 9 March 2013.

7 Ibid., 14 March 2010.

8 Ibid., 12 June 2013.

9 SS-Waffen or SS-men is an abbreviation of the paramilitary group Schutzstaffel (meaning "protective echelon" in German), who were the main armed security men of the Nazi Party.

10 Abel Bruce, personal communication, 12 June 2013.

11 Potlaches in Dakelh ghuni, the language of the Dakelh.

12 UNESCO, "Text of the Convention for the Safeguarding of the Intangible Cultural Heritage" (ICH Convention), preamble.

13 Government of Canada, "Implementing the United Nations Declaration on the Rights of Indigenous Peoples Act."

14 UNDRIP, Articles 11.1 and 31.1, respectively.

15 Pawlowska-Mainville, "Asserting Declarations."

16 Joanna Cicha-Kuczyńska, Counsellor to the Republic of Poland on the application of the UNESCO 2003 ICH Convention, personal communication, Garbatka-Zbyczyn, 16 September 2022.

17 Pitawanahwat. "Anishinaabemodaa Pane Oodenang—A Qualitative Study," 259.

18 Hart, "Brief Reflections on Sharing Circles."

19 Richard Morrison, personal communication, 17 August 2018.

20 Ken Douglas, personal communication, 14 March 2010.

21 Marcel Valiquette, personal communication, 17 March 2010.

22 Abel Bruce, personal communication, 12 March 2015.

23 The document distinguishes between the Creator (also translated to Lord) as Gaa-debenjiged and the Great Spirit as Gizhe-Manidoo.

24 Pimachiowin Aki, *Nomination for the Inscription* (2016), 13.

25 Richard Morrison, personal communication, 17 August 2018.

26 Ibid.

27 Ibid.

28 Barton et al., "Value Expression in Decision-Making."

29 I use the term "heritage language" to refer to [grand]parental language(s) and/or languages of one's own heritage(s). Expressions such as "traditional language" do not work because languages are evolving and contemporary; "parental language" is also problematic, as a parental language may be different than the heritage language. For example, while the parents may speak a dominant language such as English, the native tongue of the grandparents may be different. It is important to note that dominant languages such as English, French, Spanish, or Mandarin are heritage languages too.

30 UNESCO, "Oral Traditions and Expressions," 3.

31 The linguistic difference between English and Anishinaabemowin here is not an indication of cultural differences, because someone who identifies as Anishinaabe may not speak the language and hence may not perceive these structurally linguistic and epistemic distinctions, especially since there are often no particular reasons why something is considered animate or inanimate (or both for different regions), or male or female, or neutral. All languages are special and reflect a unique way of seeing the world. Also, the animate/inanimate distinction many be spiritual for some or merely linguistic for others, so while rocks are animate (and viewed as "grandfathers" by Richard), water, *nibi*, interpreted as the source of life, is considered inanimate.

32 "Le recensement des langues."

33 Farfan, "Keeping the Fire Alive."

34 RCAP, "Summary of Recommendations Volumes 1–5," 1.7.2 and 3.5.6.

35 *Canadian Encyclopedia*, "Languages in Use in Canada."

36 Aird and Fox, *Indigenous Living Heritage in Canada*, 10.

37 UNDRIP, Article 13.1.

38 TRC, Calls to Action, Calls 14–15.

39 See Bellrichard, "Budget's Indigenous Languages Funding 'Insufficient' to Support Revitalization Work"; and Canada, Indigenous Languages Act.

40 Please see the First Voices website, https://www.firstvoices.com/.

41 UNESCO, Information Sheet: "Language Policy," 2.

42 Ibid.

43 Ibid.

44 UNESCO, Intergovernmental Committee for the Safeguarding of ICH, Sixth session, Bali, Indonesia, November 2011, Nomination File no. 00530.

45 For examples of language work across the globe, see Living Tongues, https://livingtongues.org/resource-page/ (accessed 14 October 2022).

46 I am teaching Polish, French, and, to the best of my limited ability, Anishinaabemo to my children. Transmitting my heritage and "in-law tongue" as a first language to my children includes the strategic avoidance of English books and audiovisual media, creativity to translate content, and unrelenting persistence. This permits my children to speak Polish as a first language, with French and Anishinaabemowin as second, and English as their third (although the last three continually alter). Living away from Anishinaabe territories, I am cognizant of the fact that my children will not speak fluent Anishinaabemowin from childhood. Anishinaabemo-learning for our entire family means time spent placing Anishinaabemowin words throughout the house, money to buy books and music, as well as taking language courses. We have also made use of children's French language services, like Matin-Lecture, and British Columbia's Tire-Lire program, which delivers French books, games, and other resources to the home for one month in exchange for a small annual fee. This service has been exemplary for our French-language education.

47 Statistics Canada, "The Aboriginal Languages of First Nations People, Metis and Inuit."

48 Pocius, "The Government of Canada and Intangible Cultural Heritage," 79.

49 Canada, Department of Canadian Heritage Act, Article 4.2.

50 Gauthier, "Intangible Heritage in Canada," 133.

51 Email, quoted in Pocius, "A Review of ICH in Newfoundland and Labrador."

52 Pocius, "The Government of Canada," 79–80.

53 Ibid., 80.

54 Richard Morrison and John Mainville, personal communication, 22 July 2018.

55 Likewise, Polanie is the name for Polish people, but it literally means "people of the glades."

56 Richard Morrison and John Mainville, personal communication, 22 July 2018.

57 Richard Morrison, personal communication, 22 July 2018

58 Richard said that the word literally translates to "pounding on."

59 Asch, "Concluding Thoughts and Fundamental Questions."

60 Pocius, "Government of Canada," 85; Stefano, Davis, and Corsane, "Touching the Intangible: An Introduction," in *Safeguarding Intangible Cultural Heritage*, 1–8; Pocius, "The Emergence of Intangible Cultural Heritage Policy"; and Pocius, "A Review of ICH in Newfoundland and Labrador."

61 Parmoun, *Research Report on Intangible Cultural Heritage*, 4–5.

62 As of 8 March 2023, UNESCO has verified damage to 246 sites since 24 February 2022—107 religious sites, 20 museums, 88 buildings of historical and/or artistic interest, 19 monuments, 12 libraries. UNESCO, "Damaged cultural sites."

63 For example, the Great Mosque of Aleppo, a World Heritage Site, which was built in 8th century CE and destroyed in 2012, again in 2013, and even more in 2014. The mosque is one of the oldest prayer buildings in Aleppo and the site is symbolic for Muslims and Christians. UN News, "Stop the destruction."

64 Deacon and Smeets, "Intangible heritage safeguarding."

65 Hafstein, *Making Intangible Heritage*. Paul Nadasdy also discusses a similar process for traditional ecological knowledge in "The Anti-Politics of TEK" and in "Hunters and Bureaucrats."

66 Ibid., 3.

67 Pawłowska-Mainville, Roque, and Fillion, *Conversations on Intangible Cultural Heritage*.

68 The notes made by the Intergovernmental Committee for the Safeguarding of the Intangible Cultural Heritage at its 17th session in 2022, for example, illustrate several problematic issues relating to the convention, including the process of nominating an element to the UNESCO Representative List without meaningful community involvement. Other issues also show challenges with "artificial" transnational nominations, partial information reported by a state on the nomination file, competing state ownership over an element, and with nations which are recognized for human rights violations but who submit nominations representative of democratic community consultations.

69 Ibid. In the report, Tim Curtis, the Secretary to the 2003 UNESCO Convention, acknowledged the important work being done in Canada, particularly on the East Coast, in Quebec, and in Saskatchewan.

70 Some of the publications can be found at https://www.patrimoinevivant.qc.ca/publications.

71 Le Conseil québécois du patrimoine vivant, "Annonce de la première formation professionelle en meunerie artisanale du Québec."

72 Heritage NL, "Intangible Cultural Heritage (ICH)."

73 Out of this position, Heritage Saskatchewan developed community-based living heritage projects which were modelled on the achievement of the ICH Convention's four goals for safeguarding ICH. To date, Heritage Saskatchewan has completed five projects: Coal in Coronach, the Val Marie Elevator, gee meeyo pimawtshinawn/It Was a Good Life: Saskatchewan Metis Road Allowance Memories, Covid-19 Culture, and Black and Rural Saskatchewan.

74 The report was written by folklorist Dr. Meghann Jack, with contributions from Quebec folklorist Van Troi Tran, and with advisors Dr. Gerald Pocius and Dr. Laurier Turgeon.

75 Aird, Fox, and Bain, *Recognizing and Including Indigenous Cultural Heritage in B.C.*

76 For the Cultural Plan for Calgary, see the municipal website, https://www.calgary.ca/arts-culture/cultural-plan.html. For Heritage Vancouver's list of Top10, see https://heritagevancouver.org/category/top10-watch-list/2020/ (both sites accessed 17 October 2022).

77 Pocius, "The Government of Canada," 85–92.

78 Smith, "Discourses of Heritage," 29–34.

79 Pocius, "The Government of Canada," 86.

80 Smith and Waterton, "Envy of the world"; and McCleery, McCleery, Gunn, and Hill, "Intangible Cultural Heritage in Scotland," quoted in Pocius, "The Government of Canada," 86–87.

81 UNESCO, "Text of the Convention for the Safeguarding of Intangible Cultural Heritage," Article 11a.

82 Ibid., Article 12.1.

83 Adamowski and Smyk, *Niematerialne dziedzictwo kulturowe* [Intangible Cultural Heritage], 11.

84   UNESCO, "Intangible Cultural Heritage Domains," 3.

85   UNESCO, Information Sheet: "Identification and Inventorying Policy Provisions," 3.

86   Ibid., 2.

87   UNESCO, Information Sheet: "Encouraging Community Engagement," 3.

88   UNESCO, "Requesting International Assistance."

89   UNESCO, "Drawing Up Inventories."

90   The fundamental aspect of ICH is that the element must be passed from one generation to the next. Powwows are an effective example as many dancers are taught by the older members of the family and pass their skills to the younger members of the family. I once had a student who often competed against his father and his son in the same dance. The same goes for powwow singers who, like my *niitaa*, "brother-in-law," was taught drumming by his dad and is currently teaching his children to drum.

91   Richard Morrison, personal communication, 17 July, 2018.

92   Collins, "Indonesians Tell Malaysians 'Hands Off Our Batik.'"

93   UNESCO, "Guidance Note for Inventorying Intangible Cultural Heritage," 16.

94   To illustrate with a personal example, due to time and financial constraints we heavily focus on language learning (speaking, building vocabulary) in our household. It is by using the language in our daily activities that we also transmit cultural teachings, traditions, and certain rituals (with "cultural food" perhaps last on our list). Coming from different backgrounds, my spouse and I also teach some elements of dancing to our children, at which point "powwow dancing" is differentiated from "Polonez" and thus our children "categorize" the two distinct cultures in our home.

95   UNESCO, "Intangible Cultural Heritage: A Force for Sustainable Development."

96   UNESCO, Information Sheet: "Intellectual Property."

97   WTO, "TRIPS-Trade-Related Aspects of Intellectual Property Rights."

98   WIPO, "Berne Convention for the Protection of Literary and Artistic Works"; WTO, "Paris Convention."

99   UNESCO, Information Sheet: "Intellectual Property," 2–3.

100 Ibid., 1.

101 Lixinski, *Intangible Cultural Heritage in International Law*, 210.

102 UNESCO, "Traditional Knowledge of the Jaguar Shamans of Yuruparí," inscribed in 2011.

103 Bell and Paterson, *Protection of First Nations Cultural Heritage*, 9–10.

104 UNESCO, Information Sheet: "Intellectual Property," 3.

105 Schnarch, "Ownership, Control, Access, and Possession" (OCAP); WIPO, "Compilation of Information on National and Regional Sui Generis Regimes."

106 UNESCO, Information Sheet: "Intellectual Property," 2–3.

107 Ibid., 2–3.

108 Ibid., 2–3.

109 Stefano, Davis, and Corsane, *Safeguarding Intangible Cultural Heritage*.

110 WIPO, "Berne Convention"; HIPAMS, "The HIPAMS Toolkit."

111 Deacon, "Ethics, intellectual property and commercialization."

112 Yvonne and Ron Pierreroy, personal communication, 14 May 2016.

113 Richard Morrison, personal communication, 17 July 2018.

114 Harrison, "The Kwagiulth Dancers."

115 For example, Heritage-Sensitive Intellectual Property and Marketing Strategies (HIPAMS) is an organization based in India that assists communities in developing countries to overcome the challenges associated with marketing ICH. This includes shielding ICH holders against misappropriation, over-commercialization, misuse, misrepresentation, and lack of attribution, and facilitating the development of their own IP-related frameworks. To reduce economic marginalization, some communities may opt for development through benefit-sharing and contractual agreements. HIPAMS provides starting points for communities to begin ICH economic-based work in ways that ensures reciprocal benefits to bearer communities and ICH holders, as well as to any external partners.

116 UNESCO, "Ethical Principles for Safeguarding Intangible Cultural Heritage."

117 Governments must offer legal assistance and support for developing professional ethics and adequate statutory protection, especially in cases where commercial companies approach communities. Priorities and tools for safeguarding in tandem with market success may offer multiple avenues to mitigate risks and maximize economic benefits. This includes evaluating the skills and values associated with a specific ICH element, adopting heritage-sensitive marketing approaches, and using legal and ethical strategies to help promote and protect community interests in the marketplace. Different options and opportunities will depend on the needs and self-determination of each community. The HIPAMS, India, "Toolkit" is a useful resource for communities exploring heritage-sensitive marketing approaches.

118 Abel Bruce, personal communication, 13 March 2013.

CHAPTER THREE: "THE LAST ONE TO KNOW"

1 Richard Morrison personal communication, 3 July 2016.

2 Ibid., 17 July 2018.

3 "Energy," Encyclopedia Brittanica.

4 Richard Morrison, personal communication, 3 July 2016.

5 Richard refers to Midewewin as the Grand [Sacred] Medicine Society.

6 Richard Morrison personal communication, 3 July 2016.

7 Ibid., 17 July 2018.

8 Ibid.

9 TRC, Calls to Action.

10 TRC, Calls to Action, Calls 62.ii and iii.

11 Pawlowska-Mainville and Pierreroy, "Duni zuz 'utilnilth, 'Tanning Moose-Hide.'" Black, "Schooling the World"; Bhola, "Reclaiming Old Heritage for Proclaiming Future History."

12 Labrador, "Integrating ICH and Education."

13 Pawlowska-Mainville and Pierreroy, "Duni zuz 'utilnilth, 'Tanning Moose-Hide,'" 93.

14 UNESCO, "Text of the Convention for the Safeguarding of Intangible Cultural Heritage," Article 14 as well as the "Operational Directives for the Implementation of the Convention for the Safeguarding of the Intangible Cultural Heritage" both encourage ICH-based education.

15 RCAP, "Summary of Recommendations Volumes 1–5", 3.5.6.

16 TRC, Calls to Action, Call 63.iii.

17 See National Centre for Collaboration on Indigenous Education, "Story Search."

18 Pawlowska-Mainville and Pierreroy, "Duni zuz 'utilnilth, 'Tanning Moose-Hide,'" 93.

19 Copeland, "European Democratic Citizenship, Heritage Education and Identity," Labrador, "Integrating ICH and Education," 27.

20 Labrador, "Integrating ICH and Education," 28.

21 Freire, *Pedagogy of the Oppressed*, 81.

22 Pawlowska-Mainville and Pierreroy, "Duni zuz 'utilnilth, 'Tanning Moose-Hide,'" 95.

23 Labrador, "Integrating ICH and Education," 27.

24 The term is often used in the context of giving birth to a child.

25 Richard Morrison, personal communication, 3 February 2015.

26 Russell Lambert, personal communication, 18 July 2008.

27 Rose Klippenstein, personal communication, 22 March 2015.

28 Although a few community members in Poplar River said that all Anishinaabe food is "land food," many distinguished between store-bought food and "our" food. *Aki[iwi] miijim* was understood to be food from the land, or obtained by hunting, fishing, trapping, and gathering. A distinction between everyday food and food eaten at feasts, *wikongewin*, was also made. Elder Frances Valiquette, also talked about *ashandiwin*, the food rations that were handed out by the Canadian government in the 1960s and 1970s that taught people "learned helplessness." For a details discussion on this food system, please see Pawlowska-Mainville, "Aki miijim, 'Land Food.'"

29 Indigenous Food Systems Network, "Home Page."

30 Pawlowska-Mainville, "Asserting Declarations," 378.

31 Noel Bruce, personal communication, 15 March 2012. Tester and Kulchyski, *Tammarniit (Mistakes)*.

32 Pawlowska-Mainville, "Aki miijim, 'Land Food,'" 61.

33 Alex Mitchell, from Poplar River Elders Interviews and Histories, quoted in Poplar River First Nation, *Asatiwisipe Aki Management Plan*, 14.

34 Mariah is also called ling.

35 Ken Douglas, personal communication, 23 July 2008.

36 Ibid., 19 March 2010.

37 Ibid.

38 Abel Bruce, personal communication, 18 March 2010.

39 Ibid.

40 Ibid.

41 Many *akiwenziyag* pronounced lynx as "lynk," and since this was very noticeable and distinct among the Elders, I have decided to keep their "sound" in the transcriptions.

42 Abel Bruce, personal communication, 18 March 2010.

43 Ibid.

44 Walter Nanawin, personal communication, 16 July 2008.

45 Noel Bruce, personal note, 2015.

46 Quoted through Noel Bruce, personal note about knowledge from the late Elder Alex Mitchell, 2015.

47 Noel Bruce, personal note, 2015.

48 Pimachiowin Aki, *Nomination for the Inscription* (2016), 14.

49 Abel Bruce and Albert Bittern, quoted in Pimachiowin Aki, *Nomination for the Inscription* (2016), 47 (5–13 November 2013).

50 Abel Bruce, personal communication, 18 March 2010.

51 Jean Nanawin, personal communication, 27 July 2008.

52 Ken Douglas, personal communication, 19 March 2010.

53 Pawlowska-Mainville, "Aki miijim, 'Land Food,'" 70.

54 Adrian Tanner, the anthropologist working with the Cree in Quebec discusses this system in Tanner, *Bringing Home Animals*.

55 Ken Douglas, personal communication, 19 March 2010.

56 Some community members also used the term *mashkosiiminan*.

57 Pimachiowin Aki, *Nomination for the Inscription* (2016), 27.

58 Usher, "Evaluating Country Food in the Northern Native Economy."

59 Ernest C. Bruce, personal communication, 14 October 2009.

60 Abel Bruce, personal communication, 16 March 2013.

61 At other times a shot is made only after the animal has made eye contact with the hunter. This was common for the Shuta Got'ine Mountain Dene and shared with me during my time there in 2010 & 2011, David Etchinelle, personal communication, 14 August 2010.

62 Hallowell, *Contributions to Ojibwe Studies*, 30–32.

63 Ibid., 31.

64 "One time, the Mean Old Man accumulated lots of animals that he trapped. One winter, he caught a lot of animals. He caught mink, beaver, and rabbits. One by one, he was skinning them. He skinned the mink violently; he skinned the beaver roughly. He threw the beaver body down and proceeded to tear the skin off the rabbit. Suddenly, as the Mean Old Man was pulling the skin off the rabbit, the rabbit escaped from him. He did not have his skin on. The skinless rabbit jumped from under his hands and escaped into the bush. For several months, [Mean Old Man] checked his traps for the wild animals every morning and every evening. He found nothing. But the people would say, 'There is a lot of rabbit this winter.' But the old man did not catch any rabbit. And he did not catch any muskrat. And the old man did not catch any beaver. He looked around Mukadewa and Crane Creek. He went hungry, and he was angry. Consequently, he starved."

65 Abel Bruce, personal communication, 12 March 2013. This is a paraphrased story in which Abel repeated the name "Mean Old Man" frequently, as if to instil the man's bad behaviour in the listener. The Mean Old Man refers to an actual person and this is a true story.

66 Abel Bruce, personal communication, 12 March 2013.

67 Abel Bruce and Norman Bruce, quoted in Pimachiowin Aki, *Nomination for the Inscription* (2016), 56.

68 Sahlins, *Stone Age Economics*. Diamond Jenness discusses the exchange of the gift in *The Life of the Copper Eskimos*; and John Dowling talks about the gift in "Individual Ownership and the Sharing of Game." Both Hallowell and Tanner address the exchange of the gift in hunting societies. Rauna Kuokkanen talks about the gift in *Reshaping the University*.

69 Rose Klippenstein, personal communication, 22 March 2015.

70 Abel Bruce, personal communication, 12 March 2013.

71 Ibid.

72 Ken Douglas, personal communication, 14 March 2013.

73 UNESCO, Information Sheet: "Gender Equality Policy," 2–3.

74 UNESCO, "Intangible Cultural Heritage and Gender," 6.

75 Ibid., 4.

76 UNESCO, Information Sheet: "Gender Equality Policy," 2–3.

77 UNESCO, Universal Declaration on Cultural Diversity.

78 UNESCO, Universal Declaration of Human Rights.

79 United Nations Human Rights: Office of the High Commissioner, Convention on the Elimination of All Forms of Discrimination against Women (1979).

80 UNESCO, "Intangible Cultural Heritage and Gender," 4.

81 Please see Fact Sheet No. 23, "Harmful Traditional Practices Affecting Health of Women and Children"; and IPPF, "Harmful Traditional Practices Affecting Women and Girls."

82 Ibid.

83 UNESCO, "Text of the Convention for the Safeguarding of Intangible Cultural Heritage," Preamble and Article 2.

84 Ali, "Violence against the Girl Child," 3–7.

85 Ali, "Violence against the Girl Child."

86 LaRocque, "Re-examining Culturally Appropriate Models," 76.

87 Ibid., 84.

88 While it does not create any new rights, Section 25 of the Constitution acts like a mechanism for the reconciliation of conflicts between the rights outlined in the Canadian Charter of Rights and Freedoms and the rights outlined in the Constitution Act of 1982.

89 Paula Gunn Allen, quoted in National Sexual Violence Resource Center, Sexual Assault in Indian Country, 2.

90 Kuokkanen, "Self-Determination and Indigenous Women's Rights," 239.

91 Ibid., 239. See also Denetdale, "Chairmen, Presidents, and Princesses"; Green, "Canaries in the Mines"; and Martin-Hill, "She No Speaks."

92 UNESCO, "Intangible Cultural Heritage and Gender," 9.

93 Ibid., 3.

94 Ibid., 9.

95 Ibid., 8.

96 UNESCO, Operational Directives for the Implementation of the Convention for the Safeguarding of the Intangible Cultural Heritage, Chapter IV, articles 102 & 162 and especially Chapter VI.1.4 article 181, and UNESCO, "Intangible Cultural Heritage and Gender," 2, both encourage careful deliberation around role of gender in ICH.

97 Despite the spread of universal faiths and historical conquests that led to the eradication and modification of various belief systems and practices, these spheres continue to be valued in many regions of the world.

98 UNESCO, "Activities in the Domain of Women and Intangible Heritage." The question whether "domestic" implies a lesser status in society, or if women's work was traditionally valued as highly as men's, or if the devaluation was potentially a legacy of colonialism or patriarchy is continuously debated. Please see Georgieva, Alonso, Dabla-Norris, and Kochhar et al., "The Economic Cost of Devaluing 'Women's Work'"; as well as Hollows, *Domestic Cultures*, which explores the production of domestic labour.

99 UNESCO, "Intangible Cultural Heritage and Gender," 5.

100 Community member #2, personal communication, 2010.

101 Community member #1, personal communication, 2021. This quote is from our shared project initiated in 2020.

102 Tobias, "Chief Kerry's Moose," and "Living Proof" rarely features women as "land users," and Povinelli, "Labour's Lot" also discusses the gender limitation in her fieldwork.

103 UNESCO, "Intangible Cultural Heritage and Gender," 6.

104 UNESCO, Intergovernmental Committee for the Safeguarding of the Intangible Cultural Heritage, Sixth session, Bali, Indonesia, November 2011, Nomination file no. 00530.

105 Agronomist, "Kobieta na bacówce," 28 November 2011.

106 Plan International, "The Maasai Elder Advocating to End Female Genital Mutilation," 26 February 2021.

107 Marcel Valiquette, personal communication and notes, 14 July 2008.

108 Cultural identity is convoluted in the modern world as linguistic and racial identities add another layer to cultural diversity through a shared struggle or affinity. For example, individuals from North and/or French-speaking Africa, France, Antilles and Quebec (i.e., from different cultures) can create affinities through a francophone identity in North America. Likewise, specific Indigenous communities often create alliances based on their shared political identity as Indigenous people (albeit composed of different cultures and language groups); people from a particular racial identity (who may also be from different cultures and ethnic backgrounds) can also create coalitions. In all these instances, there is a cultural diversity of people from different backgrounds and/or geographical regions of the world, who are united by some form of affinity, and providing depth to the notion of diversity. Navigating the complexities around culture, heritage, location, and historical factors permits an ICH custodian to extend and simultaneously limit the conditions for ICH transmission. This mosaic of identity junctions consequently impacts who the heritage inheritors may be.

109 State recognition and regulation of Indian status is done through the Indian Act in Canada. The nearly 150-year-old document, designed for a particular group of people, created complex issues and multifarious understandings of who is an Indigenous/ Aboriginal/"Indian"/Native in Canada. Indigenous communities are also establishing their own definitions. For a discussion on the issues of power related to recognition, acknowledgement, and difference, see Coulthard, *Red Skin, White Masks*.

110 Pawłowska-Mainville, "Accessing and Transmitting."

111 Jones, *Protecting Historic Architecture and Museum Collections*; and Lafrenz Samuels and Rico, *Heritage Keywords*.

112 See Shariatmadari, "Why It's Time to Stop Worrying about the Decline of the English Language." Although the article discusses teen slang and the role of technology in the English language, the author also recognizes the irrational fear over the decline of "proper" English and forms of communication.

113 Mauss, "Les Techniques du Corps."

114 For discussions on cultural and collective memory, see Halbwachs, "The Collective Memory"; and McLeod, *Cree Narrative Memory*. For a discussion on "habitus," see Bourdieu, *Outline of a Theory of Practice*.

115 Albert Bittern, personal communication, 23 July 2008.

116 Ibid.

117 Frances Valiquette, personal communication, 25 July 2008.

118 Bourdieu and Wacquant, *An Invitation*, 43.

119 See the 2019 article by *Canadian Immigrant*, "Anglicize your name as a newcomer? Yes or no?"

120 Richard Morrison, personal communication, 16 June 2015. "'Nish" is a shorter, colloquial term for Anishinaabe(g).

121 For a discussion on romanticism, see Doxtator, *Fluffs and Feathers*; LaRocque, *Defeathering the Indian*, and *When the Other Is Me*; and Francis, *The Imaginary Indian*. Bernard Perley also uses humour and metaphoric anecdotes to explore the intersections of narrative, language, and identity as an element of critical Indigeneity in Perley, "Living Traditions."

122 It is important to point out that linguistic knowledge does not guarantee familiarity of culture. For example, in some circumstances, my plurilingualism makes me special; in others, that makes me Anishinaabekaaza, "acting" or pretending to be Anishinaabe (and I've also been called a "pretendian" and "Indian lover"). While I don't need a reason to learn Anishinaabemowin other than that I find the language beautiful and interesting, I wish my children, who have Anishinaabe heritage, would be so fluent in Anishinaabenowe, "the sound and natural tones of Anishinaabe," that it would not be so special in our home. *Ambegin n'gii Anishinaabemtaagwazi* (I wish I sounded like I spoke Anishinaabe). Putting up Anishinaabe words all over our house, hurriedly translating terms with a worn-out dictionary permanently placed in our kitchen makes Anishinaabemowin special. But so is speaking English fluently in Poland.

123 Richard Morrison, personal communication, 3 July 2016.

124 Ibid.

125 Ibid., June 2020.

CHAPTER FOUR: "CLEAN ENERGY, THEY SAY"

1 Noah Massan, personal conversation, 14 December 2013.

2 See *Keeyask Generation Project: Environmental Impact Statement*, supporting volume, *Socio-Economic Environment, Resource Use and Heritage Resources*, part 3, "Heritage Resources," 1-42–1-44.

3 Our group included several Elders from Makeso Sakahican, Indigenous activists from Grassy Narrows and northern Manitoba, and Dr. Peter Kulchyski, Dr. Stephane McLachlan, and me.

4 Pawlowska-Mainville and Massan, "'The Flooders' and 'the Cree.'"

5 Manitoba Hydro, "Keeyask Generating Station Produces First Electricity for Manitoba Grid."

6 Noah Massan personal communication, 7 December 2014; and CFLGC, Interviews, 2013.

7 Noah Massan, personal communication, 14 October 2013.

8 Noah Massan and Ivan Moose, personal conversation, 14 October 2013; and CFLGC, Interviews.

9 CFLGC, Interviews; Kulchyski, "Oohcinewin"; York Factory First Nation, "Kipekiskwaywinan—Our Voices"; and Fox Lake Cree Nation, "FLER" also discussed the term in detail.

10 Fox Lake Cree Nation Negotiations Office, "Ninan," 384, quoted in Pawlowska-Mainville, "Aski Atchimowina."

11 CBC News, "Allegations of Sexual Abuse, Racism Revealed." The Inninuwak harvesters and community members also discussed this behaviour in CFLGC, Interviews.

12 Ivan Moose, in CFLGC, Interviews, 12 September 2013.

13 Christine and Jack Massan, in CFLGC, Interviews, 13 June 2013.

14 Noah Massan, in CFLGC, Interviews, 12 September 2013.

15 Noah Massan, personal communication, 14 October 2013.

16 Noah Massan and Ivan Moose, in CFLGC, Interviews, 12 September 2013. This is also discussed in Pawlowska-Mainville, "Aski Atchimowina," 14.

17 Fox Lake Cree Nation, "Fox Lake Environmental Report," 48; and Fox Lake Cree Nation Negotiations Office, "Ninan," 88.

18 Noah Massan, personal communication, 6 December 2013.

19 A number of scholars working on impact assessments have pointed out the challenges of Indigenous people in the process; these include Booth and Skelton, "Industry and Government Perspectives"; Usher, "Traditional Ecological Knowledge"; Notzke, Aboriginal Peoples and Natural Resources; Stevenson, "Indigenous Knowledge in Environmental Assessment"; Wismer, "The Nasty Game"; Whitelaw, McCarthy, and Tsuji, "The Victor Diamond Mine"; Baker and McLelland, "Evaluating the Effectiveness"; and Paci, Tobin and Robb, "Reconsidering the Canadian Environmental Impact Assessment Act."

20 Canada, Impact Assessment Act, 2(c)i–ii.

21 Canada, Impact Assessment Act, 2(iii).

22 CFLGC, Interviews.

23 Pawlowska-Mainville in conversation with Massan, "'The Flooders and 'the Cree,'" 154.

24 CEC, Manitoba Keeyask Hearings, vol. 26, 11 December 2013.

25 Noah Massan, personal communication, 11 December 2013.

26 Catherine Beardy and Nora Wavey in Fox Lake Cree Nation Negotiations Office, "Ninan," 321, quoted in Pawlowska-Mainville, "Aski Atchimowina," 13–14.

27 CFLGC, Interviews; and Fox Lake Cree Nation, "Fox Lake Environmental Report."

28 Manitoba CEC, Report on Public Hearing, 54–55.

29 CBC, "Endangered Salamanders and Skinks Are Sexy Too."

30 Noah Massan, personal communication, 6 December 2013.

31 CFLGC, Interviews.

32 Atleo, Tsawalk, xii.

33 Noah Massan, personal communication, 14 July 2013.

34 Jack and Christine Massan, in CFLGC, Interviews, 13 June 2013.

35 A few scholars show the tragic consequences of relocations, including Tester and Kulchyski, Tammarniit (Mistakes); Bussidor and Bilgen-Reinart, Night Spirits; Waldram, "Native People and Hydroelectric Development"; and Hewitt, "Exploring."

36 Manitoba CEC hearings, Keeyask Project, Transcripts, Mazurat and McIvor, vol. 15, 2013, 3347–56, selections.

37 Noah Massan, in CFLGC, Interviews, 14 June 2013.

38 Noah Massan, personal communication, 8 July 2018.

39 Noah Massan, personal communication, 14 October 2013.

40 Pawlowska-Mainville in conversation with Massan, "'The Flooders' and 'the Cree,'" 165.

41 As a former employee of the Fox Lake Cree Nations Negotiations Office, I am aware of Hydro Manitoba's relationship with the Inninuwak, and Hydro's ignorance of their concerns over many activities occurring in their territory. For example, my own reports and recommendations that lagoons from work camps can be effectively processed prior to their release into streams were met with no feedback.

42 Noah Massan, personal communication, 14 October 2013.

43 Noah Massan, personal communication, 6 January 2014.

44 Noah Massan, CFLGC cross-examination at the Manitoba CEC, Keeyask Hearings, vol. 25, 10 November 2013, pg. 5824.

45 Noah Massan, personal communication, 8 January 2014.

46 Pawlowska-Mainville, Presentation to the BC Utilities Commission.

47 I submitted Expert Reports/Feedback on the immense importance of including intangible cultural heritage in Environmental and Regulatory Reviews to the Canadian Environmental Assessment Agency in 2017. I also submitted a report attesting to the need to include the ICH framework in the Site-C Dam to the Province of British Columbia as well as presented before the British Columbia Utilities Commission during their consultations in 2017.

48 Barton et al., "Value Expression in Decision-Making."

49 Canada, Impact Assessment Act, Preamble.

50 Noah Massan, personal communication, 14 October 2013.

51 Noah Massan, personal communication, 14 October 2013.

52 Noah Massan, personal communication, 18 July 2018.

CHAPTER FIVE: "THE LAND WILL STAND FOR YOU"

1 For example, the National Indigenous Economic Development Board (NIEDB) reported in 2019 that the recorded unemployment rate for First Nations men on reserve (30 percent) was nearly double that of the total Indigenous population (17.6 percent), and more than triple that of the non-Indigenous population (7.9 percent). NIEDB, Indigenous Economic Progress Report, 22–23.

2 Abel Bruce, personal communication, 17 March 2013.

3 Abel Bruce, personal communication, 17 March 2013.

4 Yvonne Pierreroy, personal communication, 5 May 2016.

5 UNESCO, Information Sheet: "Economic Development," 1.

6 Pawlowska-Mainville, "Aki miijim, 'Land Food,'" 5.

7 UNESCO, Information Sheet: "Economic Development," 9.

8 Cominelli and Greffe, "Intangible Cultural Heritage."

9 UNESCO, "Le Samoa, Fine Mat and Its Cultural Value."

10 UNESCO, quoted in Pawlowska-Mainville et al., "Tree-beekeeping and Apiary in Poland."

11 Saturo Hyoki, "Safeguarding Intangible Cultural Heritage in Japan."

12 Noriko Aikawa-Faure, "Excellence and Authenticity."

13 Yunnan Exploration, "Tie-Dying Skills of Bai Ethnic Minority in Dali."

14 Su and Fang, "Commodifying Intangible Cultural Heritage in Contemporary China," 30.

15 Inuit artists in Pangnirtung sell their unique art, crafts, and carvings through the community-

based, not-for-profit Uqqurmiut Centre for Arts and Crafts, which was founded in 1990 to "promot[e] and preserv[e] local culture [and] artistic heritage" of the community. Uqqurmiut, "About the Uqqurmiut Centre."

16 Ernest C. Bruce, personal communication, 22 July 2008.

17 Byron Mitchell, personal communication, 18 July 2008.

18 Freddie Bruce, personal communication, 6 July 2008.

19 Ibid.

20 Ernest C. Bruce, personal communication, 5 March 2010.

21 Abel Bruce, personal communication, 16 March 2012.

22 Ibid.

23 Ibid.

24 Ibid.

25 Ibid.

26 Ray, *Indians in the Fur Trade*; Burch and Ellanna, *Key Issues in Hunter-Gatherer Research*; Martin, *Keepers of the Game*; Innis, *The Fur Trade in Canada*; Van Kirk, *Many Tender Ties*; and Manore and Miner, *The Culture of Hunting in Canada* all address the topic of hunting in Canada.

27 Ernest C. Bruce, personal communication, 22 July 2008; Abel Bruce, personal communication, 16 March 2010; Stanley Bittern, personal communication, 5 July 2008.

28 Community member #3, personal communication, 18 July 2008.

29 Sometimes Abel used the term *izhitwaawin* or *Anishinaabe'itwaawin*; one time he distinguished *izhitwaawin* as "the cultural way of life/do it is a cultural or spiritual way" and *Anishinaabe'itwaawin* as the "Indian way of life."

30 Noel Bruce, personal communication and written notes, 2010.

31 Ken Douglas, personal communication, 19 March 2010.

32 Walter Nanawin, personal communication, 2008.

33 Noah Massan, personal communication, 15 June 2018.

34 Abel Bruce, personal communication, 19 March 2013.

35 Ibid.

36 Ibid.

37 Ernest C. Bruce, personal communication, 22 July 2008.

38 Feit, "Hunting and the Quest for Power," 193.

39 Ibid., 197–99.

40 Pawlowska-Mainville, "Experts and Professionals."

41 World Wildlife Fund, "Payments for Ecosystem Services."

42 Indigenous Circle of Experts, *We Rise Together*, 6.

43 Albert Bittern, personal communication, 22 July 2008.

44 Rose Klippenstein, personal communication, 22 March 2015.

45 Noel Bruce, personal communication, 17 July 2008.

46 Indigenous Climate Hub, "About—Indigenous Community-Based Climate Monitoring Program."

47 ICCA Consortium, "Website Home Page."

48 Indigenous Circle of Experts, *We Rise Together.*

49 David Suzuki Foundation, Tribal Parks and Indigenous Protected and Conserved Areas.

50 Tribal Parks Gathering, 14–19 March 2016 organized by the Tribal Parks, "Tla-o-qui-aht Tribal Parks" and the Indigenous Community Conserved Areas (ICCAs) Consortium, https://www.iccaconsortium.org/ (accessed 6 March 2023). For example, the Qqs Society does their own monitoring of the coast and land: https://www.qqsprojects.org/projects/coastwatch/.

51 Tribal Parks Gathering, 18 March 2016.

52 Abel Bruce, personal communication, 17 March 2012.

53 Amah Mutsun community member, class presentation for INTS 498/FNST 416/606/POLS 498/698, University of Northern British Columbia, 11 October 2018. For the work being carried out to revive Amah Mutsun land and resource knowledge, please see Amah Mutsun Tribal Band, www.amahmutsunlandtrust.org (accessed 6 March 2023).

54 Noah Massan, personal communication, 21 July 2018.

55 Noah Massan, personal communication, 7 January 2014.

56 Some voices at the CEC hearings argued this, particularly the Pimicikamak expert witnesses who questioned the description of science and Aboriginal Traditional Knowledge (ATK) having "different worldviews, arguing instead that science is a methodology, rather than a worldview. The conflict of worldviews in this case is not between science and ATK, but rather between an economic growth imperative and a traditional worldview that seeks to protect the land." Manitoba CEC, Report on Public Hearing, 43.

57 Noah Massan, personal communication, 7 January 2014.

58 Pawlowska-Mainville, "Asserting Declarations."

59 Shewell, *Enough to Keep Them Alive*, 8.

60 Ibid., 319–21 and 334–36.

61 Desmarais and Whitman, "Farmers, Foodies and First Nations."

62 Morris writes that a lot of Indigenous people complained that promises made at the time of signing were unfulfilled. Morris, *The Treaties of Canada*, 72.

63 Richard Morrison, personal communication, 3 July 2016.

64 Ibid.

65 Ibid.

66 Borrows, "Frozen Rights in Canada," and *Recovering Canada*; Benton-Banai, *The Mishomis Book*; Henderson, *First Nations Jurisprudence*; Henderson, Benson and Findlay, *Aboriginal Title and the Constitution*; and Craft, "Reading beyond the Lines" all discuss Indigenous jurisprudence from an Indigenous perspective.

67 Usher and Bankes, *Property, the Basis of Inuit Hunting Rights*, 13.

68 UNDRIP, Article 25.3. The document, which Canada adopted in 2016, asserts that states "shall give legal recognition with due respect to the customs, traditions and land tenure systems of the Indigenous peoples concerned."

69 The ILO Indigenous and Tribal Peoples Convention (No. 169) as well as the Convention for Biological Diversity both recognize Indigenous and community *sui generis* rights as land governance systems.

70 UNESCO, Information Sheet: "Intellectual Property," 2.

71 Abel Bruce, personal communication, 18 March 2010. While the reference to Catholic

mass and the Creator in the same sentence may seem like a contradictory statement, it is also a demonstration of living culture. For Elders like Abel, Walter, and Ken, the church has been adopted into their cultural world views and lived realities as much as trapping, the fur trade, the HBC, and the telephone.

72 Stanley Bittern, personal communication, 15 July 2008.

73 Abel Bruce, personal communication, 18 March 2010.

74 *R. v. Badger*, Supreme Court of Canada, 1996.

75 Abel Bruce, personal communication, 18 March 2010.

76 Ibid.

77 Walter Nanawin, personal communication, 15 March 2010.

78 Ernest C. Bruce, personal communication, 14 October 12009.

79 Macklem, *Indigenous Difference and the Constitution of Canada*, 183.

80 Pimachiowin Aki, *Nomination for the Inscription* (2012), 127.

81 Craft, *Breathing Life into the Stone Fort Treaty*.

82 Canada, Constitution Act, Section 35.

83 *R v. Van der Peet*, Para. 11.

84 Ibid., decision, emphasis added.

85 Ibid., decision.

86 *R. v. Van der Peet*.

87 See Borrows, "Frozen Rights in Canada"; and Asch, "Concluding Thoughts and Fundamental Questions."

88 Borrows, "Frozen Rights in Canada," 63.

89 Although I am using the interpretation of Aboriginal rights as discussed in the 1990s, I am applying the ICH framework to a contemporary context, where the discussion revolves around Indigenous rights, hence the term 'Indigenous.'

90 UNESCO, "Text of the Convention for the Safeguarding of Intangible Cultural Heritage," Article 11.

91 UNESCO, Information Sheet: "Constitution," 2.

92 Ibid., 2.

93 UNESCO, Information Sheet: "Culture Policy," 4.

94 Republic of Latvia, "Intangible Cultural Heritage Law."

CONCLUSION

1 Bell and Patterson, "Introduction."

2 *R. v. Van der Peet*.

3 UNESCO, Information Sheet: "Providing Support for Policy," 7.

4 Scholars have already laid the groundwork for such initiatives. For such a recommendation, see Pocius, "The Government of Canada," 72.

Bibliography

Adamowski, Jan, and Katarzyna Smyk (eds). *Niematerialne dziedzictwo kulturowe: Źródła, wartości, ochrona* [Intangible cultural heritage: Origins, values, protection]. Lublin-Warsaw: Wydawnictwo Uniwersytetu Marii Curie-Skłodowska and Narodowy Instytut Dziedzictwa [Marie Curie-Skłodowska University Press and National Heritage Institute], 2013.

Agronomist. "Kobieta na bacówce. [Woman at the shepherd's territorial hut]." 28 November 2011. https://agronomist.pl/artykuly/kobieta-na-bacowce (accessed 14 June 2021).

Aikawa-Faure, Noriko. "Excellence and Authenticity: 'Living National (Human) Treasures' in Japan and Korea." *International Journal of Intangible Heritage* 9 (2014): 38–51.

Aird, Karen, and Gretchen Fox. *Indigenous Living Heritage in Canada*. First Peoples' Cultural Council and Fox Cultural Research, April 2020.

Aird, Karen, Gretchen Fox, and Angie Bain. *Recognizing and Including Indigenous Cultural Heritage in B.C.* First Peoples' Cultural Council, September 2019. https://indigenousheritage.ca/wp-content/uploads/2020/08/FPCC-ICH-Policy-Paper-190918-WEB-_2.pdf (accessed 12 May 2021).

Aird, Karen and Gretchen Fox. Indigenous Living Heritage Canada. First Peoples Cultural Council, May 2020. Ottawa, ON: Canadian Commission for UNESCO's IdeaLab. https://fpcc.ca/resource/indigenous-living-heritage-in-canada/(accessed 15 May 2021).

Ali, Shamima. "Violence Against the Girl Child in the Pacific Island Region." United Nations DAW (Division for the Advancement of Women) in collaboration with UNICEF, Expert Group Meeting on Elimination of All Forms of Discrimination and Violence against the Girl Child. Florence, Italy, 25–28 September 2006. https://www.un.org/womenwatch/daw/egm/elim-disc-viol-girlchild/ExpertPapers/EP.14%20%20Ali.pdf (accessed 21 May 2021).

Anderson, Kim. *Life Stages and Native Women*. Winnipeg: University of Manitoba Press, 2011.

Archibald, Joanne. *Indigenous Storywork*. Vancouver: UBC Press, 2008.

Asch, Michael. "Concluding Thoughts and Fundamental Questions." In *Protection of First Nations Cultural Heritage*, edited by Catherine Bell and Robert K. Paterson, 394–411.Vancouver: UBC Press, 2009.

Atleo, Richard. *Tsawalk: A Nuu-Chah-Nulth Worldview*. Vancouver: UBC Press, 2004.

Baker, D.C., and J.N. McLelland. "Evaluating the Effectiveness of British Columbia's Environmental Assessment Process for First Nations' Participation in Mining Development." *Environmental Impact Assessment Review* 23, no. 5 (2003): 581–603.

Barton, David, and Rebecca Chaplin-Kramer, Elena Lazos Chavero, Meine van Noordwijk, Liliana Bravo-Monroy, Stefanie Engel, Thomas Hahn, et al. "Value Expression in Decision-Making." In *Methodological Assessment of the Diverse Values and Valuation of Nature of the Intergovernmental Science-Policy Platform on Biodiversity and Ecosystem Services*, edited by P. Balvanera, U. Pascual, M. Christie, B. Baptiste, and D. González-Jiménez, chap. 4. IPBES secretariat, Bonn, Germany: IPBES Secretariat, 2022. https://doi.org/10.5281/zenodo.6522261.

Battiste, Marie Ann, and James Youngblood Henderson. *Protecting Indigenous Knowledge and Heritage: A Global Challenge*. Saskatoon: Purich Publishers, 2000.

Bell, Catherine E., and Paterson, Robert K., (eds.). "Introduction." 3–14. *Protection of First Nations Cultural Heritage: Law, Policy, and Reform*. Vancouver: UBC Press, 2009.

Bellrichard, Chantelle. "Budget's Indigenous Languages Funding 'Insufficient' to Support Revitalization Work, Says B.C. Advocate." CBC News, 22 March 2019. https://www.cbc.ca/news/indigenous/indigenous-languages-budget-funding-1.5066806 (accessed 12 May 2021).

Benton-Banai, Edward. *The Mishomis Book: The Voice of the Ojibway*. Minnesota: University of Minnesota Press, 1988.

Berkes, Fikret. *Sacred Ecology*. 2nd ed. New York: Routledge Press, 2008.

Besio, Mariolina. "Conservation Planning: The European Case of Rural Landscapes." In *Cultural Landscapes: The Challenges of Conservation*, 60–67. World Heritage Papers 7. Paris: UNESCO World Heritage Centre, 2003.

Bhabha, Homi. *The Location of Culture*. London: Routledge Press, 1994.

Bhola, Harbans. "Reclaiming Old Heritage for Proclaiming Future History: The Knowledge-for-Development Debate in African Contexts." *Africa Today* 49, no. 3 (2002): 2–21.

Black, Carol (Director). *Schooling the World*. [Film], 2010.

Booth, Annie, and Norm Skelton. "Industry and Government Perspectives on First Nations' Participation in the British Columbia Environmental Assessment Process." *Environmental Impact Assessment Review* 31, no. 3 (2011): 216–25.

Bordo, Jonathan. "Jack Pine—Wilderness Sublime or the Erasure of the Aboriginal Presence from the Landscape." *Journal of Canadian Studies* 27, no. 4 (1992–93): 98–128.

Borrows, John. "Frozen Rights in Canada: Constitutional Interpretation and the Trickster." *American Indian Law Review* 22, no. 1 (1997/98): 37–64.

———. *Recovering Canada: The Resurgence of Indigenous Law*. Toronto: University of Toronto Press, 2002.

Bourdieu, Pierre. *Outline of a Theory of Practice*. Cambridge: Cambridge University Press, 1977.

Bourdieu, Pierre, and Loïc J.D. Wacquant. *An Invitation to Reflexive Sociology*. Chicago: The University of Chicago Press, 1992.

Brosius, J.P. "What Counts as Local Knowledge in Global Environmental Assessments and Conventions?" In *Bridging Scales and Knowledge Systems: Concepts and Applications in Ecosystem Assessment*, edited by Walter V. Reid, Fikret Berkes, Thomas Wilbanks, and Doris Capistrano, 129–44. Washington: Island Press, 2006.

Burch, Jr., Ernest, and Linda J. Ellanna. *Key Issues in Hunter-Gatherer Research*. Oxford: Berg, 1996.

Bussidor, Ila, and Üstün Bilgen-Reinart. *Night Spirits: The Story of the Relocation of the Sayisi Dene*. Winnipeg: University of Manitoba Press, 1997.

Cadena, Marisol de la. *Earth Beings: Ecologies of Practice across Andean Worlds*. Durham, NC: Duke University Press, 2015.

Cajete, Gregory. *Native Science: Natural Laws of Interdependence*. Santa Fe: Clear Light Publishers, 2000.

Cameron, Christina, and Mechtild Rössler. "World Heritage and Indigenous Peoples: The Evolution of an Important Relationship." *World Heritage* 62 (February 2012): 45–51.

Canada. "Basics of Environmental Assessment." https://www.canada.ca/en/ environmental-assessment-agency.html (accessed 18 May 2018).

———. Constitution Act, 1982.

———. Department of Canadian Heritage Act, 1995. https://laws-lois.justice. gc.ca/eng/acts/C-17.3/page-1.html (accessed 12 May 2021).

———. "Government of Canada Supports Indigenous Languages in Quebec." https://www.canada.ca/en/canadian-heritage/news/2018/11/government- of-canada-supports-indigenous-languages-in-quebec.html (accessed 15 May 2021).

———. Impact Assessment Act, 2019. https://laws-lois.justice.gc.ca/eng/ acts/I-2.75/page-1.html?txthl=indigenous#s-2. (accessed 2 May 2021).

———. "Implementing the United Nations Declaration on the Rights of Indigenous Peoples Act." https://www.justice.gc.ca/eng/declaration/index. html (accessed 29 October 2022).

———. Indigenous Languages Act, 2019. https://laws-lois.justice.gc.ca/eng/ acts/I-7.85/page-1.html (accessed 30 May 2021).

Canadian Encyclopedia. "Languages in Use in Canada." Historica Canada. Published 7 February 2006; updated 21 October 2020. https://www. thecanadianencyclopedia.ca/en/article/languages-in-use (accessed 15 May 2021).

Canadian Immigrant. "Anglicize your name as a newcomer? Yes or no?" by Ramya Ramanathan, 3 January, 2019. https://canadianimmigrant.ca/ living/community/anglicize-your-name-as-a-newcomer-yes-or-no (accessed 11 March 2023).

Carrier Linguistic Society, and A. Pawlowska-Mainville, assistant ed. *Nak'azdli Medical Pocket Phrasebook.* Carrier Linguistic Society, 2016.

CBC News. "Which endangered species should we save? Humans face tough choices about what lives—and what dies." CBC News, 22 July 2022. https://www.cbc.ca/news/science/endangered-species-choose- extinction-1.6527673 (accessed 18 February 2023).

CBC News. "Allegations of Sexual Abuse, Racism Revealed in Report on Hydro Projects' Impacts in Northern Manitoba." CBC News, 21 August 2021.

https://www.cbc.ca/news/canada/manitoba/abuse-racism-report-hydro-1.4793749. (accessed 21 May 2021).

CEC (Clean Environment Commission), Manitoba Keeyask Hearings, Transcripts, vol. 26, 11 December 2013.

Ceklarz, Katarzyna. "Tradycja i Kultura—inwentaryzacja dziedzictwa kultury wołoskiej: Raport z inwentaryzacji dziedzictwa kulturowego 'Tradycja i Kultura'" ["Tradition and Culture-Inventory of Wallachian Cultural Heritage: Report on the inventory of heritage 'Tradition and Culture'"]. Małopolska: Interreg, Polska-Słowacja, n.d. https://szlakwoloski.eu/app/default/files-module/local/documents/inwentaryzacja%20Kultura%20i%20Tradycja%20Ma%C5%82opolska-skompresowany.pdf. (accessed 11 March 2023).

CFLGC (Concerned Fox Lake Grassroots Citizens). Interviews for the Keeyask Project. Concerned Fox Lake Grassroots Citizens, 2013–14.

Cole, Douglas. *Captured Heritage*. Vancouver: UBC Press, 1995.

Collins, Nick. "Indonesians Tell Malaysians 'Hands Off Our Batik.'" *Telegraph*, 5 October 2009. https://www.telegraph.co.uk/expat/expatnews/6251806/Indonesians-tell-Malaysians-Hands-off-our-batik.html.

Cominelli, Francesca, and Xavier Greffe. "Intangible Cultural Heritage: Safeguarding for Creativity." *City, Culture and Society* 3, no. 4 (2012): 245–50.

Le Conseil québécois du patrimoine vivant. "Annonce de la première formation professionnelle en meunerie artisanale du Québec." 1 July 2022. https://www.patrimoinevivant.qc.ca/actualites/annonce-formation-meunerie (accessed 14 October 2022).

Cook-Lynn, Elizabeth. "American Indian Intellectualism and the New Indian Story." In *Natives and Academics: Researching and Writing about American Indians*, edited by Devon A. Mihesuah, 124–31. Omaha: University of Nebraska, 1998.

Copeland, Tim. "European Democratic Citizenship, Heritage Education and Identity." 2006. *Strasbourg: Council of Europe*. https://rm.coeint/0900001680927395 (accessed 11 March 2023).

Coulthard, Glen. *Red Skin, White Masks: Rejecting the Colonial Politics of Recognition*. Minneapolis: University of Minnesota Press, 2014.

Craft, Aimée. *Breathing Life into the Stone Fort Treaty: An Anishinabe Understanding of Treaty One*. Saskatoon: Purich Publishing, 2013.

———. "Reading beyond the Lines: Oral Understandings and Aboriginal Litigation." Public Interest Law Centre, December 2013 (accessed 10 May 2021).

Cruickshank, Julie. *Life Lived Like a Story: Life Stories of Three Yukon Native Elders*. Vancouver: UBC Press, 1991.

Davidson-Hunt, Iain, Nathan Deutsch, and Andrew M. Miller. *Pimachiowin Aki Cultural Landscape Atlas: Land That Gives Life*. Winnipeg: Pimachiowin Aki Corp., 2013.

David Suzuki Foundation. *Tribal Parks and Indigenous Protected and Conserved Areas: Lessons from B.C. David Suzuki Foundation*. August 2018. https://davidsuzuki.org/wp-content/uploads/2018/08/tribal-parks-indigenous-protected-conserved-areas-lessons-b-c-examples.pdf.

Deacon, Harriet. "Ethics, intellectual property and commercialization of cultural heritage." *Pravovedenie* 64 (2020): 93–111.

Deacon, H., and Smeets, R. "Intangible Heritage Safeguarding and Intellectual Property Protection in the Context of Implementing the UNESCO ICH Convention." *Safeguarding Intangible Heritage*, edited by Laurajane Smith and Natsuko Akagaw, 36–53. Routledge, 2019.

Denetdale, Jennifer Nez. "Chairmen, Presidents, and Princesses: The Navajo Nation Gender, and the Politics of Tradition." *Wicazo Sa Review*, 21, no. 1 (2006): 9–28.

Desmarais, Annette, and Hannah Wittman. "Farmers, Foodies and First Nations: Getting to Food Sovereignty." Paper presented at "Food Sovereignty: A Critical Dialogue." International Conference, Yale University, New Haven, CT, 14–15 September 2013. https://www.iss.nl/sites/corporate/files/3_Desmarais_Wittman.pdf (accessed 10 May 2021).

Disko, Stefan, and Helen Tugendhat. *World Heritage Sites and Indigenous Peoples' Rights*. IWGIA Document 129. Copenhagen: IWGIA, Forest Peoples Programme, and Gundjeihmi Aboriginal Corporation, 2014.

Dowling, John. "Individual Ownership and the Sharing of Game in Hunting Societies." *American Anthropologist* (1968): 502–7.

Doxtator, Deborah. *Fluffs and Feathers: An Exhibit on the Symbols of Indianness: A Resource Guide*. Brantford, ON: Woodland Cultural Centre, 1992.

Dzieje, Portal Historyczny. "Muzeum Tatrzańskie chce wpisania Góralskiej kultury na listę UNESCO [Tatra Museum wants to put Highland culture on UNESCO list]." https://dzieje.pl/dziedzictwo-kulturowe/muzeumtatrzanskie-chce-wpisania-goralskiej-kultury-na-liste-unesco (accessed 15 May 2021).

Eigenbrod, Renate. *Travelling Knowledges: Positioning the Im/Migrant Reader of Aboriginal Literatures in Canada*. Winnipeg: University of Manitoba Press, 2005.

Encyclopedia Brittanica. "Energy." https://www.britannica.com/science/energy (accessed 3 December 2020).

Farfán, José Antonio Flores. "Keeping the Fire Alive: A Decade of Language Revitalization in Mexico." Centro de Investigaciones y Estudios Superiores en Antropología Social, n.d. FloresFarfan_final_.pdf (d1wqtxts1xzle7.cloudfront.net).

Feit, Harvey. "Hunting and the Quest for Power." In *Native Peoples: The Canadian Experience*, edited by R. Bruce Morrison and C. Roderick Wilson, 181–223, 2nd ed. Toronto: McClelland and Stewart, 1995.

Fixico, Donald. *That's What They Used to Say*. Norman: University of Oklahoma Press, 2017.

Fox Lake Cree Nation. "FLER: Fox Lake Environmental Report." 2012.

Fox Lake Cree Nation Negotiations Office. "Ninan." Unpublished manuscript. 2012.

Francis, Daniel. *The Imaginary Indian*. Vancouver: Arsenal Pulp Press, 1992.

Freire, Paulo. *Pedagogy of the Oppressed*. Introduction by Donaldo Macedo. London: Bloomsbury Publishing, 1967.

FSC (Food Secure Canada). "What Is Food Sovereignty." FSC website, n.d. http://foodsecurecanada.org/who-we-are/what-food-sovereignty (accessed 2 February 2014).

Gauthier, Antoine. "Intangible Heritage in Canada: Political Context, Safeguarding Initiatives, and International Cooperation." In *Building and Sharing ICH Information*, ICHCAP 2011 Expert Meeting Report, 131–42. Jeonju, Republic of Korea. http://www.ichcap.org/eng/ek/sub8/pdf_file/03/2011_Expert_Meeting_Report.pdf (accessed 27 June 2017).

Geniusz, Mary Siisip. *Plants Have So Much to Give Us, All We Have to Do Is Ask: Anishinaabe Botanical Teachings*. Edited by Wendy Makoons Geniusz and illustrated by Annmarie Geniusz. Minneapolis: University of Minnesota Press, 2015.

Georgieva, Kristalina, Cristian Alonso, Era Dabla-Norris, and Kalpana Kochhar. "The Economic Cost of Devaluing 'Women's Work.'" *IMF Blog*, October

2019. https://www.imf.org/en/Blogs/Articles/2019/10/15/blog-the-economic-cost-of-devaluing-women-work (accessed 1 February 2023).

Green, Joyce. "Canaries in the Mines of Citizenship: Indian Women in Canada." *Canadian Journal of Political Science* 34, no. 4 (2001): 715–38.

Halbwachs, Maurice. *On Collective Memory.* Chicago: University of Chicago Press, 1992, originally published in 1952.

———. "The Collective Memory." In *The Collective Memory Reader*, edited by Jeffrey K. Olick, Vered Vinitzky-Seroussi, and Daniel Levy, 139–49. Oxford: Oxford University Press, 2011.

Hallowell, Irving. *Contributions to Ojibwe Studies: Essays, 1934–1972.* Edited with introductions by Jennifer S.H. Brown and Susan Elaine Gray. Lincoln: University of Nebraska Press, 2010.

Harrison, Klisala. "The Kwagiulth Dancers: Addressing Intellectual Property Issues at Victoria's First Peoples Festival." *World of Music* 44, no. 1 (2002): 137–51.

Hart, Michael. "Brief Reflections on Sharing Circles and Indigenous Worldviews and Empowerment." *Circle Talk* 2, no. 1 (2006): 51–53.

Henderson, James Sakej Youngblood. *First Nations Jurisprudence and Aboriginal Rights.* Saskatoon: Native Law Centre, University of Saskatchewan, 2006.

Henderson, James Youngblood, M. Benson, and I. Findlay. *Aboriginal Title and the Constitution of Canada.* Scarborough, ON: Carswell, 2000.

Heritage NL (Heritage Foundation of Newfoundland and Labrador). "What Is ICH?" 2008. https://www.mun.ca/ich/media/production/intangible-cultural-heritage/media-library/what_is_ich.pdf (accessed 12 May 2018).

Hewitt, Kate. "Exploring Indigenous-Led Collaborative Stewardship in a Watershed Context: Perspectives from the Nechako Headwaters." MSc Thesis, University of Northern British Columbia, 2019.

HIPAMS (Heritage-Sensitive Intellectual Property and Marketing Strategies). "About HIPAMS India." http://hipamsindia.org/ (accessed 31 March 2021).

———. "The HIPAMS Toolkit." HIPAMS, 2021.

Hollows, Joanne. *Domestic Cultures.* Maidenhead, UK: Open University Press, McGraw-Hill Education, 2008.

Hulan, Renee, and Renate Eigenbrod. *Aboriginal Oral Traditions.* Winnipeg: Fernwood Publishing, 2008.

Hyoki, Satoru. "Safeguarding Intangible Cultural Heritage in Japan: Systems, Schemes and Activities." https://www.researchgate.net/profile/Satoru-Hyoki/publication/267851229_Safeguarding_Intangible_Cultural_Heritage_in_Japan_Systems_Schemes_and_Activities/links/575ed01008ae9a9c955f7ffa/Safeguarding-Intangible-Cultural-Heritage-in-Japan-Systems-Schemes-and-Activities.pdf (accessed 13 May 2016).

ICCA Consortium (Indigenous Peoples' and Community Conserved Areas and Territories. Website home page. 2014. http://www.iccaconsortium.org (accessed 18 February 2014).

ICOMOS (International Council of Monuments and Sites). "Authenticity and Outstanding Universal Value." Webinar and workshop, 20 January 2021 and 10–12 March 2021.

Indigenous Circle of Experts. *We Rise Together: The Indigenous Circle of Experts' Report and Recommendations.* March 2018. https://static1.squarespace.com/static/57e007452e69cf9a7af0a033/t/5ab94aca6d2a7338ecb1d05e/1522092766605/PA234-ICE_Report_2018_Mar_22_web.pdf (accessed 1 February 2023).

Indigenous Climate Hub. "About—Indigenous Community-Based Climate Monitoring Program." https://indigenousclimatehub.ca/indigenous-community-based-climate-monitoring-program/ (accessed 20 May 2021).

Indigenous Food Systems Network. "Home Page." https://www.indigenousfoodsystems.org/ (accessed 14 March 2023).

Innis, Harold. *The Fur Trade in Canada: An Introduction to Canadian Economic History.* Toronto: University of Toronto Press, 1999.

ILO (International Labour Organization). "International Labour Standards on Indigenous and Tribal Peoples." 1988. http://www.ilo.org/global/standards/subjects-covered-by-international-labour-standards/indigenous-and-tribal-peoples/lang--en/index.htm.

IPPF (International Planned Parenthood Federation). "Harmful Traditional Practices Affecting Women and Girls." December 2012. https://www.ippf.org/resource/harmful-traditional-practices (accessed 10 May 2021).

IUCN (International Union for Conservation of Nature). "Gender-Based Violence and Environment Linkages (GBV-ENV Center)." https://genderandenvironment.org/agent-gbv-env/ (accessed 14 October 2022).

Jenness, Diamond. *The Life of the Copper Eskimos*. Report of the Canadian Arctic Expedition, 1913–1918, vol. 12. Ottawa: F.A. Acland, Printer to the King's Most Excellent Majesty, 1922.

Johnston, Basil. *Ojibway Heritage*. Toronto: McClelland and Stewart, 1976/2008.

Jones, Barclay, ed. *Protecting Historic Architecture and Museum Collections from Natural Disasters*. Boston: Butterworth-Heinemann, 1986.

Keeyask Hydropower Limited Partnership. *Environmental Impact Statement*. https://keeyask.com/project-timeline/environment-assessment-process/environmental-licensing-process/.

Kulchyski, Peter. *Oohcinewin*. A Report for the Manitoba Clean Environment on behalf of Concerned Fox Lake Grassroots Citizens. January 2014.

Kuokkanen, Rauna. "Self-Determination and Indigenous Women's Rights at the Intersection of

International Human Rights." *Human Rights Quarterly* 34, no. 1 (2012): 225–50.

LaRocque, Emma. *Defeathering the Indian*. Agincourt, AB: Book Society of Canada, 1975.

———.".Re-examining Culturally-Appropriate Models in Criminal Justice Applications." In *Aboriginal and Treaty Rights in Canada: Essays on Law, Equality, and Respect for Difference*, edited by Michael Asch, 75–96. Vancouver: UBC Press, 1997.

———. When the Other Is Me: Native resistance discourse, 1850–1990. Winnipeg: University of Manitoba Press, 2010.

Lawrence, Bonita. *"Real" Indians and Others: Mixed-blood Urban Native Peoples and Indigenous Nationhood*. Vancouver: UBC Press, 2004.

Lafrenz Samuels, Kathryn, and Trinidad Rico, eds. *Heritage Keywords: Rhetoric and Redescription in Cultural Heritage*. Colorado: University Press of Colorado, 2015.

Lazos-Chavero, Elena, Agnieszka Pawlowska-Mainville, David González-Jiménez, Mariana Cantú-

Fernández, and Simone Athayde. "Philosophies of Good Living and Values of Nature: Power and Uncertainties in Decision-making to Achieve Social-environmental Justice in the Americas." *Current Opinion in Environmental Sustainability*, forthcoming in 2023.

Manore, Jean, and Dale Miner, eds. *The Culture of Hunting in Canada*. Vancouver: UBC Press, 2007.

Martin, Calvin. *Keepers of the Game: Indian-animal Relationships and Fur Trade*. Berkeley: University of California Press, 1978.

Martin-Hill, Dawn. "She No Speaks and Other Colonial Constructs of 'The Traditional Woman.'" In *Strong Women Stories: Native Vision and Community Survival*, edited by Kim Anderson and Bonita Lawrence, 106–20. Toronto: Sumach Press, 2003.

Mauss, Marcel. *Sociologie et anthropologie*. Paris: Les Presses universitaires de France, 1968.

———. "Les Techniques du Corps." *Journal de Psychologie* 32, nos. 3–4 (15 March–15 April 1936).

McCleery, Alistair, Alison McCleery, Linda Gunn and David Hill. "Intangible Cultural Heritage in Scotland: One Nation, Many Cultures." In *Sharing Cultures*, edited by Sérgio Lira, Rogério Amoêda, Cristina Pinheiro, João Pinheiro and Fernando Oliveira, 141–54. Barcelos: Green Lines, 2009.

McLachlan, Stephane. *Deaf in One Ear and Blind in the Other: Science, Aboriginal Traditional Knowledge, and the Implications of Keeyask for the Socio-Environment*. A Report for the Manitoba Clean Environment Commission on behalf of Concerned Fox Lake Grassroots Citizens. January 2014.

McLeod, Neal. *Cree Narrative Memory*. Saskatoon: Purich Publishing, 2007.

McNeil, Kent. "Indigenous Law and Aboriginal Title." Osgoode Legal Studies Research Paper Series 183, 2017.

Morris, Alexander. *The Treaties of Canada with the Indians of Manitoba and the North-West Territories: Including the Negotiations on Which They Were Based*. Toronto: Belfords, Clark, 1880; Calgary: Fifth House Publishers, 1991.

Nadasdy, Paul. "The Anti-Politics of TEK: The Institutionalization of Co-Management Discourse and Practice." *Anthropologica* 47, no. 2 (2005): 215–32.

———. *Hunters and Bureaucrats*. Vancouver: UBC Press, 2003.

National Centre for Collaboration on Indigenous Education. https://www.nccie.ca/search/ (accessed 29 May 2021).

National Sexual Violence Resource Center. *Sexual Assault in Indian Country: Confronting Sexual Violence*. National Sexual Violence Resource Center,

2000. https://www.nsvrc.org/sites/default/files/Publications_NSVRC_
Booklets_Sexual-Assault-in-Indian-Country_Confronting-Sexual-
Violence.pdf (accessed 2 May 2018).

NIEDB (National Indigenous Economic Development Board). *The Indigenous
Economic Progress Report*, 2019. Gatineau, QC: NIEDB, 2019. http://
www.naedb-cndea.com/wp-content/uploads/2019/06/NIEDB-2019-
Indigenous-Economic-Progress-Report.pdf (accessed 1 May 2021).

Notzke, Claudia. *Aboriginal Peoples and Natural Resources in Canada*. Concord,
ON: Captus Press, 1994

Nyéléni International Movement for Food Sovereignty. *Declaration of Nyéléni*. 27
February 2007. https://nyeleni.org/IMG/pdf/DeclNyeleni-en.pdf
(accessed 11 March 2023).

Paci, C., A. Tobin, and P. Robb. "Reconsidering the Canadian Environmental
Impact Assessment Act: A Place for Traditional Environmental
Knowledge." *Environmental Impact Assessment Review* 22, no. 2 (2002):
111–27.

Parmoun, Yadollah. *Research Report on Intangible Cultural Heritage (ICH): Basics
and History*. Library and Archives Canada, 2017. https://www.mun.ca/
ich/media/production/intangible-cultural-heritage/media-library/
resources/ICH_Report_Basics_and_History.pdf (accessed 11 March
2023).

Pawłowska-Mainville, Agnieszka. "Accessing and Transmitting Living Heritage in
a Multiple-Heritage Family Context." Submitted to Intantilis
International Research Group 8 December, 2022 for group collection
publication.

———. "Aki miijim, 'Land Food' and the Sovereignty of the Asatiwisipe
Anishinaabeg Boreal Forest Food System." In *Indigenous Food Sovereignty*:
Concepts, Cases, and Conversations, edited by Priscilla Settee and Shailesh
Shukla, 57–82. Toronto: Canadian Scholars, 2019.

———. "Aski Atchimowina and Intangible Cultural Heritage." Expert Report
and Presentation to the Clean Environment Commission of Manitoba on
the Keeyask Generating Station on Behalf of the Concerned Fox Lake
Grassroots Citizens, participant. CEC Manitoba, 2014.

———. "Asserting Declarations: Supporting Indigenous Customary Governance
in Canada through Intangible Cultural Heritage." *"Patrimonio": Economía
cultural y educación para la paz* (MEC-EDUPAZ) 1, no. 19 (2021): 346–
81.

———. "Cannibalizing the Wiindigo: The Wiindigog in Anishinaabeg and Oji-Cree Boreal forest Landscapes and its Re-presentations in Popular Culture." *Literatura Ludowa: Journal of Folklore and Popular Culture* 66, no. 22 (2022): 51–69.

———. "Engaging *Dibaajimowinan*, 'Stories': Community-Based Research at Asatiwisipe Aki, Manitoba." In *Practising Community-based Participatory Research: Stories of Engagement, Empowerment, and Mobilization*, edited by Shauna MacKinnon, 127–43. Vancouver: Purich Press, 2018.

———. "Escaping the 'Progress Trap': UNESCO World Heritage Site Nomination and Land Stewardship through Intangible Cultural Heritage in Asatiwisipe First Nation, Manitoba." PhD diss., University of Manitoba, 2014.

———. "Experts and Professionals": Intangible Cultural Heritage Custodians and Natural Resource Management in Poland and Canada. *New Metropolitan Perspectives*. Special Issue on Post Covid Dynamics: Green and Digital Transition, between Metropolitan and Return to Villages Perspectives. Springer Lectures Notes in Networks and Systems 482(2022): 2383–92.

———. Presentation to the BC Utilities Commission on Site-C Dam, 29 September 2017.

———. "Using the Global to Support the Local." MA thesis, University of Manitoba, 2009.

Pawlowska-Mainville, Agnieszka, in conversation with Noah Massan. "'The Flooders' and 'the Cree': Challenging the Hydro Metanarrative Using Achimowinak, 'Stories.'" *In Our Backyard: Keeyask and the Legacy of Hydroelectric Development*, edited by Aimee Craft and Jill Blakley, 147–71. Winnipeg: University of Manitoba Press, 2022.

Pawlowska-Mainville, Agnieszka, and Yvonne Pierreroy. "Duni zuz 'utilnilth, 'Tanning Moose-Hide': Weaving Dakelh (Indigenous) Intangible Cultural Heritage Transmission with Academia." *Journal of Intangible Heritage* 15 (2020): 90–101.

Pawłowska-Mainville, Agnieszka, Lucas dos Santos Roque, and Barbara Fillion. *Conversations on Intangible Cultural Heritage*. Canadian Commission for UNESCO, 2023.

Pawlowska-Mainville, Agnieszka, et al. "Tree-Beekeeping and Apiary in Poland: Report in Response to the IPBES-ILK Dialogue, Methodological Values Assessment," 18 March 2021.

Perley, Bernard. "Living Traditions: A Manifesto for Critical Indigeneity." In *Performing Indigeneity: Global Histories and Contemporary Experiences*, edited by Laura Graham and H. Glenn Penny. Omaha: University of Nebraska Press, 2014.

Pimachiowin Aki. *Nomination for the Inscription of Pimachiowin Aki on the World Heritage List*. Pimachiowin Aki World Heritage Site Project, 2012.

———. *Nomination for the Inscription of Pimachiowin Aki on the World Heritage List*. Pimachiowin Aki World Heritage Site Project, 2016.

Pitawanahwat, Brock. "Anishinaabemodaa Pane Oodenang—A Qualitative Study of Anishinaabe Language Revitalization as Self-Determination in Manitoba and Ontario." PhD diss., University of Victoria, 2009.

Plan International. "The Maasai Elder Advocating to End Female Genital Mutilation." 2 February 2021. https://plan-international.org/kenya/case-studies/the-maasai-elder-advocating-to-end-female-genital-mutilation/ (accessed 21 October 2022).

Pocius, Gerald L. "The Government of Canada and Intangible Cultural Heritage: An Excursion into Federal Domestic Policies and the UNESCO Intangible Cultural Heritage Convention." *Ethnologies* 36, no. 1–2 (2014): 63–92.

———. "A Review of ICH in Newfoundland and Labrador," Intangible Cultural Heritage Update 16 (May 2010): 43–45. In Heritage Foundation of Newfoundland and Labrador, "Information and Reflection on the Approach, Strategy and General Vision on Documenting and Inventorying Intangible Cultural Heritage in Newfoundland and Labrador," n.d.

———. "The Emergence of Intangible Cultural Heritage Policy in Newfoundland and Labrador." *Newfoundland Quarterly* 103, no. 1 (2010): 43–45.

Poplar River First Nation. *Asatiwisipe Aki Management Plan*. Updated version, May 2011. https://pimaki.ca/wp-content/uploads/Poplar-River-First-Nation-Land-Use-Plan.pdf (accessed 18 May 2016).

Posey, Darrell, and Graham Dutfield. *Beyond Intellectual Property*. Ottawa: International Development Research Centre, 1996.

Povinelli, Elizabeth. *Labor's Lot: The Power, History, and Culture of Aboriginal Action*. Chicago: The University of Chicago Press, 1994.

Ray, Arthur R. *Indians in the Fur Trade: Their Role as Trappers, Hunters, and Middlemen in the Lands Southwest of Hudson Bay 1660–1870*. Toronto: University of Toronto Press, 1974.

"Le recensement des langues." Last modified 20 October 2020. https://www.axl.
    cefan.ulaval.ca/Langues/1div_recens.htm (accessed 15 May 2021).

Regalado, Antonio. "More Than 26 Million People Have Taken an At-Home
    Ancestry test." *MIT Technology Review*, 11 February 2019. https://www.
    technologyreview.com/2019/02/11/103446/more-than-26-million-
    people-have-taken-an-at-home-ancestry-test/ (accessed 12 October 2022).

R. v. Badger. Supreme Court of Canada (1996). https://scc-csc.lexum.com/scc-
    csc/scc-csc/en/item/1366/index.do (accessed 1 February 2023).

R. v. Van der Peet. Supreme Court of Canada (1996). http://scc-csc.lexum.com/
    scc-csc/scc-csc/en/item/1407/index.do (accessed 20 January 2016).

Report of the Royal Commission on Aboriginal People (RCAP), 1996.

Republic of Latvia. *Intangible Cultural Heritage Law* [Nemateriālā kultūras
    mantojuma likums]. 2016. https://likumi.lv/ta/en/en/id/285526-
    intangible-cultural-heritage-law (accessed 12 March 2023).

Sahlins, Marshall. *Stone Age Economics.* Chicago: Aldine-Atherton, 1972.

Sartre, Jean-Paul. *Critique of Dialectical Reason.* Vol. 1 (1960), edited by Jonathan
    Ree, translated by Alan Sheridan-Smith, and with a foreword by Fredric
    Jameson. London: Verso, 2004.

Schechner, Richard, and Sara Brady. *Performance Studies: An Introduction.*
    London: Routledge, 2013.

———. *Performed Imaginaries.* London: Routledge, 2014.

Schnarch, Brian. "Ownership, Control, Access, and Possession (OCAP) or Self-
    Determination Applied to Research: A Critical Analysis of Contemporary
    First Nations Research and Some Options for First Nations
    Communities." *International Journal of Indigenous Health* 1, no. 1 (2004):
    80–95.

Shariatmadari, David. "Why It's Time to Stop Worrying about the Decline of the
    English Language." *Guardian*, 15 August 2019. https://www.theguardian.
    com/science/2019/aug/15/why-its-time-to-stop-worrying-about-the-
    decline-of-the-english-language (accessed 21 October 2022).

Shewell, Hugh. *Enough to Keep Them Alive.* Toronto: University of Toronto Press,
    2004.

Simpson, Leanne Betasamosake. *Dancing on Our Turtle's Back: Stories of
    Nishnaabeg Re-Creation, Resurgence, and a New Emergence.* Winnipeg:
    Arbeiter Ring Publishing, 2011.

Slattery, Brian. "The Constitutional Dimensions of Aboriginal Title." *Supreme Court Law Review: Osgoode's Annual Constitutional Cases Conference* 71, no. 1 (2015): 45–66.

———. "The Generative Structure of Aboriginal Rights." In *Moving Toward Justice: Legal Traditions and Aboriginal Justice*. Conference Proceedings, edited by John D. Whyte, 595–600. Saskatoon: Purich Publishing, 2008.

Smith, Laurajane. "Discourses of Heritage: Implications for Archaeological Community Practice." *Nuevo Mundo Mundos Nuevos*, "Questions du temps présent," 5 October 2012. https://doi.org/10.4000/nuevomundo.64148 (accessed 14 May 2021).

Smith, Laurajane, and Emma Waterton. "The Envy of the World?': Intangible Heritage in England." In *Intangible Heritage*, edited by Laurajane Smith and Natsuko Akagawa, 289–302. London: Routledge, 2009.

Smith, Laurajane and Natsuko Akagawa. *Intangible Heritage*. New York: Routledge, 2009.

Statistics Canada. "The Aboriginal Languages of First Nations People, Metis and Inuit." https://www12.statcan.gc.ca/census-recensement/2016/as-sa/98-200-x/2016022/98-200-x2016022-eng.cfm (accessed 12 May 2021).

Stefano, Michelle L., Peter Davis, and Corsane Gerard, eds. *Safeguarding Intangible Cultural Heritage*. Woodbridge, ON: Boydell Press, 2012.

Stevenson, M.G. "Indigenous Knowledge in Environmental Assessment." *Arctic* 49, no. 3 (1996): 278–91.

Su, Junjie, and Da Fang. "Commodifying Intangible Cultural Heritage in Contemporary China." *'Patrimonio': Economía cultural y educación para la paz* (MEC-EDUPAZ) 1, no. 19 (2021): 9–37.

Tanner, Adrian. *Bringing Home Animals*. St. John's, NL: Memorial University Press, 1979.

Tatrzański Park Narodowy. "Dziedzictwo Kulturowe w Tatrach. [Cultural Heritage in the Tatra Mountains]." 10 April 2013. https://tpn.pl/poznaj/dziedzictwo/dziedzictwo-kulturowe-w-tatrach (accessed 15 May 2021).

Taylor, Diana. *The Archive and the Repertoire: Performing Cultural Memory in the Americas*. Durham, NC: Duke University Press, 2003.

te Heuheu, Tumu, Merata Kawharu, and Ariihau Tuheiava. "World Heritage and Indigeneity." *World Heritage* 62 (February 2012): 8–18. https://unesdoc.unesco.org/ark:/48223/pf0000215774.

Tester, Frank, and Peter Kulchyski. *Tammarniit (Mistakes): Inuit Relocation in the Eastern Arctic 1939–63*. Vancouver: UBC Press, 1994.

Tobias, Terry, The Union of BC Indian Chiefs (UBCIC) and Ecotrust Canada. *Chief Kerry's Moose, A Guidebook to Land Use and Occupancy Mapping, Research Design and Data Collection*. EcoTrust Canada and UBCIC, 2000.

———. *Living Proof, The Essential Data-Collection Guide for Indigenous Use-and-Occupancy Mapping*. EcoTrust Canada and UBCIC, 2009.

Tribal Parks. "Tla-o-qui-aht Tribal Parks." https://tribalparks.com (accessed 18 February 2023).

TRC (Truth and Reconciliation Commission of Canada). *Calls to Action*. Winnipeg: Truth and Reconciliation Commission of Canada, 2015.

Turner, Nancy. *Ancient Pathways, Ancestral Knowledge*. Montreal: McGill-Queen's University Press, 2014.

UNDRIP (United Nations Declaration of the Rights of Indigenous Peoples). United Nations, 2008. http://www.un.org/esa/socdev/unpfii/documents/DRIPS_en.pdf (accessed 13 November 2013).

UNESCO. "Activities in the Domain of Women and Intangible Heritage." UNESCO. https://ich.unesco.org/doc/src/00160-EN.pdf (accessed 19 May 2021).

———. "Atikaki/Woodland Caribou/Accord First Nations (Pimachiowin Aki)." https://whc.unesco.org/en/list/1415 (accessed 14 October 2010).

———. "Browse the Lists of Intangible Cultural Heritage and the Register of Good Safeguarding Practices." UNESCO: Intangible Cultural Heritage. https://ich.unesco.org/en/lists (accessed 8 May 2021).

———. Convention Concerning the Protection of the World Cultural and Natural Heritage. https://whc.unesco.org/en/conventiontext/ (accessed 15 January 2014).

———. Convention on the Elimination of All Forms of Discrimination against Women (1979). https://www.ohchr.org/en/professionalinterest/pages/cedaw.aspx (accessed 18 May 2021).

———. "Craftsmanship of Alençon Needle Lace-Making." "Safeguarding Our Living Heritage." http://www.unesco.org/culture/ich/en/RL/craftsmanship-of-alencon-needle-lace-making-00438 (accessed 21 November 2013).

———. "Cultural Landscapes." http://whc.unesco.org/en/culturallandscape/ (accessed 30 June 2014).

———. "Cultural Space and Oral Culture of the Semeiskie." Inscribed in 2008. https://ich.unesco.org/en/RL/cultural-space-and-oral-culture-of-the-semeiskie-00017 (accessed 30 April 2018).

———. "Cultural Space of the Yaaral and Degal." Inscribed in 2008. https://ich.unesco.org/en/RL/cultural-space-of-the-yaaral-and-degal-00132 (accessed 12 May 2018).

———. "Drawing Up Inventories." https://ich.unesco.org/en/drawing-up-inventories-00313 (accessed 20 May 2018).

———. Fact Sheet No. 23: Harmful Traditional Practices Affecting Health of Women and Children. UNCHR. https://www.ohchr.org/sites/default/files/Documents/Publications/FactSheet23en.pdf (accessed 18 May 2021).

———. "Ethical Principles for Safeguarding Intangible Cultural Heritage."

———. "Ethics and Intangible Cultural Heritage." https://ich.unesco.org/en/ethics-and-ich-00866 (accessed 13 May 2021).

———. "Guidance Note for Inventorying Intangible Cultural Heritage." 2018.

———. "Intangible Cultural Heritage domains." 2011.

———. "ICH Convention Operational Directives." *Basic Texts of the 2003 Convention for the Safeguarding of the Intangible Cultural Heritage*, 2022. https://ich.unesco.org/doc/src/2003_Convention_Basic_Texts-_2022_version-EN_.pdf (accessed 6 March 2023).

———. ICH Information Sheet: "Culture Policy." n.d.

———. ICH Information Sheet: "Constitution." n.d.

———. ICH Information Sheet: "Encouraging Community Engagement." n.d.

———. ICH Information Sheet: "Economic Development." n.d.

———. ICH Information Sheet: "Gender Equality Policy." n.d.

———. ICH Information Sheet: "Identification and Inventorying Policy Provisions." n.d.

———. ICH Information Sheet: "Intellectual Property." n.d.

———. ICH Information Sheet: "Language Policy." n.d.

———. Identifying and Inventorying Intangible Cultural Heritage. Infokit, 2011.

———. Information Sheet: "Providing Support for Policy." n.d.

———. "Intangible Cultural Heritage." http://www.unesco.org/culture/ich/index.php?lg=en&pg=00011&RL=00438 (accessed 3 November 2013).

———. "Intangible Cultural Heritage: A Force for Sustainable Development." UNESCO, Media Services. http://www.unesco.org/new/en/media-services/in-focus-articles/intangible-cultural-heritage-for-sustainable-development/ (accessed 16 May 2021).

———. "Intangible Cultural Heritage and Gender." 2015.

———. Intergovernmental Committee for the Safeguarding of the Intangible Cultural Heritage, Sixth session, Indonesia, 2011. Nomination File no. 00530. UNESCO, Nomination files for inscription in 2011 on the List of Intangible Cultural Heritage in Need of Urgent Safeguarding (item 8 on the agenda) - intangible heritage - Culture Sector - UNESCO (accessed 15 May 2021).

———. Intergovernmental Committee for the Safeguarding of the Intangible Cultural Heritage, Seventeenth session, Rabat, 2022. https://ich.unesco.org/en/17com. (accessed 23 March 2023).

———. "Kihnu cultural space." https://ich.unesco.org/en/RL/kihnu-cultural-space-00042 (accessed 21 April 2018).

———. "The Operational Guidelines for the Implementation of the World Heritage Convention." WHC.21/01, 31 July 2021. http://whc.unesco.org/en/guidelines. (accessed 6 March 2023).

———. "Oral Traditions and Expressions Including Language as Vehicle of the Intangible Cultural Heritage." https://ich.unesco.org/en/oral-traditions-and-expressions-00053 (accessed 24 May 2021).

———. "Periodic Report No.01049/Russian Federation." Intergovernmental Committee for the Safeguarding of the Intangible Cultural Heritage, Ninth Session, 24–28 November 2014. https://ich.unesco.org/en/state/russian-federation-RU?info=periodic-reporting (accessed 12 May 2018).

———. "Places of Memory and Living Traditions of the Otomí-Chichimecas People of Tolimán: the Peña de Bernal, Guardian of a Sacred Territory." http://www.unesco.org/culture/ich/en/RL/places-of-memory-and-living-traditions-of-the-otomi-chichimecas-people-of-toliman-the-pena-de-bernal-guardian-of-a-sacred-territory-00174 (accessed 26 October 2013).

———. "Purpose of the Lists of Intangible Cultural Heritage and of the Register of Good Safeguarding Practices." https://ich.unesco.org/en/purpose-of-the-lists-00807 (accessed 8 May 2021).

———. "Requesting International Assistance." http://www.unesco.org/culture/ich/en/requesting-assistance-00039 (accessed 20 May 2016).

———. "Safeguarding without Freezing." http://www.unesco.org/culture/ich/en/safegurding-00012 (accessed 13 May 2021).

———. "Le Samoa, Fine Mat and Its Cultural Value." https://www.unesco.org/archives/multimedia/document-4926 (accessed 15 May 2018).

———. [ICH convention] "Text of the Convention for the Safeguarding of the Intangible Cultural Heritage." http://www.unesco.org/culture/ich/en/convention (accessed 13 May 2021).

———. *Third Session of the Intergovernmental Committee.* 8 November 2008. http://www.unesco.org/culture/ich/en/3com.

———. "Tongariro National Park—World Heritage List." http://whc.unesco.org/en/list/421. (accessed 20 April 2014).

———. "Traditional Knowledge of the Jaguar Shamans of Yuruparí." https://ich.unesco.org/en/RL/traditional-knowledge-of-the-jaguar-shamans-of-yurupari-00574 (accessed 13 May 2021).

———. "Traditions and Practices Associated with the Kayas in the Sacred Forests of the Mijikenda." https://ich.unesco.org/en/USL/traditions-and-practices-associated-with-the-kayas-in-the-sacred-forests-of-the-mijikenda-00313 (accessed 21 April 2018).

———. Universal Declaration of Human Rights. http://portal.unesco.org/en/ev.php-URL_ID=26053&URL_DO=DO_TOPIC&URL_SECTION=201.html (accessed 15 May 2021).

———. Universal Declaration on Cultural Diversity. http://portal.unesco.org/en/ev.php-URL_ID=13179&URL_DO=DO_TOPIC&URL_SECTION=201.html (accessed 18 May 2021).

———. "Le Vieux Lunenburg." http://whc.unesco.org/fr/list/741/ (accessed 1 March 2014).

———. World Heritage Centre. "The Criteria for Selection." https://whc.unesco.org/en/criteria/ (accessed 20 May 2018).

———. International Expert Workshop on Integrity and Authenticity of World Heritage Cultural Landscapes." Organized by World Heritage Committee and ICOMOS-Canada. 12 December 2007.

———. *Report and Recommendations on Integrity and Authenticity of World Heritage Landscapes.* Recommendations, Aranjuez, Spain: UNESCO.

———. "37th Session of the World Heritage Committee (37 COM), Decision 37 COM 8B.19," 2013:175 §b.

———. "Targeted destruction of Ukraine's culture must stop: UN experts." 23 February 2023. https://www.ohchr.org/en/statements/2023/02/targeted-destruction-ukraines-culture-must-stop-un-experts (accessed 16 March 2023).

UN News. "'Stop the destruction,' UN officials urge in peal to save Syria's cultural heritage." 12 March 2014. https://news.un.org/en/story/2014/03/463782 (accessed 16 March 2023).

Uqqurmiut. "About the Uqqurmiut Centre for Arts and Crafts." http://www.uqqurmiut.ca/UCAC.html (accessed 2 May 2018).

Usher, Peter. "Evaluating Country Food in the Northern Native Economy." *Arctic* 29, no. 2 (1976): 105–20.

———. "Traditional Ecological Knowledge in Environmental Assessment and Management." *Arctic* 53, no. 2 (2000): 183–93.

Usher, Peter, and N.D. Bankes. *Property, the Basis of Inuit Hunting Rights—A New Approach*. Ottawa: Inuit Committee on National Issues, 1986.

U.S. NEWS. "10 Countries with the Richest Histories." Updated 14 December 2017. https://www.usnews.com/news/best-countries/articles/2017-12-14/the-10-countries-with-the-richest-histories-ranked-by-perception (accessed 1 May 2021).

Van Kirk, Sylvia. *Many Tender Ties: Women in Fur-trade Society, 1670–1870*. Norman: University of Oklahoma Press, 1980.

Waldram, James B. "Native People and Hydroelectric Development in Northern Manitoba, 1957–1987: The Promise and the Reality." *Manitoba History* 15 (1988). https://www.mhs.mb.ca/docs/mb_history/15/hydroelectricdevelopment.shtml (accessed 11 March 2023).

White Earth Wild Rice. http://realwildrice.com/ (accessed 12 April 2021).

Whitelaw, G.S., D.D. McCarthy, and L. Tsuji. "The Victor Diamond Mine Environmental Assessment and the Mushegowuk Territory First Nations: Critical Systems Thinking and Social Justice." *Canadian Journal of Native Studies* 30, no.1 (2012): 83–116.

Wikipedia. "Culture of Italy." Updated 14 May 2021. https://en.wikipedia.org/wiki/Culture_of_Italy (accessed 24 May 2021).

WIPO (World Intellectual Property Office). "Berne Convention for the Protection of Literary and Artistic Works." https://www.wipo.int/treaties/en/ip/berne/ (accessed 20 May 2021).

————. "Compilation of Information on National and Regional Sui Generis Regimes for the Intellectual Property Protection of Traditional Knowledge and Traditional Cultural Expressions." 18 January 2021. https://www.wipo.int/export/sites/www/tk/en/resources/pdf/compilation_sui_generis_regimes.pdf (accessed 20 May 2021).

Wismer, S. "The Nasty Game: How Environmental Assessment Is Failing Aboriginal Communities in Canada's North." *Alternatives Journal* 22, no. 4 (1996): 10–17.

Withers, Paul. "Fishery Growth Has Had Positive Impact on First Nations in the Maritimes: Report." CBC News, 1 October 2020. https://www.cbc.ca/news/canada/nova-scotia/maritime-first-nations-hold-commercial-fishing-licenses-1.5745492.

World Health Organization. "Food Security." http://www.who.int/trade/glossary/story028/en/ (accessed 30 January 2014).

World Wildlife Fund. "Payments for Ecosystem Services." https://wwf.panda.org/discover/knowledge_hub/where_we_work/black_sea_basin/danube_carpathian/our_solutions/green_economy/pes/?#:~:text=Payments%20for%20Ecosystem%20Services%20is,with%20subsidies%20or%20market%20payments (accessed 10 May 2021).

WTO (World Trade Organization). Paris Convention, 1967. https://www.wto.org/english/tratop_e/dispu_e/repertory_e/p2_e.htm (accessed 16 May 2021).

————. "TRIPS-Trade-Related Aspects of Intellectual Property Rights." https://www.wto.org/english/tratop_e/trips_e/trips_e.htm (accessed 20 May 2021).

York Factory First Nation. "Kipekiskwaywinan—Our Voices." York Factory First Nation, 2012.

Yunnan Exploration. "Tie-Dying Skills of Bai Ethnic Minority in Dali." https://www.yunnanexploration.com/tie-dyeing-skills-of-bai-ethnic-minority-in-dali.html (accessed 25 May 2021).

Index

aki miijim (land food): cooperation needed to harvest, 138–39; and ecology, 137; goodness of, 136–38; as ICH, 142–44, 218, 226–27; K. Douglas's enjoyment of, 133–34; as medicine, 134–35; Poplar River view of, 261n28; as a relationship, 141

akiwenziyag: and acts of resistance to cultural homogenization, 22–23; and aki miijim, 134–35; appropriation of their knowledge, 117; author's interpretation of, 24; and belief everyone can learn ICH, 160; belief in human's place in world, 137; and bush skills, 80, 146; and customary governance, 220, 221; depth of wildlife knowledge of, 211–13; described, 6; and dreams, 140; and food system as ICH, 20–21; on gender roles, 152–53; harvesting skills of, 212; how ICH discourse can be used to their advantage, 19, 23, 198–99; ICH manifested in stories and traditions, 20; idea of making them conservation officers, 213–15, 216–17; importance of stories to, 131; and ji-ganawendamang Gidakiiminaan, 49; lack of interest in debates of authenticity and integrity, 101; land-culture connection of, 18; and limitations on land use, 57; map of territories, 25; and mino-bimaadiziwin, 84–87; at odds with nature/culture dichotomy, 43; on resource stewardship and sovereign food system, 226–27; and respect for animals, 142, 143; responsibilities as ICH custodians, 230–32; on secrecy and traditional knowledge, 71; sense of duty, 157; songs of, 88; strength and determination of, 74; and Thunderbirds, 55; and tie of stories to land, 73; trust of memory over written history, 72–73; understanding of interest

in their culture, 158, 160; view knowledge systems as creative genius, 44; view of heritage, 17; view of land rights, 221–24; view of trapping life, 206–8

Amah Mutsun, 216

animals: disrespect towards, 142–43, 183, 184, 212, 217, 262n64; how they control hunting, 140–41; learning from, 144; N. Massan's concern for, 188–89

Anishinaabeg: connection to land, 219–20; and cultural heritages of, 81; food systems of, 132; home of, 34–35; importance of stories to, 61; language of as ICH, 84; nominates Pimachiowin Aki for World Heritage Site, 35–36; R. Morrison sharing teachings of, 121–23, 162–63; set of beliefs and knowledges of, 47–50; view of land food, 261n28; view of successful hunt, 139

Anishinaabemowin, 257n46, 265n122

at-risk heritage, 13, 99, 146, 158

appropriation/misappropriation of ICH, 108, 111, 112, 114, 117, 260n115

authenticity, 14, 44–45, 101

Baltic Sea, 13, 24, 51

batik case, 108

Beardy, Johnny, 182

beaver, 133–36, 188–89, 193, 206, 208, 212

Belize, 90, 227

Berens, John, 66

Bittern, Albert, 157–58, 214

Bittern, Gordy, 210–11

Bittern, Stanley, 222

Bolivia, 87, 90, 227

Brazil, 11, 104, 227

British Columbia, 100

Bruce, Abel: and beaver, 134–35; death, 235; and dreams, 140; eagerness of to pass on his skills, 211–12, 215–16; and food distribution, 141–42; on his connection to land, 221–22; and ICH, 6; on land rights, 222; and learning women's skills, 153, 155; mean old man story, 140–41; and medicines, 134, 135–36; and *mino-bimaadiziwin*, 85; nature of his stories, 131; photos, 76, 79, 134, 143; and preparing tobacco, 143, 144; sharing stories with author, 28, 61, 79–80; story of conservation officer, 73–74; in T. Douglas's story, 208; tobacco harvesting of, 26; and traplines, 49, 63–64; as trapper, 131, 199, 204–6, 209–11; trapping stories of, 75–78, 116–17; on youth's lack of bush skills, 145

Bruce, Albert, 61, 76, 210
Bruce, Ernest, 212, 223–24
Bruce, Freddie, 203–4
Bruce, Noel, 29, 136–37, 208, 214–15
Bruce, Norman, 141–42
Bruce, Philip, 76, 206
Bruce, Willie, 7, 29, 209, 211
Burkina Faso, 227
bush skills, 80, 143–44, 145, 209, 223–24

Calgary, City of, 100
Canada: endorses UNDRIP, 81, 269n68; food rationing by government, 261n28; local development of ICH in, 98–100, 202–4; and mixed-heritage sites, 41; plea for need to re-evaluate ICH, 231, 232–33; and preservation of Indigenous languages, 89; and ratifying the ICH Convention, 15–16, 31, 92–96, 97, 100–101, 230, 233; three Calls for Action to, 233–34; training/courses in ICH management, 125
caribou: disappearance of, 170, 172–73; disrespect toward, 217; effect of hydro development on, 176–77, 178, 180, 189, 194; hunting of, 58, 132, 141–42, 223; N. Massan challenges Manitoba Hydro on, 183–85; poaching, 182
CEC (Manitoba Clean Environment Commission) hearings: and argument over science v. traditional knowledge, 269n56; and compensation program, 180; and disagreement on existence of caribou in Keeyask area, 184–85; ICH brought up during, 187; inaccurate information from Manitoba Hydro in, 177–78; intervenors at, 168; Keeyask Environmental Impact Statement and

rebuttal, 169–70, 175, 177; and map showing heritage sites, 165–67; time limitations of, 186
China, 90, 125, 152, 202
colonialism, 80, 146, 155, 263n98
commercialization of ICH, 113, 260n115, 260n117
commodification of craftmanship/skill, 112, 202
Concerned Fox Lake Grassroots Citizens (CFLGC), 168, 169, 180–81, 184
Le Conseil québécois du patrimoine vivant, 99
conservation officer story, 73–74
Crane Creek, 58
cultural diversity, 7–8, 19, 23, 147
cultural protocols, 21, 138, 143, 215
customary governance: background of mistreatment which makes necessary, 218–19; basis of, 221–22; elements of, 231; and ICH, 227; as Indigenous right, 217, 218

Dakelh Elders, 83, 100, 114, 126–28, 249n58, 250n68
documentation of cultural heritage: advantages for Indigenous Canadians of, 104–5; difficulties in, 105–6; and disputes over origins of ICH, 108–9; example of inventory card, 241–43; ICH Convention methods of, 20, 101–4; and impact assessments, 187–88; importance for safeguarding ICH, 232–33; and inventory guidelines, 244–45; textualization and ethics of, 107–8; training in, 125; and transmission, 106–7, 230; as way of organizing knowledge, 109–11
doodemag, 49–50
Douglas, Ken: on *aki miijim*, 138; and food, 133–34; importance of trapping to, 84; on lack of bush skills by young, 145; stories of, 64–67, 133, 208–9
Douglas, Tom, 208
dreams, 139, 140

eco-cultural tourism, 203, 204
ecology, Indigenous view of, 137
education, 123–28
environmental assessment review, 168, 169–70, 177

environmental impact assessments. *See* impact assessments (environmental)

Environmental Impact Statement (EIS), 167, 169–70, 183

Esperanto, 90

ethics, 107–8

Europe, 41–42

fasting, 119–21, 128–30

female genital mutilation, 147, 152

First Peoples' Cultural Council (BC), 89, 100

fishing: cooperation needed in, 139; as demanding occupation, 67; effect of hydroelectric development on, 172; by Hydro workers, 177, 182; and K. Douglas, 133; licences, 224; stories, 66; and *Van der Peet* case, 225, 226

folklore, 10, 16, 95

food distribution, 141–43

food systems: and hydroelectric development, 172–73; as ICH, 20–21, 132, 137; Indigenous, 132–35, 226; and Indigenous on Western diet, 218; in *Van der Peet* case, 226

Fox Lake Cree, 167, 168–69, 175, 176

Garifuna, 90

gender: on changing roles of, 155; and colonialism, 263n98; and natural segregation of ICH, 149–50; as point of contention in ICH, 146–49; powwows and, 161; R. Morrison's crossing of line on, 162; transmission of gender roles, 151–53; and women's deference to men as experts in ICH, 150–51

Górale, 52, 147, 152

health care, 78–79

Hee Biki ritual, 112

Heritage Act, 93

Heritage Foundation of Newfoundland and Labrador, 99

Heritage Saskatchewan, 99–100, 258n73

Heritage-Sensitive Intellectual Property and Marketing Strategies (HIPAMS), 260n115

Hezhen Yimakan storytelling, 91, 152

human rights, 147–49

hunting: animals control of, 140–41; compared to trapping, 207–8; cooperation needed in, 139; and disrespect to animals, 142–43; and

dreams, 139, 140; effect of hydroelectric development on, 172–73; and survival skills, 143–44; what's needed for success in, 139–41, 262n61. *See also* caribou; trappers/trapping life

ICH Convention (UNESCO's 2003 Convention): addressing loss of ICH elements, 124; Canada's failure to ratify, 15–16, 31, 92–96, 97, 100–101, 230, 233; and definition of ICH, 9; and documentation of cultural heritage, 20, 101–4; encouraging educational programs in ICH, 125; examples of link between culture and land by, 51–52; and five domains of ICH, 9–10, 102–3; how it advanced ICH discourse, 8–9, 229; and identity politics, 156; and principles of safeguarding ICH, 13–14, 227; and push for recognition of Indigenous plans and programs, 81; recent problems relating to, 258n68; recognition of Canada's Indigenous Peoples in, 80; situation in nations which failed to ratify, 96–97; and strengthening language development, 89, 90–91; understanding of customary governance by, 221; used as framework by provinces, 99, 100; and view of gender and human rights, 147; World Heritage Committee's unfamiliarity with, 39

identity politics, 155–56, 160, 264n108

immersive pedagogy, 129, 131

Impact Assessment Act (IAA), 173–74, 187–88, 234

Impact Assessment Agency of Canada, 173, 186–87

impact assessments (environmental), 168, 169–70, 177, 186–88, 267n47

India, 37, 114, 186

Indian Act, 264n109

Indigenous and Tribal Peoples Convention, 221

Indigenous Community Conserved Areas (ICCAs), 215

Indigenous Languages Act, 94

Indigenous Languages and Cultures Program, 94

Indigenous Peoples of Canada: advantages of documenting ICH for, 104–5; and belief of who controls land, 221–22; disappearance of cultural elements of, 7–8; examples of cultural heritages, 81–

83; food systems of, 132–35, 226; history of mistreatment of, 218; how World Heritage Sites criteria do not apply to, 44–45; human rights concerns about traditions of, 148–49; and ICOMOS's attempt to change criteria for, 45–46; and lack of consultation on ICH Convention ratification, 95–96; Manitoba Hydro's ignoring knowledge of, 182, 184–85; prohibition of cultural traditions, 80; recognized by ICH Convention, 80; role in Impact Assessment Act, 174; and social capital of being an Elder, 158–60; transmission of ICH from men to women, 152–53; values of unfamiliar to World Heritage Committee, 39; and *Van der Peet* case, 224–27. *See also* Anishinaabeg; Inninuwak; trappers/trapping life

Indigenous Protected and Conserved Areas, 215

Indonesia, 108

industrial development, 217. *See also* Keeyask hydroelectric development

Inninuwak: effect of hydroelectric development on, 169–70, 171–79; and hydro compensation program for, 179–82; Hydro employees disrespect of, 183, 184, 194; importance of documentation to, 187; Keeyask project's ignorance of, 30–31; as knowledge holders, 212; and *mino-pimatisiwin*, 87; reaction to N. Massan's testimony, 185; relations with Manitoba Hydro, 158, 267n41; view of customary governance, 218

intangible cultural heritage (ICH): appropriation of, 108, 111, 112, 114, 117, 260n115; benefits of compiling inventories of, 186–88; benefits of safeguarding, 8, 234; bureaucratization of, 97–98; can be non-conscious or deliberate, 15; Canada's lack of interest in, 93; commercialization of, 113, 260n115, 260n117; community-centred approach to transmission, 15, 16; conflict with human rights and, 147–48; connection to tangible heritage, 17–18; considered rights based on *Van der Peet* case, 226–27; and deference of women to men as experts in, 150–51; depth of trappers knowledge on wildlife, 212–13; difficulties in transmission of, 145–46,

160–61; divide between scholars and locals on, 14–15; documentation of, 104–11; economic benefits of, 198–202; examples of global policy on, 227–28; exploitation of, 114, 115; fluid traditional relations of, 153, 155; and focus on at-risk culture, 156, 157; food systems as, 20–21, 132, 137; four ways of understanding, 13; fragility of, 6–7; funding of, 100–101, 233; and gender, 22, 146–51; how it can be used by Indigenous Peoples, 19, 23; how stories form a part of, 62–63; and idea of making Indigenous conservation officers to safeguard, 213–14, 216–17; and identity politics, 155–56, 230; and impact assessments, 186–88, 267n47; impact of resource development on, 185–88; and Indigenous self-determination, 230; intellectual property considerations of, 111–16; intergenerational loss and rebuilding of, 154–55; international scale of, 229; and language preservation, 84, 88–92; left out of Impact Assessment Act, 174; livelihoods in as method of transmission, 215–16; living heritage as preferred term for, 16–17; and local community development in Canada, 98–100, 202–4; loss of in some communities, 216; loss of with hydroelectric development, 170–73; mixed-heritage custodians of, 156; national lists and registers of, 11; need for legal analysis/resolution of, 98, 227, 228, 232; need for policy making in environmental impact assessments, 21–22; not considered in Keeyask hydro project assessment, 174, 176–77; outsiders in control of, 146; portability of, 18; and powwows, 9, 13, 83, 106; recommendation for safeguarding of, 232–33; and redrawing of natural resource management practices, 22; role in understanding treaty rights, 221; role of education in, 123–28; role to play in future, 230–31; and special people, 156–57; strength of from Elders, 157–60; and sweat ceremony, 197–98; three Calls for Action on in Canada, 233–34; transmission of, 9, 144, 151–53, 211–12, 259n90, 259n94; from trapping, 206; UNESCO's five domains of, 9–10, 102–

3. *See also* documentation of cultural heritage; ICH Convention (UNESCO's 2003 Convention)
Intangible Cultural Heritage Fund, 104
intellectual property (IP), 111–16, 260n115
intermittent harvesting, 205–6
International Council of Monuments and Sites (ICOMOS), 45–46
inventories. *See* documentation of cultural heritage
Ivan (CFLGC member), 171

Japan, 201
ji-ganawendamang Gidakiiminaan, 47–50, 85, 106, 205, 226, 227

Keeyask Cree Nations, 168
Keeyask hydroelectric project: benefits program from, 179–82; and damage to environment of, 177–79; effect on Indigenous groups of, 169–73; evidence of its destruction, 188, 190–93, 194; hearings on, 165–67, 168; ignores cultural effects of in impact assessment, 174–75; and lack of mention of Inninuwak culture, 30–31; and Valued Environmental Components (VECs), 175–77
Keeyask Hydropower Limited Partnership (KHLP), 165, 168
Keeyask Impact Benefits Agreement, 179–82
Kichi Sipi (Nelson River), 165, 168, 178–79
Kihnu Cultural Space, 51
kitayatisuk: acts of resistance to cultural homogenization, 22–23; author shares concerns of at CEC meeting, 187; author's interpretation of, 24; and cultural mode of production, 158; and customary governance, 221; described, 6; economic benefits of ICH for, 217; effect of hydroelectric project on, 176, 180–85; and food system as ICH, 20–21; idea of turning into conservation officers, 214, 216; importance of ICH discourse to, 19; knowledge of land, 73, 212–13; land-culture connection of, 18; map of territories, 25; and *mino-pimatisiwin*, 87; and responsibilities as ICH custodians, 230–32; on secrecy and traditional knowledge, 71; on sovereign food system, 226; trapping life of, 207–8; troubles with Manitoba Hydro, 169–70, 172;

view of heritage, 17; view of knowledge system as creative genius, 44
Klippenstein, Rose, 130, 214
Korea, 12, 125
Kwakwaka'wakw Nation, 115
Kyrgyzstan, 103

Lambert, Russell, 130
land: connection to culture, 18, 51–52; and getting youth interested in, 214–15; Indigenous belief of who controls, 221–22; R. Morrison's connection to, 219–20; sacredness of keeping, 137; stories of connection to, 72–73; and trauma of relocating, 181
land food. *See aki miijim* (land food)
land rights, 222–24
language, 84, 88–92, 94, 265n122
Latvia, 125, 228
List of Intangible Cultural Heritage in Need of Urgent Safeguarding, 10–12, 91, 152
Lithuania, 90, 105, 125
little birds story, 68
living heritage as preferred term, 16–17, 248n41
lynx, 69, 135, 204, 209–11

Madagascar, 113
Mainville, John, 143, 144
Malaysia, 108, 125
Manitoba, Government of, 35, 37
Manitoba Hydro: challenged by N. Massan on caribou, 183–85; and compensation program for Cree/Inninuwak, 179–82; documents from collected by N. Massan, 30; evidence of hydro development damage, 190–93, 194; ignores Indigenous knowledge, 182, 184–85; illegal and disrespectful activities of, 182–83, 184, 188, 189, 194, 212, 217; N. Massan's confrontation with security guard of, 194–96; N. Massan on, 158; as partner in Keeyask project, 168; plan for transmission line, 35; questioned about Keeyask, 177, 187; and relations with Inninuwak, 267n41; sees ICH as irritations, 174; as source of problems for Indigenous groups, 169–73; truth of clean energy claims by, 177–79; and Valued Environmental Components, 175–77

manoomin (wild rice), 66, 106, 115, 138–39, 200

Massan, Christine, 172, 180–81

Massan, Jack, 172, 180–81, 182

Massan, Noah: and catching sturgeon on Nelson River, 182; at CEC hearings, 165–66, 168, 187; challenges Manitoba Hydro on caribou, 183–85; concern for animals by, 188–89; confrontation with Hydro security guard, 194–96; death, 235; experience working for hydro, 183; as Hydro watchdog, 217; and Hydro workers' disrespect, 183, 188, 189, 194, 212, 217; and ICH, 7; passes Hydro files to author, 30; and pipe from R. Morrison, 26, 144; as trapper, 158, 169, 188, 209; view of Keeyask hydro development, 170–71, 172–73, 175, 176, 177–78

Mean Old Man stories, 140–41, 262n64

medicines, 113, 134–37, 172

Midewewin, 80, 82, 122, 161–63

mino-bimaadiziwin, 84–87

mino-pimatisiwin, 87, 170, 172, 175, 185

Mitchell, Alex, 133

Mitchell, Byron, 203

mooshide tanning course, 126, 127

Morrisseau, Norval, 83

Morrison, Richard: on being an Elder, 159–60; and ceremonial drum songs, 115; on changing ICH gender roles, 155; connection to author, 26; death, 235; on the Four Directions, 161–63; and ICH, 6; as ICH teacher, 124, 125; and *mino-bimaadiziwin*, 85–87; and original linguistic descriptions, 94–95; photos, 3, 125, 128, 220; and pipe making, 2–4, 26; on pipe-smoking, 5; preparing a sweatlodge ceremony, 107–8, 197–98; preparing for fasters, 119–21, 128–29; shares Anishinaabe teachings, 121–23; and spirit plate, 142; trip home, 1–2; view of his connection to land, 219–20; view of recording Indigenous stories, 71

Mukatewasipe River (Black River), 58, 61, 75–76, 116–17, 255n1

Nanawin, Jacob, 58, 59

Nanawin, Jean, 56, 57, 136, 203

Nanawin, Sarah, 59

Nanawin, Walter: and creation story, 52–53; death, 235; as historian, 68–69; keeping an eye on differences in landscape, 55–60; on land rights, 223; on medicine, 136; passes material to author, 29–30; photos, 52, 56, 59; qualities as storyteller, 67–72; and Sasquatch, 55–56; and Thunderbirds, 54–55; and trapping, 209

Nanowin, Charlie, 58

nature/culture dichotomy, 43–44

Newfoundland and Labrador, 99

Off-Setting Program, 179–82

Ontario, Government of, 37

oral literacy, 61–62

oral traditions, 62–63

Otomí-Chichimecas People, 11, 51

Ottertail Lake, 120

owls, 60

Papua New Guinea, 110–11, 147

Peru, 90

Pewanowinin, Chief, 58

Philippines, 113

Pimachiowin Aki: and community development, 202–4; description of, 37; development of, 214–15; on Heritage Site culture-to-nature spectrum, 42–43; and *ji-ganawendamang Gidakiiminaan*, 85; nomination as World Heritage Site, 35–36, 37–38; translation of, 47

pipes/pipe-smoking, 2–4, 5–6, 94–95

place making, 50, 64

Poland, 26–27, 103, 142

Polonez, 84

Poplar River, 34–35, 36, 46–47, 202–4

Poplar River First Nation, 19–20, 35

potlaches, 82–83

powwows: as element of many Indigenous cultures, 109–10; gender diverse, 161; and ICH, 9, 13, 83, 106; transmission of, 259n90

Quebec, 98–99

Representative List, 10–12

residential schools, 1, 126, 205

Royal Commission on Aboriginal People (RCAP), 16

sacred traditional knowledge, 96

Sápmi People, 114

Saskatchewan, 99–100

Sasquatches, 55–56

Section 35 of the Constitution Act, 224
spirit plate, 142
stories/narratives: A. Bruce shares with author, 28, 61, 79–80; experience of listening to W. Nanawin relate, 69–71; and family, 131; and Hezhen Yimakan storytelling, 91; how they define land, 72–73; how they form part of definition of ICH, 20, 62–63; as Indigenous life and knowledge, 61–62; and K. Douglas, 64–67, 133, 208–9; loss of, 173; Mean Old Man, 140–41, 262n64; and pipe-smoking, 5–6; stored in the bones, 6; of trapping from A. Bruce, 75–78, 116–17; of W. Nanawin, 56–60, 70–72
sturgeon, 172, 177, 182
sweatlodge ceremony: attempt to record, 107–8; at Elder's Lodge, 65; as ICH element, 81; preparing for, 197–98; R. Morrison teaches, 124; used as metaphor for taking care of land, 219
Syria, 97

The Terrible Summer (Wagamese), 24
throat singing, 12, 82, 186
Thunderbirds, 54–55, 68, 72, 83, 253n54
tobacco offering: A. Bruce's story of, 63–64; to Beings, 71; at campsite by A. Bruce, 131; for harvesting sweetgrass, 220; K. Douglas's stories of, 64, 66–67; for killed deer, 144; and trapping, 212
tourism, 13, 112, 202, 203, 204
trappers/trapping life: of A. Bruce, 75–78, 116–17, 131–32, 199, 204–6, 209–11; compared to hunting, 207–8; effect of Keeyask hydroelectric development on, 175; as hard work, 116–17, 130–31, 199, 208, 209, 211; and K. Douglas, 84, 208–9; knowledge of environment of, 206–7; N. Massan and, 158, 169, 188, 209; as part-time work today, 158; and trapping lynx, 209–11; wealth of knowledge involved in, 211–13
Treaty 5, 68, 222
treaty rights/land claims, 95, 221
tree beekeeping, 201, 267n10
Truth and Reconciliation Commission (TRC), 16, 89, 123–24

Ukraine, 96–97
UNESCO (United Nations Educational, Scientific and Cultural Organization):
and authenticity, 14; definition of oral tradition, 62–63; efforts at cultural preservation, 7; and five domains of ICH, 9–10, 102–3; and human rights, 147, 148; and IP protection, 111; view of ICH economic benefits, 200
UNESCO World Heritage Sites, 35–38, 39, 40, 41–42, 44–45
United Nations Convention on Biological Diversity, 221
United Nations Declaration on the Rights of Indigenous Peoples (UNDRIP), 15, 81, 89, 221, 269n68

Valiquette, Frances, 29, 47, 152–53, 158, 261n28
Valiquette, Jim, 208
Valiquette, Marcel, 85, 208
Valued Environmental Components (VECs), 175–77
Van der Peet, Dorothy, 224–25
Van der Peet, R. v, (1996), 224–26
Vancouver, City of, 100
Venezuela, 103, 104, 109, 227
vision quest, 119

wolves, 60, 208–9
women, 22, 146–49, 150–53, 155, 263n98.
See also gender
World Heritage Committee, 38–39, 41, 42, 45, 251n9
World Heritage Sites. See UNESCO World Heritage Sites
World Intellectual Property Organization (WIPO), 113

Zafimaniry People, 113
Zayed Complex for Herbal and Traditional Medicine Research Centre, 113

Printed in the USA
CPSIA information can be obtained
at www.ICGtesting.com
CBHW030617130224
4305CB00002B/66

9 781772 840452